Under the Radar During Camelot

Under the Radar During Camelot

MY FRONT ROW SEAT TO HISTORY

A Memoir

LAYTE BOWDEN

Cover design: Jeff Brandenburg
Interior design: Jeff Brandenburg
Proofreader: Kathy Fesq
Publishing advisor: David Carr

Published by Figleaf Ltd.
Miami, Florida, USA
amartistic@gmail.com

First printing, 2013
Printed in the United States of America

IN MEMORY OF HUGH SIDEY
1927–2005

The *Time Magazine* White House correspondent who possessed a moral
compass not so often expressed in reporting, or by journalists of this
young twenty-first century is terribly missed by all who knew him.

He was an Iowa man who never lost his bearings in a Capitol City
fraught with lies, deceit and personal agendas. His sense of humor kept
so many of us in a good mood despite the sometimes grueling travel on
the White House Press Charters all over the world.

He exacted a promise from me to tell my unusual relationship with
President Kennedy and finally I have done so.

CONTENTS

PREFACE

Much of my life has been lived in what now seems a CIRCUS atmosphere. Perhaps you look back at a more serene life because by happenstance, or choice, you didn't enter the tent that featured life's unending carnival of events as I did.

I totally understand that many readers will not relate to my experiences, and many will question my truthfulness in describing my life shared with the famous people now residing in history. I can only say that *nothing* I have written here was exaggerated or misrepresented and is totally true to my memories and diaries of these years.

This was not written in judgment or criticism of anyone with whom I shared my experiences. It is a straightforward personal description of my extraordinary life. I am grateful that I was gifted the opportunity to know such interesting and accomplished people in this lifetime. I am also thankful that I was blessed to visit the many other countries of our world and to witness the variety of their cultures and environments.

I don't pretend for a moment that I accomplished one feat worthy of a Wikipedia mention, but by serendipity, I found myself personally witnessing some of the most important events of the 1960's. I think many of you will really enjoy reliving those years with me. Hopefully reading this will enlighten those much younger than I who only know the sixties from history books.

Aside from the perhaps shocking, often funny stories I relate, you will also refresh or learn for the first time factual information that could win you a night on JEOPARDY!

INTRODUCTION

JFK White House Charter
El Paso, Texas, June 1963

"Wherever she went, including here:
it was against her better judgment."

—DOROTHY PARKER

How this beautiful day would end was quite beyond my imagining. As I closed the entry door of our Pan Am Charter at Andrews Air Force Base in the early morning of June 5th, a lovely breeze kissed my face. Our Boeing 707 jet would follow President Jack Kennedy in Air Force One en route to Colorado Springs. He was scheduled to address the Air Force Academy's graduating class of 1963 on one of the most beautiful campuses in America.

Following his speech at the Academy, JFK was to visit NORAD (the North American Aerospace Defense Command) located in the southwestern side of the city. I hadn't realized that this command post was established in 1958 in partnership with Canada to safeguard all of North America's air space. I would have so loved to tour the facilities hidden within the Cheyenne Mountain, but it is so secret and hi-tech that I would, of course, have needed a top security clearance.

The Presidential party arrived early that same evening in El Paso. We checked into the rather drab El Cortez Hotel. This was not as grandiose as the establishments where the President usually resided while traveling. I had just changed from my Pan Am uniform into a pair of comfortable slacks and plopped down on my bed to stretch my tired legs, when the phone rang from several floors above mine in the hotel.

I answered and JFK's cheerful voice inquired, "Hi, what did you think of my speech to those handsome young studs at the academy today?"

"I think you were a terrific inspiration to the guys. Your speech almost inspired me to sign up and serve my country!" I told him. "It must be a great feeling to know that you inspire young people everywhere you go."

"Layte, I'd like to inspire you and some of your crew to join me in my suite for a couple of drinks to unwind from the day. Pierre and a couple of my other aides are here, so George is mixing up a large batch of daiquiris."

"That sounds like fun, Jack. I'll call the gals and we'll come up as soon as we're organized."

The stewardesses, several of whom had never personally met the President, were excited with the opportunity to actually talk with him. A little later, the seven of us exited the elevator and the Secret Service escorted us to his suite. We entered the living room to find Pierre Salinger, Jack Kennedy's Press Secretary, puffing on his ever-present cigar while searching for some good music on the radio. Two other aides were also there just chatting.

There were snacks spread around the living room tables, and George Thomas, the President's loyal valet, immediately began serving us daiquiris from a silver tray. He was a terrific bartender and made the meanest daiquiri on the continent. George was always present and always invisible. His absolute loyalty to this President was clearly obvious. That was a common thread that ran through Kennedy's inner circle. Both men and women relished being around JFK and made that time comfortable and stimulating, or whatever the occasion deemed necessary.

A few minutes later, the door from one of the bedrooms opened and Jack Kennedy joined us following his meeting with Texas Governor John Connolly. He brightened the room with his smile and became our enthusiastic host. We had spirited discussions about the highlights of the day and the travels awaiting us. He loved hearing stories about the chaotic unplanned "happenings" on our press plane and what we heard people saying about him at airports or in the crowds where he spoke. He loved gossip period.

When it was time for everyone to leave, Jack took my elbow and asked if I would stay for a few extra minutes. It would have been much smarter if I had excused myself due to exhaustion, but I didn't suspect what was to follow. I had been alone in a room with him several times, including his bedroom in the White House. Never once was he inappropriate with me. Our mutual friend (and my boss), Senator George Smathers, was the wedge that had always kept me in the safe zone from this voraciously woman hungry man.

When he walked into his bedroom, I followed and sat down in a comfy easy chair and propped my shoeless feet on the edge of the bed.

"Pierre told me the Press Corps is really happy about the crew change on their charters and feels the cabin atmosphere is much more relaxed with the stewardesses you chose," JFK related.

Then he surprised me by saying, "You know you could be a real help to me by leaving Pan American before my next campaign to work with Pierre in the White House Press offices. You've built a good rapport with those fellows, and I need all the good press I can get during the next election."

"I would love that as a job! I've become quite fond of some of them, and Pierre is one of my favorite people. It might surprise him that I have tremendous typing speed! But Jack, even for a desk in the White House, I won't be an ornament or a plaything for you. I think you know that." I said. "If you mean a *serious* work job, then I'd love it."

"Perfect," he said as he leaned over and began shuffling some papers on the desk. Suddenly, he rose fully to his 6'1" frame, stepped measurably toward me and lifted me from the chair. The cadence in his voice turned seductive, and I felt incapacitated. We had never kissed excepting on the cheek and truthfully at this point, I was very curious. Slowly his lips brushed mine and then with more passion than I expected, he embraced me. This initial intimacy made me shiver. Presidential power and aura personified, I had always been in total control of myself around him, but this unbalanced me. His lips had intensity and warmth without exhibiting impatience.

I forgot for a moment that previously I thought he was *not* the most sensual man I had ever met. He would almost prove me wrong before his second kiss aroused feelings in me that also awakened my brain. I knew I had to curb this INSTANTLY.

I tried to pull away and said, "Jack, this can't go any further. This is totally my fault for staying longer, but I need to leave now! *Please* let me go."

But he became forceful, backing me onto the bed. What ensued was a wrestling match, and it became much too rough for me. In a moment like this, with bodies entwined, a force was flowing through us both. I suddenly knocked him sideways quite hard, and it threw him off balance and off the bed and into the wall. A terrible thud followed as his body hit next to the dresser. When I looked at him, he was grimacing in pain. I absolutely panicked! And unknown to me at the time, so did the Secret Service agents who were listening with devices on the other side of the bedroom wall.

"Jack, my God are you all right?" I jumped from the bed, dropped down beside him and asked, "Should I call for help? Please, PLEASE say something."

He said nothing during the longest moment of my life. Then with a deep laugh, he declared, "You *really are* something!"

After the next intake of breath he said, "Let's not mention this little episode to George, okay?"

With a smile of great relief, I told him that Senator George Smathers would be the last person I would tell. Had he succeeded in seducing me, I'm sure that my boss would have been the first to hear it from Jack's own lips. Gamesmanship had existed in their relationship for years, and was one reason JFK had been attentive to me since the first day I met him in 1959.

The next morning in the hotel's breakfast café, I shared a table with a few agents and learned that the previous night there had been a good deal of scurrying about and much indecision in the neighboring room of the Presidential Suite. The advance people secured and wired the President's rooms so the secret service agents could monitor his safety. They told me when they overheard the wrestling on the bed and then the loud thud against the wall, followed by silence and my panicking voice, they almost broke in to make sure the President was not seriously injured. One agent even said he wanted to help *me* before I so physically defended myself. Of course he didn't dare do so. The agents knew that I hadn't put myself in that position before, but since I had done so this particular night they had to let it play out. They were very relieved to hear Jack Kennedy's laugh, however, and figured everything was *okay*.

As time would tell, everything was *not* okay. I had hurt him more than we realized, and his back pain became extremely severe after that night. He never mentioned our wrestling match to me again, and only later did I learn the seriousness of his increased pain from other mutual friends.

At the time, I was unaware that I had been assigned a Secret Service code name. If you spend much time around a sitting President, the agents need code names for security and secrecy sake. I learned later that mine was "Mrs. Black." This became almost prophetic considering what came to pass on November 22, 1963.

"Death cancels everything but truth."

—MARK TWAIN

When the President returned to Washington, his pain was so great from our skirmish that night in El Paso, that his doctors had to design a stronger back brace for him. It resembled a corset with heavy cords that had to be tightened one by one until it held him as straight as a ramrod.

THIS is the brace he wore in the motorcade on November 22, in Dallas.

The writer James Reston, Jr. writes an interesting article on why the second bullet killed the President. He explained the details of the *corset* for the Houston Chronicle in 2004 in an article entitled, "JFK and the Corset that helped kill a President."

This journalist wrote, "But this simple device imparted a fate almost Mephistophelean in its' horror to the sequence of events in Dallas 41 years ago."

Sally Bedell Smith wrote a very well researched book entitled, "Grace and Power" that was released in March of 2005. She asked TIME Magazine's Hugh Sidey about a story that had been circulating for years. The exact details never accompanied the rumors.

Years after the assassination, I had confided the incident to Hugh, and below is an excerpt from her book, which comes closest to the truth.

"JFK had been suffering from a flare-up of painful back spasms that may have originated during his overnight stay at the Hotel Cortez in El Paso on June 6. Hugh Sidey later heard from a woman in the presidential entourage that Kennedy had hurt himself in an amorous skirmish with her. "He either came into her room or he asked her to his room," Sidey recalled. "They were sitting on the bed and he wanted to have sex. She wrenched to pull herself away, swung her arms, pushed him against the wall and he injured his back."

Ms. Bedell continued, *"On the evening of June 7, journalist Alistair Cooke watched for a full minute as Kennedy grabbed the arms of his chair to "force himself in a twisted, writhing motion to his feet" before two navy officers could help him to his quarters on the KITTY HAWK. In the White House several days later documentary filmmaker Robert Drew caught JFK "moving awkwardly and pushing his knuckles into his cheek, then pressing them into his teeth, as he rocked back and forth."*

Hugh Sidey represented Time Magazine in the White House Press, and I admired him more than anyone else. He was in every way a gentleman and a bright, humorous, sensitive man—the kind they grow in Iowa. He had known my story for years, but never disclosed my name, or the exact circumstances.

I received a long email from Hugh in April 2004 and an excerpt from it reads, *"Yes, Grace and Power is a good Kennedy book. Sally Bedell Smith spent about eight hours with me going over anything I could dredge out of my mind. She was after your story on the back brace, but that is our secret and so remains until you tell it."*

The Early Years

*"Writing a book is an adventure:
it begins as an amusement, then it
becomes a mistress, then a master
and finally a tyrant."*

—Sir Winston Churchill

My family history is hazy to me on my mother's side. Grandma Grace grew up in the same western Pennsylvania town where I was born. She was lucky enough to marry *above her station* in life. I never met my grandfather because he died much too young from pneumonia. I heard many stories about him from my mother, Jean, who adored him. She told me he became very successful in co-designing the open-hearth method of heating steel. She was born into a beautiful household on Lake Erie, with live in servants.

We didn't learn that my mother was adopted until she was about thirty-five. That revelation came about when my grandmother was so angry with her for marrying my stepfather several years earlier, that she spewed forth the news quite spitefully. Although she knew her brother William thirteen years her senior was adopted, Jean was shocked and terribly hurt. After talking to a few aunts and uncles and dredging up all we could from family during those years, we think we discovered the true story.

In Cleveland, my grandfather was rich and powerful enough to *get things done.* We know my grandmother checked into the local hospital, emerged with a baby girl and a birth certificate listing Grace and William Yost as her parents. Outsiders couldn't have known that my grandmother was infertile, but I knew in my years with her that she was one *cold fish* sexually speaking. They had a beautiful live in maid at that time, and we are pretty certain that she was the birthmother. Official documents were probably created to accommodate my grandfather's wish that he keep his own child.

After my grandfather died of pneumonia, my grandmother sold out her inherited half of the business patent to his partner. We could have had wonderful trust funds if she hadn't been so foolish. I suppose it seemed like a fortune to her at the time, but she still managed to blow through it at record speed.

"There was a star danced,
and under that was I born."
—WILLIAM SHAKESPEARE

I didn't think of Grandma as particularly attractive, but she did seem to have her way with men. Naval Captain Phillips came into her life soon after widowhood and they married. He had two daughters about my mother's age, and the three girls were bundled off to private schools. At one point they went to Virginia Intermont College where the rules were extremely strict for women. Smoking was a definite no-no on campus.

Mother related to me, "several of us would shut ourselves in a bathroom, light up a single cigarette, each take a puff, very quickly blow the smoke into the toilet and immediately flush! It wasn't exactly a Chesterfield moment, but we were scared to death of being caught."

Grandfather Phillips also succumbed to pneumonia within a few years. At least that gave my mother the opportunity to transfer up to Penn State, which was near Grandma's hometown, Tyrone, Pennsylvania. This university was coed and less strict on rules for women. She was thrilled until my grandmother, a published songwriter, insisted that she study music and, in particular, the piano.

"Mother, you know I hate playing the piano and I love mathematics. Why can't I major in what I find interesting? And you know math is my best subject, even if I am a girl!"

"Jean, you're accomplished on the piano and I simply won't allow you to simply drop it. I know what's best for you and what in the world would you do with a degree in mathematics?"

The control management from Grandma hit a wall this time. My mother became defiant and quit school after her sophomore year. What goes around comes around in many families, and ours was no exception. Mother married the son of an upholsterer and farmer back in Tyrone. My dad was a good-looking Tyrone Power (no pun intended) movie star type and I was lucky to get my deep brown eyes and dark brown hair from him.

Jean was pretty in an aristocratic, well-bred sort of way. She wasn't sexy looking, but had great legs. I was lucky again with those genes. Where I inherited my need for a double D bra is still a mystery in the family. There were lots of A's and B's until I came along. This inheritance did not make itself evident however until the summer before I entered college.

Dad was a little too good looking for the health of the marriage and too popular with the ladies in this very small (everyone knew what was happening with everyone else) town. He couldn't even be located to get home the morning of my arrival into this world.

That special morning my mother called out to hers, "Mother, water is gushing out of me, please come and help."

"Good Lord, Jean, get off that toilet and get into your bed immediately. I think your water has broken, and your child is about to come out! Are you having pains?"

"Yes, I'm in agony," she screamed as she got into bed.

Grandma called the doctor and he arrived shortly after I did!

Thank Heaven Gramma Phillips was with my mother when her water broke, or I might have landed on my head in a bathroom fixture similar to the one into which Jean blew her cigarette smoke while at college! For me that would have been quite an austere arrival to usher in my adventurous life.

> *"Life was so much easier*
> *when boys had cooties."*
> —SALLY ERICKSON CRAWFORD

My timing has always made living more interesting. Entering this world on Christmas Eve in 1936 has caused my birthday celebrations to be lost in the whirlwinds of the huge celebration the following day for Jesus' birth, or more special because that holiday of the year is so joyous. I often exclaim to my girlfriends, "Do you realize how incredibly lucky we are that we were born at this exact time in the history of our country?" Any date on my birth certificate that year would have been just fine with me.

My mother decided that emotionally she could no longer stay married to my philandering father. She and my grandmother moved me at the age of one to Miami, Florida, where Jean found a job in the auditing department at Sears and Roebuck.

After a year she was transferred to the Ft. Lauderdale store, and moved there. We certainly needed that thirteen-dollar weekly paycheck because my dad contributed nothing for our support, After she contacted the Army, they sent her $10 a week garnished from his wages. *Wow*, time to jive it up with all that extra money.

Lauderdale in the forties was more a town than a city. We didn't always lock our front doors or our parked cars. There was an actual *downtown* and malls had not yet been created. Sometimes I would hang out with my grandmother's friend, Charlie Gross, at the local Stock Exchange on Andrews Avenue. We watched the workers chalking in the latest price of each stock on a huge blackboard. It was so large they used ladders to reach the columns near the ceiling. I was quite fascinated watching all the erasing and re-recording of the prices as they were called out by another man from a telephone. It was a terribly primitive method. Thinking back, I wish I had asked Mr. Gross to buy me just ten Coca Cola shares of stock as a gift. He was quite well off financially and would have been delighted to do it. I certainly would be a richer woman today.

World War Two had begun, and one memory bounces out from that period for me. Everything was rationed, absolutely everything. I'll never know how mother saved enough for my bicycle with real rubber wheels, since rubber was so vital for the war effort. Her greatest coup, one that made me a big deal in our neighborhood, was in securing a huge box of Double Bubble Gum—each sugary lump—100 strong, wrapped and twisted in colorful paper. This box was more valuable than 100 gold nuggets to a kid, and I felt I now had real power on the street. Talk about rationing, I distributed packets ever so slowly to my friends to make my popularity last.

In those days, we lived at the 'Mary D' apartments, in a one bedroom on the second floor. The bells I remember most vividly from that time were from the Good Humor truck. It was hotter than Hades most of the year, so the Good Humor Man was heaven sent as far as all the children on my block were concerned.

As kids, ages didn't matter all that much under thirteen. We all climbed trees, built forts and loved playing in the rain together. I started early liking *cute* boys. Don Kimbro was a year older than me and lived a couple of houses away. I guess I must have become a pest to him, because late one day he yelled at me, "I'm going to flush your head down the toilet, and I'm not kidding."

In shock, I turned and ran faster than I ever had to our second floor apartment. I was sobbing uncontrollably by the time I reached my mother.

"I hate him—I just hate him," which is what all girls say when they find out that *special* boy doesn't like them.

My mother spoke with Donald's mother and that was the end of our *relationship*. We returned to being just playmates.

"Comfort zones are most often
expanded through discomfort."
—PETER MCWILLIAMS

We had *no* refrigeration then, which meant that we needed the ice truck. The ice man delivered a large square chunk of ice to us several times a week to keep our *icebox* cold. We could never have envisioned the fancy refrigerators of today, whose door windows spit out all the cubes you need when you touch a button. I think the worst of it then however, was trying to sleep through the 90 to 100 degree summer nights. In Florida, the humidity was unbearable and my sheets were always damp from my body when I awoke each morning for school. No one ever hears me talk about the *good old days* when it comes to human comfort and luxuries.

I remain forever grateful to Freon for making air conditioning possible in the overheated south. It didn't occur to most people then that creating comfortable living even during the dead heat of summers in the deep south, would also lead to the huge migration of northerners to Florida and to the southernmost states.

Project this population shift into politics. We all watched as the electoral vote expanded to Florida in particular. We had ten electoral votes in 1960 and after the 2010 census, our state tied New York's 28, making us both a powerful third behind California and Texas. It's quite fascinating really, when you can connect the dots from little "ole" Freon to Capitol Hill and the White House!

"A journey is best measured in
friends, rather than miles."
—TIM CAHILL

My grandparents on Dad's side in Warriors Mark were heart broken about my parents divorce. Mary and Charlie were good strong German stock, which is why I was Christened in the Lutheran Church. They really liked my mother and hated losing our geographical closeness to Tyrone when we moved to Miami.

With World War II well underway, my dad was scheduled to join his army unit abroad. He would be sent off to Europe where he stepped in a hole while walking guard duty around his base camp and broke his leg. Not much hope there for the Medal of Honor in our family.

Before he left the states, he wanted to see his only daughter. In 1943, my real *adventuress* travels began when I was put on a train in Ft. Lauderdale for Washington, D. C. with dozens of stops all along the east coast. I was only seven years old, and my mother dressed me properly, packed my little bag, pinned my purse strap to my coat and fastened a note for the "Traveler's Aid" in my purse. This was the name given to the people who looked out for unaccompanied minors in those days.

Can you imagine any loving mother today putting a sweet little seven-year-old girl on a train filled with hundreds of troops going off to war, or putting her on *any* train alone? You might now have to put your children on a non-stop airplane and then worry yourself sick until they arrive with family or camp officials to meet them. Mothers now have good reason to worry about sending their children to school for the day on a school bus. That's part of what I mean about being lucky enough to be born at the exact time in America that I was.

On that train, I was very lucky to have all those troops aboard. By the time the train left the station, they were homesick for their moms, girl-friends and little sisters. Many of them were too young to have wives. In our car, they all absolutely *adopted* me. I left with twelve dollars zipped inside my purse, and I departed the train in Washington with over twenty. The guys taught me how to play card games. Certainly they let me win more often than I should have! They also bought my meals and all the candy and treats that were being sold up and down the aisles. I knew *then* that I would always love traveling!

It was exciting to go to Washington because it meant I would visit my father for the first time since the divorce. Gib and my "grandpap" met me at the beautiful Union Station. We took another train to Tyrone. It was to be the first of my happy summers spent on the farm.

"The secret of genius is to carry the spirit
of the child into old age, which means
never loosing your enthusiasm."

—ALDOUS HUXLEY

I wasn't born into a life of privilege, even though my mother's thirteen dollar paycheck bought much more in those days than now. I didn't realize there were ski resorts in America then and summer camps for the children of the rich. For me, summers always meant going north to the farm in Warriors Mark, a few miles outside Tyrone and seventeen miles from Penn State.

My grandparents lived with their oldest daughter, Aunt Grace, and her family next to a beautiful old stone Methodist Church in the green Allegheny Mountains. There were only two roads. It was very easy to find the center of town because that's where they crossed. Aunt Grace had two boys and two girls, I fit exactly into the regimented two year separation slot for each, between the youngest son and their youngest daughter.

I loved being with my cousins because at home I had no brothers or sisters to share that *it's us against the world* attitude that siblings develop. Since Grandpa lived with those *wild Indians*, as he sometimes referred to my cousins on the farm, he unfairly favored his Florida granddaughter, at least while I was there. I'm sure in his heart he loved us equally. But my oldest cousin Jack, whom I absolutely adored, referred to me sarcastically at every opportunity as, "The Princess."

"Well, the Princess is here again. What has the Princess been up to this past winter? Would the Princess like more corn on the cob?" I would giggle and hope he secretly thought I was worth having around.

All my summer memories of the farm are good. I learned to milk a cow, call in the pigs and scoot the eggs out from under the chickens. When you accidentally stepped in a fresh pile of cow droppings, it was called *"cutting your foot."* When the piles got hard, we used them as base markers for our softball games. It was a real working farm and I still miss the rich flavor of the beefsteak tomatoes and the tender corn that grew tall and sweet by the Fourth of July.

One year, we got into big time trouble when my cousin Eugene got several of us behind the barn and taught us how to roll the dried corn silk in toilet paper, so we could smoke it.

Wow, did those suckers go up with an initial flame. The fact that smoking cigarettes never became a habit that I acquired probably dates back to that very day. Thank you Eugene! Evidently I inhaled because I got really sick. I threw up several times and was sent straight to bed, which meant missing the best cookout party of the summer that July Fourth.

The only rich folks I knew in Warriors Mark were the Harpsters. They owned several businesses and the only soda shoppe in town. It was a real treat when their kids would invite us over to Harpster's Manor for the day. They had hundreds of acres, and their children were allowed to drive a couple of old Model T Fords around the dirt roads on their property. That was quite exciting for us as 11 and 12 year olds.

One day we were invited to stay over for dinner, and in the middle of what I thought was a delicious chicken dish, one of my cousins asked what meat we were eating. When old man Harpster told us it was rattle snake, I couldn't touch another bite. But, in their family—he'd shoot 'em—the cook cooked 'em—and they all ate 'em! I personally never stayed over there for supper again.

> *"If you can't get rid of the skeleton in*
> *your closet, you'd best teach it to dance."*
> —George Bernard Shaw

Years following the depression in the thirties and forties, the future *Venice of America* named Ft. Lauderdale, looked more like swamp land on all the islands bordering the Intercoastal. Unique arched cement bridges connected them to Las Olas Boulevard, but they were not drivable due to so much deterioration. Alligators lived there in large numbers. It would have been difficult to envision the multimillion-dollar mansions that now stand majestically side-by-side surrounded by manicured landscaping. I imagine some of those alligators ended up as shoes and handbags that accessorized the women who eventually moved there.

Mother married my stepfather Henry Grady Bowden from Georgia when I was in the fifth grade. My grandmother hated him from the word go, and I was soon to learn that her vibes were not off tune. "Gig" was pretty good to me, but he was an alcoholic with a mean disposition after downing a fifth of anything. He was really a son of a bitch to my mother because she earned more money than him and his ego was fragile.

This was my first exposure to an alcoholic. A Jekyll changing into Mr. Hyde doesn't have to make him a murderer. Booze creates such an alteration in the personality that Hyde can appear as many difficult characters.

Gig found the most incredible places to hide liquor bottles outside. His workshop was in the garage, separate from our house. Some nights he made as many as ten trips out there for tools, until he staggered to bed. I wondered who he thought he was fooling as Mother and I would simply roll our eyes.

He wrecked a couple of our cars. I was lucky he never abused me unless you count the times I had no choice but to watch him assault my mother. One evening he actually chased her around the house with a large butcher knife. I don't think he would ever have used it as he really was just a cowardly bully bathed in liquor. All of us are *coming from somewhere* and my stories pale compared to so many others I've heard. However, I have to admit, it soured my outlook on marriage as a happy state of being.

While in the army, Gig had gone into Normandy on one of the first waves during the Second World War, and almost everyone in his division was killed except him. He was so shell shocked, however, they had to hospitalize him for a couple of years. That is where he learned to crochet and knit to quiet his nerves. As I mentioned earlier, there was little hope for the Medal of Honor in my family.

> *"Young people are in a condition like*
> *permanent intoxication, because youth*
> *is sweet and they are growing."*
>
> —ARISTOTLE

When the economy did come back and air conditioning became available for a decade, Lauderdale became the fastest growing city in the United States. Today there is no downtown as such, but they have a cleverly developed River Walk and Performance Center. Buying good real estate price wise, is almost impossible excepting by the rich. Shopping malls had not yet been conceived when I was in high school, and we had no idea of the luxury that would be available to a generation following ours. We hung out at the bowling alley and especially at the beach. What you can't imagine, you can't miss having.

Our house was really tiny and my bedroom was about ten feet by eight. I learned to be a neat freak because if I tossed a sweater on my bed, the whole space looked a mess! As an only child with a working mother, I created my own little dream world in which I lived in luxury. As a child, I used my paper dolls to attend fancy balls and travel all over the world in couture fashions. When I became a young woman however, I lived a far more glamorous life than my paper dolls. As a teenager I read movie magazines with passion, not ever desiring to become an actress, but concentrating on the handsome movie actors. In my case, those daydreams would evolve into reality as well.

Dating was so simple in the early fifties. There were so many rules that girls didn't have the dilemma of making too many decisions on their own. There was a special area at the beach a little north of the main hotels, where simply everyone parked. Most of us double dated because we were lucky that one out of two boys could get his dad's car for the evening. We still necked and made out pretty innocently with four to six in a car. There weren't many secrets in the romance department. It was certainly the Sandra Dee era, at least for many of us.

Our proms were in the gymnasium with the large round mirrored sphere hanging high above us. It tossed sparkling light specks in all the spaces around us while I swooned over Nat King Cole songs during the slow dances. For me at that time, Frank Sinatra was further down on my favorite singers' list.

Even if my parents had not been very strict with me, I would never have questioned a rule, authority, or statement from *anyone taller* than me. My youth was quite insulated. Current events weren't discussed much at the dinner table. My parents didn't discuss social issues, or politics at home, but stood in line for hours to vote, only to cancel out one another's choices year after year.

People of color were not even allowed to walk on the sidewalks downtown after dark and lived in a district apart from us. Those students went to Dillard High School. We were the Flying L's of Fort Lauderdale High. That was the *way it was,* and I didn't question it. I had no idea that when black people traveled in the south, they were unable to use public restrooms or eat at restaurants. I cannot even explain today how I could have been so oblivious to the realities of segregation and the terrible pain it caused so many. I should have walked with a white cane. I was so blind to what was happening around me.

On one occasion, my stepfather invited two well dressed black gentlemen to our house to discuss the sale of a small boat he owned and kept in the side yard. They sat on the porch, and he came inside to ask my mother to bring them some ice tea. She suddenly became rattled, but managed to fix the tea and serve them. After they left, all hell broke loose.

"Gig, why ever would you bring those men to our home with Layte and me here?"

"I didn't mean to upset you," he responded. "They just wanted to see the boat and I think they're going to buy it. I'm sorry. It won't happen again."

He left while mother was literally scouring the ice tea glasses. I'd never seen her show such prejudice. She was working herself into an absolute dither. Suddenly in a trembling rage, she flung open the cupboard door to the trash bin and threw all three glasses into it—where they shattered into dozens of shards.

"The Hell with it," she said slamming the cupboard closed.

"Mother, what in the world are you thinking? They're people, just like us and they couldn't have been more polite!"

"Well, young lady, you just don't understand. They are *not* just like us and don't you forget that!"

I closed the door to my room and lay on my bed for a long time trying to figure out how this very loving woman, who had never even discussed black people with me, could fly into such an ugly frenzy. She *was* raised in the north, but she definitely had a terrible problem with prejudice.

In the future we would have several personal blowouts because I never accepted her strong feelings about the black race. I would intentionally describe how much I admired and liked "those" people who shared my adult life. "Deal with it," I would tell her. Today I would be more patient with her because I have come to understand it is where you are coming from that forms who you are, and a person has to work through that to have a fair outlook on so many things. Sadly, my mother wasn't able to overcome her prejudice.

"Intensity is so much more
becoming in the young."
—JOANNE WOODWARD

I loved my high school days. Of course as in most any school, there was the in crowd, and as a freshman, I wasn't in it. Luckily for me, one of the more popular boys took a liking to me in my sophomore year and suddenly I seemed to be accepted. Everyone referred to us as Mayhue's crowd. Susan Mayhue's father owned several large liquor stores around town and had enough money to host some rather special parties for us at the Coral Ridge Yacht Club.

As one of the *poorer* girls, I would never have been able to go to such dressy dances, or even see the inside of the Yacht Club, without invitations to these affairs. It seemed to me most girls were rich excepting me, Jeanne DeShields and Patti Murphy. Many others drove their own convertibles and lived in beautiful homes on one of the Intercoastal waterways. It was not a problem for me. Life was good. Life was very good.

Mother was a devoted Miami Hurricanes football fan in those days, and I evidently inherited that gene too. She and my stepfather took me to many of the Hurricane games. In high school, I tried out for the cheering squad, but didn't make it. I did manage to hurt my back, which was the beginning of a lifetime of spinal pain for me. The best consequence was that I learned to understand the game that helped me become Co-Sports Editor of our high school newspaper.

Athletes always appealed to me more than the other boys. I went from dating "Inky" on the football team to "Pinky" on the basketball team. My real crush all through high school, however, was Bill Huegele. He was our star basketball player and later received a scholarship to North Carolina. I would end up sitting home almost every New Year's Eve because I would wait and hope Bill would ask me out. Any date with him usually depended on whether Jeanne DeShields was available or not. Later in my life, when any of my stepchildren would talk to me about a *broken heart*, I would tell them my Huegele story.

By the time we were in college, he asked me to marry him during a summer vacation. The moral of this being, just because you can't have exactly what you want exactly when you want it, doesn't mean you won't have the opportunity in the future. I didn't mention that by then you would have probably grown into a different person and would want someone or something else you might not be able to have!

I had no idea then what an idyllic life we led during high school. Girls were girlfriends and not bitches to one another. We had slumber parties where we shared our secrets and planned out our lives together. The guys as a whole respected a *no* when it was said. Friendship and support of one another was always prevalent. The only future knowledge I wish we had known was the damage we were doing to our skin. We spent hundreds of hours on the beach without protecting ourselves. We worshipped the sun, and I couldn't count the painful burns we all acquired. That is the only damage I can recall from living our young lives in paradise.

Florida State University
1954–1958

*"To those of you who received
honors, awards and distinctions, I
say well done. And to the C students,
I say you too may one day be
President of the United States."*

—GEORGE W. BUSH

It was the fall of 1954 and Florida State University became my new world. Including graduate students, our total enrollment was about 6,000 that year. Absolutely *no* drinking was allowed on campus by any coed, a carry over from the days when it was Florida State College for Women. Ivy covered brick buildings on gently rolling hills was not the Florida I had always known. After living in Miami and Ft. Lauderdale, this looked like an Ivy League school to me, but the curriculum was hardly Harvard's.

Later, when people in the north learned where I got my degree, they asked if my major was underwater basket weaving. Thank you very much, but I "degreed" in journalism and marketing and upon graduation in 1958 was offered the grand sum of $40.00 a week to work for the Jacksonville, Florida paper. Thank you *not* so very much.

Dormitory life was fairly typical for a southern university in the mid fifties. No men were ever allowed past the reception area on the first floor. At five minutes before 10 pm on weeknights, the supervisor blinked the lights and blew a whistle. That meant you had five minutes to finish the goodnight with your date.

On weekends they really kicked back, and we could stay out until midnight. The forbidden raised the level of passion for me. That last kiss goodnight became quite intensified knowing the front door would lock—no matter which side of it I was on—one minute after the deadline. The fear factor of having to go to the Dean's office in order to seek readmission always trumped my passionate side.

Before I pledged Kappa Alpha Theta and lived in the sorority house, Barbara "Burke" Burkhardt, my high school friend, was my roommate in the dormitory. One night when we were talking about how friendly our campus was I asked, "Burke, do you think anyone in this school smokes marijuana?"

"Hell, no. The students are so clean cut, I'm surprised Ivory Soap doesn't film all their commercials here."

"This campus is absolutely perfect for a sexually repressed girl like me. I suppose most all the other females here are still virgins too." I said believing it.

"Well now wait a minute, Layte, I wouldn't go that far. Most of our crowd at home had really strict parents, but lots of these students are *from out of state* ya *know.*"

> *"My mother sent me to college not to*
> *get a good job, but to get a degree that*
> *would help me land a husband who was*
> *a higher class businessman!"*
>
> —LAYTE BOWDEN

By my sophomore year, I was wearing Ham Bisbee's ATO Fraternity pin. As number 81, he played end on the Seminole football squad, and I loved football players! He had very dark hair and thick eye lashes shading his burnt umber eyes. His laugh was always filled with honest amusement.

We were good together and spent most of our fun time as part of a "Big Eight" on campus along with my sorority sisters Nella Kelley, Jeani Kitchens and Caryl James, and their date mates, Ron Schomburger, Jim Webb and Bill Cullom. The Culloms and Schomburgers are still two of the happiest married couples I know, but Jeani and I married outside the pack.

Ham often complained, "Bowden, my legs are skinnier than yours!"

"True Bubba (as he was known then), but one thing I'm lucky to have is a good pair of legs. Look at it this way—you can slide right out of low tackles on the run with skinny legs like yours. That's a good thing for an end."

His roommate was "Buddy" Reynolds. Today better known as Burt, the actor.

And our Quarterback was Lee Corso, or today's Mr. ESPN on college campuses.

We drifted apart by my junior year, but always remained friends.

In 1948, when Florida State School for Women finally turned coed and morphed into Florida State University, we still had too many women for the amount of young men attending in 1954. But the guys we did have were cool to me, and I didn't have a problem finding an entertaining intelligent fellow to date.

> *Scientists have found the gene for*
> *shyness. They would have found it years*
> *ago, but it was hiding behind a couple of*
> *other genes."*
>
> —JONATHAN KATZ

Bob Crenshaw, however, was the epitome to me. I first saw him during my freshman orientation week while he was giving a speech at Westminster House. I had never seen any young man so handsome other than a movie star. His smile was contagious and his inconceivably perfect sky blue eyes would augment everything he said.

It was more than an instant secret crush, it was an unspoken obsession I tucked away in a deep chamber of my heart. He was an upper classman when I arrived and became Vice President of the Student Body and Captain of the football team. I felt I had little chance of attaining a simple lunch date with him. I learned if you dream it and believe it, it can happen. He dated one of my sorority sisters, so I did get to know him. Then early in my junior year, he asked me out. After graduating the year before, he joined the Air Force and was stationed at flight school nearby in Bainbridge, Georgia. It was an easy drive across the border from Tallahassee, and he and I could easily visit back and forth.

One weekend I drove up with my sorority sister Beverly Perkins, who was dating Jack Conley, a pilot friend of his. When we arrived, Bob was still flying at 20,000 feet. The guys in the control tower beside the landing field told us to come on up. Things were obviously much *looser* in those days at an air force training field. They thought it would be funny if I talked him down. The flight controller handed me the speaker, told me what to say, and I got on the earphones to do the job—much to Bob's surprise. When he jumped down from his T-33 trainer's wing, my heart made several of those flip flops it produces when you're excited. He was as handsome in his pilot jumpsuit as he ever was in a Seminole football uniform. His smile alone liquefied my emotions.

"Hey, you're pretty professional sounding over the horn. I think you ought to join up and handle the control tower. Your voice sounds much better than these guys," he yelled at me while slinging his helmet by its' strap.

"Ah yes, I'm pretty talented especially when being fed the technical terms by a pro!" I answered back.

He slipped his arms around me, dropping the helmet to the ground, and lifted me off the ground to kiss me. "I'm starving. Why do you always give me an appetite when I see you?"

He looked over his shoulder, "Hey, Beverly, as soon as Jack and I change, let's hit that restaurant we went to last weekend."

I was so innocent then, and this story might reveal how much so. Some weeks later, we spent a weekend with a married couple Bob knew in Miami. They went to bed early leaving us privacy in the living room. Since virginity had been pounded into my head, I could at least get high on necking. After one very passionate kiss he said, "I love you, Layte. We'd be so good together."

"And I think you have to be the most perfect man I've ever met."

"Sure that's me, Mr. Perfect."

He added, "I love this moment and I love you too." I suddenly had a transcendent moment that took me by surprise. Could I possibly be receiving a promise this wonderful for my future?

"Hey, why the tears?"

"Because, Bob, just two years ago, I would have thought this night absurdly impossible."

He kissed me so sweetly on top of my nose, and then walked with me down the hall to my room. Of course, we had separate bedrooms. The house was so terribly quiet, and I desperately needed to use the bathroom. I thought, "Oh my gosh, he'll hear me use the toilet."

This is before I learned to turn the water faucet full force to block any toilet flushing. Well, I just couldn't do it. How silly was it after sharing intimate necking that I went to bed with a full bladder and suffered, until exhaustion finally put me to sleep. That takes shy to a pathetic level. Sophistication of any sort for me would be achieved many moons in the future.

*"We're not here for a long time. We're
here for a good time!"*

—STEVE MORAN

My junior year, while Bob and I were seeing one another as often as the Air Force permitted, his ATO Fraternity sponsored me as their candidate for FSU's Homecoming Queen. It was much more a popularity vote than a beauty contest, although the five finalists were usually very pretty. I confess that it thrilled me when I won, especially after being only runner-up to my now sorority sister, Patti Murphy, in high school. At halftime of the Homecoming Game, I was crowned with a stunning pure white-feathered Indian headdress. White mink tails cascaded from the headband glittering with crystals, and the feathers floated down my back as the Seminole Queen.

My parents didn't drive up to Tallahassee for homecoming because there was a big football game scheduled for the Hurricanes in Miami. Their season tickets for 25 years were with the same group of people. When they arrived at the Orange Bowl and neared their seats, several friends called out, "Jean, what are you and Gig doing *here*? Why aren't you in Tallahassee tonight?"

Before mother had a chance to react, a couple of people pulled out the Miami Herald. On the front page, the headline over my picture read,"Hometown Girl Being Crowned Homecoming Queen at Florida State University Tonight."

"Well," Mother told me later, "I just sat down and cried through most of the game because we weren't with you. But sweetheart, it just never occurred to me that you would win."

I never told her how crippling that statement was to me for years. I wanted so much to please my mother. I couldn't escape the "mommy, mommy watch me" stage that most children pass through in a healthy manner.

This was the fifties, when girls thought being Queen of something or other was special. Whereas now when I return to my alma mater, the young women I talk with are studying to become a marine biologist, or how to climb high on a corporate ladder. My senior year when I won the "Miss FSU" beauty contest, it was very anticlimactic because it wasn't an honor I received from my fellow students on campus. I also thought several of the young women were much prettier than I. Mother was more pleased when I was elected to Who's Who in American Colleges and Universities than as some "Queen of the May."

Life was a happy merry go round at Florida State and the music was beautiful. The Village Vamps "tapped" me, and I joined the girls who dressed all in black and acted as official campus hostesses for every important school affair. It certainly saved me buying tickets for plays and other functions!

I ran for Senior Women's Judiciary with the main purpose of voting to keep girls *IN* school. It's hard to believe that a young woman could be expelled for taking one drink of her date's beer on campus, but it was a fact. I guess many people thought I was a goody two shoes however, because when I would enter a fraternity party, I would see beverage glasses shifting from the girls' to the guys' side of the table. I hated that, and even though I didn't drink, I wanted to blast out, "I'm on *YOUR* side ladies."

There were more rules for women at FSU than my parents had for me when I lived at home, and THAT is a really big statement. We couldn't even walk across campus in Bermuda shorts to an intramural event without wearing a raincoat over them! I finally realized that's probably why I own five raincoats today. They became the fashion anchor of my wardrobe.

I did have nice clothes since Mother and I had sewn most of them. We wouldn't have been able to afford nice outfits any other way. My roommate during my junior and senior years at the Theta Sorority `House was Nella Kelley from Daytona. Looking back, she and I were fairly different excepting for our very effervescent personalities around people.

She was laid back and cool about anything while I was uptight and a worrier over everything. When the alarm rang about 7 A.M., she would roll over and light a cigarette, then head for my closet to see what she might borrow to wear that day. It got to be a running joke when someone on campus would compliment me on how well I looked in Nella's dress. She was the same as a blood sister would be to me, and I loved sharing.

> *"Love is metaphysical gravity."*
> —R. B. FULLER

Just before I was to return to Tallahassee for my senior year, Bob was on leave and visiting with me in Ft. Lauderdale. In my mind, I knew we would marry after graduation. Cren was very confident that our future would be spent together as well. But still, he surprised me with his introspection. I *was* immature and still a bit of a butterfly regarding commitment. He recognized the depth of it more than I did. Because of my mother's painful marriage to my stepfather, this total commitment thing would be a thick wall for me to climb for years.

"Layte, I've given *us* a great deal of thought. I know how much you love your life on campus, and there's no way I can get back often enough to escort you to all the social events you want to enjoy your final year. Call me crazy, but I want you to feel free to date since I think that's what you need for now. I won't call five times a week, or even write letters. I love you enough and feel secure about the strength of our relationship to even say this. You and I will benefit by this after you graduate."

"At graduation, I'll come down, and we'll build our future from there. If you need to see me before that, call Caryl or Bill and tell them. By now my sorority sister was married to his best friend Bill Cullom.

"Bob, this is crazy. I love you and I don't want to date anyone else."

"I expected you to say that, but I know differently and so do you. It's a great time of your life and no other experience will be the same once you're out in the real world. We've both been blessed with our involvement at FSU, and you have such lust for life. Go back, be your vivacious self and live it to the fullest. I know you love me, and I'm confident I won't lose you."

I couldn't believe I actually had his approval to flap my wings, fly freely for the year, and he would still be mine after graduation. He went back to his life in the Air Force, and I returned to Florida State as the butterfly he knew I needed to be.

I was absolutely not in the least interested in meeting anyone special to date. I was young and didn't know the folly of thinking in absolutes. As if on queue, an irresistible young man convinced me to go out with him. Jim Magee was lithe, tall and sexy with a killer smile. I should have done more soul searching on the spot, but in truth, there was a magnetic attraction. I certainly had no intention of kissing him goodnight on our first date. He had no intention of letting me close the sorority front door without doing so.

"Tell me you're not considering shutting this door in my face," he said smiling.

"Jim, there's too much current going through here. You make me edgy and nervous."

"Good, lets add hungry and needy to those feelings."

Very possessively, he leaned down and enveloped me in his arms before I even realized I was lifting my face to his. I'd been kissed by some great kissers, but I felt a real passion propel though me. I was actually dizzy when I finally swayed away from him with barely enough coordination to back away from the electric currents between us.

"Jim, this was just transitory emotion on my part. I know you're aware Bob Crenshaw and I were a couple all last year and even though he wants me to feel free to date and totally enjoy my senior year, I honestly don't see anyone but him in my future. I need to be honest and you need to understand this. And, I'm also not one to fall in lust quickly, but thank you for the opportunity."

"It's okay, darlin', I can handle that. No guy in this school could compete with Crenshaw. But I think we had fun tonight and I'll use my mouth for talking only, if you'll go out with me again."

I smiled, but went into the Theta House without answering. Thirty minutes later, the phone in the booth on my end of the hall began ringing. Yes, phone "booth" with a telephone land line! It was Jim and we must have talked for over an hour. This would become a pattern for us. I don't know how attraction like this happens, but we know it just does— with no valid explanation.

I can't even say it started slowly, because we were together constantly before I knew what force whacked me. He was seductive and my drug of choice all year, but I did manage to keep my virginity intact. We drove to his home, or mine, during days off from school.

I couldn't have explained my emotions to Bob and didn't understand myself how I could feel so deeply about two men at the same time. Perhaps it was because they were so completely different. Bob was even tempered, and I don't remember him ever being angry about anything. He was an up mood optimistic guy in every way.

Jim was much more emotional and demonstrative. A flare of jealousy could sear the air between us in an instant. He could be moody, but I found that challenging. Bob had been the golden boy his entire life, whereas Magee spent his younger life on tougher streets.

Jim was a good athlete in several sports and a terrific water-skier. He used the banana skis in turning circles and taught me how to ride on his shoulders. One time while we were skiing near Tampa, I was standing in shallow water with both feet balancing on my slalom ski. While waiting for the boat to pull me up, I put my left foot down in the sand for a second and accidentally stepped on a Sting Ray. Instantly it jabbed its' poison barbed tail into my foot, and it felt as though I had been bitten by a Coral Snake.

I screamed bloody murder! Our friends rushed back, got me in the boat, and we sped toward the dock. By the time we reached the car, I was in agony. The throbbing pain had moved from my foot up into my thigh. I almost passed out by the time we reached the nearest doctor's office.

Mother answered the phone in Sears' auditing department, "Hello, Jean Bowden speaking."

"Mrs. Bowden this is Dr. Morton calling from Tampa. Your daughter is in my clinic now because she was hit by a stingray while water-skiing with friends. I need to ask you if she has been immunized for lock jaw."

"Oh, my God. Is she going to all right? I don't recall her ever needing a tetanus shot before now. Is she in pain?"

"Don't worry, she'll be fine, I'll go ahead and give her the shot. I've given her enough pain medication that she will be good to go once she sleeps it off," he told Mother.

"May I speak to her?"

The Doctor handed Jim the phone. "Mrs. Bowden, I'm really sorry if we scared you with this, but Layte's going to be okay. She's sort of out of it now, but I'll have her call you tomorrow as soon as she wakes up. I called my mother and she's going to watch over her."

Poor Jean, she would get gray hair much earlier than she deserved with me as a daughter. In fact, my life stressed her to the point that in her late 40's it turned a beautiful gleaming white. Women thought she dyed her hair.

When I awakened, I learned from Jim's mother that I slept almost thirty hours. It was fortunate we were staying at his home. She took good care of me, and I actually had the nerve to water-ski for years after that. Isn't it wonderful to be twenty years old and immortal? With most of us, the fears grow as we do. And then that wonderful day arrives so many years later, if we're fortunate, when that arcane feeling burrows inside us once again, and we feel safe enough to dispel the fear of dying.

"Love, like death, changes everything."
—Elisabeth Patton

My life was perfect on this campus, but I was still quite insecure about my own capabilities. As graduation approached and I faced an unknown future with great trepidation, Bob became more and more a part of my thoughts. I felt that a future with him would give me a faithful, loving husband and a secure charmed life, probably in Miami. I had no confidence that I could make a living by supporting myself. My mother sent me to college to "get a degree, so that I'd be more appealing to a successful man as his wife!" Mother adored Bob as did I, and I also felt he represented a happy future.

There was a looming problem for me however. Could I just walk away from Jim, even though I told him at the start what my plans were for my future? It was foolish and naïve of me, or perhaps my arrogance of self to think I could control my heart's direction. I was not only young and foolish, but clueless as to the games our hearts play with our minds.

I never had the chance to go over to Bill and Caryl's to ask them to have Bob call me so that we could have a heart to heart talk. I was in the library studying for final exams when my Theta sister Beverly walked in and asked me to join her outside for a minute.

"Layte, I don't know how to tell you this to make it any easier. We just heard that Bob crashed in his jet and was killed."

"Oh my God!" The convulsions began and I went into shock. She drove me to her house in Tallahassee, and her dear sweet mother plied me with hot tea. I didn't want to see or talk to anyone and was absolutely stricken. No one in my life whom I had ever loved had died, How could I possibly believe this perfectly perfect twenty-four year old was gone forever?

Bob's oxygen system in the T-33 failed, and it took three days to dig the cockpit out of the Florida soil.

Until this happened, I hadn't realized how *deeply* I thought he was the right choice for my future. I imagine part of my emotion was simply shock. I could not endure his funeral in Miami. But I know the Governor of Florida stood in the rain with the many people who witnessed his burial. I felt terrible guilt, selfish and self centered at not having spent the past year being with him when it was possible, and I didn't feel I even had the right to attend. I couldn't face his mother or his closest friends and family.

After the shock subsided, the sorrow pervaded my entire being. Losing someone I had loved left me with the numbness that only allowed me to sleepwalk during the long days of that interminable summer. The nights were spent awakening from wretched nightmares. Jim gave me space and unselfish support, understanding that I was being torn emotionally. He, along with almost everyone who had ever known Bob Crenshaw, realized he was a rarity when compared with the finest of young men. Bob was later honored with a sports center named for him on our campus, but more importantly for those who loved him, he was a special gift to us all while he was with us.

So, here I was at twenty-one, armed only with a bachelors degree in journalism with which I didn't know what the hell to do. Certainly after that big offer of $40 a week in Jacksonville, I knew I might well need other educational skills to survive. By the end of the summer however, life unfolded itself to me again without much effort on my part.

Washington: The Pentagon

*"We are not retreating—we are
advancing in another direction."*

—General Douglas MacArthur

During the summer following graduation, my sorority sister Beverly Perkins, took a teaching job at a school in Virginia and another friend from FSU, found a job in Washington. They invited me to come up and share an apartment with them in nearby Arlington, Virginia, where they rented a comfortable two bedroom totally furnished sublet on Columbia Pike. I joined them that fall and found a job close by in the Pentagon with the Army Corps of Engineers. My secretarial work would be in Research and Development for the Signal Corps. I can only describe this period of my life as transitional. It wasn't exciting, but it helped in adjusting my psyche to deal with the mentality of governmental Washington.

My necessary expenses for an entire month were $95.00. That was a good thing because I was only going to earn $3,750 a year to start! But, with bus fare at forty cents round trip and lunch for under a dollar, you could make do. I still sewed most of my own clothes, and I needed that skill because my social life would soon be exhausting.

I started my new job with trepidation on September 28, 1958. I was hired to be the only secretary for five officers with a Colonel as the highest rank. If you are over fifty, you can appreciate the drudgery of secretarial office duties in those days. Computers were nonexistent, typewriters only! Every letter I typed had seven, *yes* seven, copies on various colors of thinner tissue-like paper. I was a good typist, but I still made mistakes and every time I made one, I had to take my little eraser and remove that error on every single copy, while blocking each sheet to keep the carbon paper from smudging the piece behind it. The dread of *that* exercise almost kept me from breathing while tapping the keys.

As if that wasn't frustrating enough, the Colonel would sign whatever I had just typed and sent me out to find the six or seven offices to get concurrence initials on what ever their copy color was. At the DOD, concurrence was the name of the game. I realized that way no *one* person could be blamed when something went wrong with a decision!

For a young woman who loved and grew up in the Florida sunshine, the Pentagon was a dungeon. You had to work for someone important to have an office on the outer ring or the inner ring with window exposure to that precious Vitamin D. It was, however, like a self-contained town. There were restaurants, shops and medical clinics located through out. A police squad and fire department were also on the Pentagon campus.

Thank heaven I only worked there for three months that fall, because the bus dropped me off inside the lower tunnel every Monday morning before daylight and picked me up after sunset every weekday. If it didn't rain on the weekend, I was blessed to enjoy the sun on Saturday and Sunday.

Every time a staff member from any Congressman's office, or certainly a Senator's aide called and said the words, "The Man wants such and such," our entire office went into a frenzy trying to get the requested information ASAP. The Congress dispensed the money and the Pentagon jumped through hoops to please the members. Capitol Hill was hallowed ground to the military establishment.

My spirits were lifted enormously when Jim Magee, in his senior year, came up from FSU to visit in October, as did Duby Ausley who was dating Beverly. We had a terrific time together just like most first time tourists probably do when they visit the Nation's Capitol. It is such a beautiful city even though we have to give credit to Frenchman Pierre Charles L'Enfant for the architectural layout.

The major avenues spread out octopus style from circles, each of which contains a monument to someone famous, usually mounted on a horse. A good map was a necessity. The streets and avenues were named after states, or simply a letter of the alphabet, even before you threw in names like Temperance Ave. I lost my way in this city more often than in Karachi, or New Delhi years later.

"Garfinkels" was *the* store for elegant fashion shopping, but of course we could only gaze at those beautiful displays. The museums and monuments we could afford, but it would take months to explore them properly.

So many young people then, as now, found Georgetown the most fun area in the city to party. The pubs along Wisconsin seemed to have been there forever and had a great sense of permanence attached to them. The Universities were in this area of the District, so the party places were to continue growing. The cobblestones remain in the street even today to remind us all that we are just passing through this historic city.

We were young and energetic, and any place at night that offered inexpensive food, dancing and singing was for us. We certainly didn't have any money to spare. Club 823, the Georgetown Club, or the Brickskeller and the chic Gaslight Club (when someone else was paying, or when we put our dollars together) were the ones we frequented.

Since my graduation, Jim had been so supportive, but more than that, we had a strong physical attraction. He could drive my temperature just short of point Celsius. I know I had loved Bob. He was so comfortable in his own skin *and* comforting to be with, but now I was living in such a *big world* away from school with such fragile confidence in myself.

I didn't realize how much I missed Jim's arms around me until I felt them again. Like a lap puppy, I couldn't keep my paws off. I had to feel his warmth and his breathing on my face. He would kiss me slowly, deeply and with so much passion, I felt like a plastic doll finally coming to life. It had been a long summer and fall until now, and we could make love magic with only our lips. He was blessed with a good mind and body, but overly blessed with a sexuality women would find irresistible during his lifetime.

"Change is the law of life. And those who
look only to the past or present are sure
to miss the future."

—JOHN F. KENNEDY

As fate would have it, our roommate Loretta Lewis knew Scotty Peek. He was a dynamic young man from Jacksonville, who was the Administrative Assistant to Senator George Smathers of Florida. Scotty's wife Lillian was in the hospital giving birth to one of their six children when Loretta invited him for dinner at our apartment. I was running a temperature, blowing a very red nose and had adorned my neck with a smelly mustard wrap for the evening meal. I looked simply stunning. No matter, meeting Scotty Peek that night would turn my small world into a large universe of fascinating experiences yet unimagined for my future.

This man was and is one of the most incredible people I have ever known. He could have been elected a Florida Senator one day, but he never had ambition for himself.

He seemed absolutely satisfied to do the best possible job, not only for Senator Smathers, but for anyone important or unimportant who asked a favor of him.

Scotty's running mate and pal on the Hill at that time was the omnipotent Bobby Baker, who as the top aid to LBJ, then the Majority Leader in the Senate, held the authority to set up many "deals." Today more people are well educated as to how the Congress works. Vote trades were and are an everyday occurrence. The public at that time saw only the outcome as the bickering and bargaining was mainly behind closed doors.

Peek was the first human I had met who actually worked on Capitol Hill. I certainly knew how exalted it was from my service in the five-sided military dungeon. That night at dinner, I asked Scotty a hundred questions about The Hill and told him, "I would just love to work there some day." He scanned my lovely presence in the flu costume and said, "Uh, if anything opens up, I'll let you know."

Surprise! A couple of weeks later he called to say that the Senator's receptionist was leaving to get married and asked if I would be interested in having her job. I cannot believe that with this wonderful opportunity, I had the nerve to tell him that my Pentagon boss had promised me Christmas week off. I asked if it would be all right if I accepted his job offer, and then started after the holidays. Cheeky really, as I did not have a master's degree in anything, so this *was* at least a good opening for me.

To my relief Scotty said, "That works for us as the Congress pretty much shuts down during the holidays anyway. You can start on January 5th."

To the guys in Army brown, I wrote a heartfelt thank you for all their kindnesses, along with my resignation. Yes! I was off to Ft. Lauderdale for the Christmas of '58, which was to offer another unexpected surprise.

*"Why should I get married and make
one man miserable when I can stay
single and make hundreds miserable?"*

—CARRIE SNOW

Jim came down to Lauderdale to be with me for the holidays, but I was preoccupied with visions of my future life on "The Hill." On Christmas Eve he presented me with a totally unexpected gift. I opened the box and he slipped the engagement ring on my finger with confidence. Looking back, it seemed the natural progression for our relationship. We were fascinated by one another on our first date, and he had been a rock for me even through my depression over Bob Crenshaw's death. Emotionally I knew I wasn't ready for a life commitment with one person at this point. Jim, with one semester left to graduate, didn't realize it, but he wasn't either.

We did love one another, and I could not dream of hurting him. That would come later.

To tell you that I was surprised, is nothing compared to the shock my mother experienced. She liked Jim very much, but didn't want me to marry while I was so young and hadn't reached the maturity to figure out who I was as a woman yet. She quit college before she graduated, married too young and that ended very badly. Knowing that both of us needed to experience more of life before making such a serious commitment, she also felt her daughter, certainly true, was still "flighty."

However, since I couldn't possibly say no to Jim, I went back to Washington in January engaged to Mr. Jim Magee of Tampa.

Capitol Hill, 1959

"Ah,—Capital Hill—Washington . . .
I've arrived at the one place where egos
are more confused and infused than
anywhere else in the world other than
Hollywood. If only I had studied to be
a psychiatrist. . . . . who knows what
I could have accomplished there."

—LAYTE BOWDEN

January 5, 1959 was a very cold day in Washington, but I didn't feel the icy wind. I was so excited to be entering the Russell Senate Office Building for the first time. It was the gateway to my new life, this impressive door at the top of beautiful marble steps on the corner of Constitution Avenue. This was most definitely a propitious time to work on "The Hill."

As my high heels clicked on the polished marble floors in the hallway from the elevator, I found my new boss' office. Senator George Smathers of Florida occupied an inside corner suite of offices on the third floor just around the corner from Senator John F. Kennedy. On the outside of the hall corner was Vice President Richard Nixon's office, which he used when attending his duties on The Hill. The Vice President presides over the Senate Chamber as its' President, and votes to break a tie should there become one on any bill. It was then and is now, a rare occasion. Of course you know that, but I had it to learn.

You can see by the aforementioned names that I landed at the most exciting corner of any office building on Capitol Hill that year. George Armisted Smathers was six feet four inches tall with deep marine blue eyes, very dark hair and he dressed elegantly. He was smooth, confident and wore his smile with ease. Simply put, he totally delighted the eyes of women. Even men were taken by his appearance of perfection and confidence. I was impressed and nervous by his imposing presence from the moment we met. As naïve as I was, I could recognize noblesse oblige in a person when I saw it.

My beginning job as his receptionist required more hours and much more skill with people than had been required of me at the Pentagon, but certainly it was more stimulating. I was outgoing, friendly and could talk conversationally with a tree. It took little extra effort to greet cheerfully any stranger who appeared at my desk.

> *"If you cannot be famous . . .*
> *at least be colorful!"*
> —ASTRONAUT CHARLES "PETE" CONRAD

I never knew who might walk through the Senator's reception office door. Anyone from Bob Hope to Billy Graham might pop in to say hello to George, their golfing buddy. Smathers was chairman of the Aviation Committee and in May of 1959, seven attractive young men appeared and told me they had an appointment with the Senator.

One advised me they were the Astronauts from Project Mercury with NASA. Yes, I saw them on the schedule, but I had only a vague idea what an astronaut was at that point. The word astronaut, along with many others pertaining to NASA, was just earning its place in our dictionaries. An entirely new vocabulary evolved along with the evolution of space exploration. It would be more than two years until the Russian, Yuri Gagarin, pierced the outer layer of our atmosphere into outer space. Less than a month later, Mercury's Alan Shepard accomplished the same fete.

As their courtesy visit progressed, I learned much more about this program and NASA. In case I could ever get on TV's Jeopardy, I memorized their names. They were Carpenter, Cooper, Glenn, Grissom, Shepard, Slayton, and Schirra. I remember them as the Magnificent Seven and brave as any pioneers in our history. It was dense of me not to request a picture with them, as it would be personally invaluable to me today. I have to settle for the honor and good fortune of having met and talked with these American heroes.

Millions of Americans stopped whatever they were doing on May 5, 1961 to watch television as Shepard's rocket penetrated the ozone layer. Alan was alone physically in the capsule that day, but he carried with him the prayers and hopes of an entire nation. Americans didn't like losing the race to be first, especially to our archenemy Russia, so the success of this mission was very important.

Sadly, Gus Grissom of the original seven was killed on a later Apollo 1 mission. His space capsule burned before leaving the launching pad at Cape Canaveral. He had been the second man in a suborbital launching of the "Liberty Bell 7" and later co-piloted an orbital flight on the Gemini 3 program. His contribution and the sacrifice of his life exemplified to me "The American Spirit" that makes this country unique in all of history.

Those who loved him must have truly missed his sense of humor. He had endeared himself to me when we met and I asked him if Gus was his real first name.

He said, "Wouldn't you make it yours, if your mother had named you Virgil?"

I countered with; "Do you think 'Gus' would actually suit me?"

John Kennedy made the space program a priority during his Presidency. We were neck and neck in that race with the Russians, and he was determined we would pull ahead. This *was*, after all, the Twentieth Century, America's Century, and we surpassed them in the technological field throughout the Cold War.

> *"It is the duty of the Patriot to protect his*
> *country from its government."*
>
> —THOMAS PAYNE

When I first saw Capitol Hill, it was awe-inspiring. From a distance, it appeared a mountain of white marble and granite. During its' two centuries of growth, it has evolved into a city within a city. Towering 288 feet above the front east plaza, is the Capitol Dome's iconic Freedom Statue. Few people realize it is the classic form of a *woman* cloaked in robes, with an eagle helmet relating to native Americans. She is a formidable lady, weighing 15,000 pounds of bronze and standing over 19 feet tall! I found this ironic in that our congress was ruled entirely by men until 1917 when Jeannette Rankin of Montana was elected to the sixty-fifth

House of Representatives. It would take until 1948 for Margaret Chase Smith of Maine to be elected to the Senate.

Not long after I started working on the Hill, the New Senate Office Building (NSOB) named after Senator Everett Dirksen was completed. Senator Smathers chose, due to his seniority, to move across the street into a suite of brand new offices.

Thinking back, patronage certainly comes to mind because of all the costly mistakes that were made during the construction of this new building. Contracts were bestowed to personal friends, or contractors who were not the best qualified to provide the new additions on the Hill. Ah, patronage was not a new concept for the government.

There was a big to do when it was discovered that the tunnel blasted underground to tie into the existing tunnel from the original Senate Offices to the Capitol was off course. It had to be reconstructed at great cost to the taxpayers.

On a smaller, but somewhat humorous scale, the waiter's jackets for the beautiful new and private United States Senators' Restaurant arrived in bright red fabric with the initials USSR, in bold gold embossing! Despite all the incompetence, our officials in Congress continued going about the people's business.

Each day for me was exhilarating and chock full of activities involving my job. As just a member of a Congressional Staff, I found myself being invited to a dozen or more not terribly significant social events each month. It gave me the opportunity to meet glib and provocative people just as interested in the political intrigues as was I.

My love for good wines had not yet been discovered. Because I never drank in college, I perfected the art of pretending to enjoy Scotch whiskey. It seemed to be the sophisticated drink of choice by the more eminent personalities. Actually, I thought it tasted like medicine and sloshed club soda in mine. Heaven forbid I had been born English and had to drink the damn stuff "neat" to fit in.

> *"All the art of living is a fine mingling of*
> *letting go and holding on."*
>
> —HENRY ELLIS

After a few months, Senator Smathers began showing more personal interest in me. When I needed to take letters in for his signature, or consult him on some other matter, he would ask me questions about my life in the past and also about my engagement to Jim. He expressed his opinion that I was rather young to be engaged. I admit his interest titillated me, but knowing he was married, I kept my responses quite restricted.

In April of 1959, when Jim came up to Washington, we spent most of his visit discussing our relationship. The geographical distance between us now made it difficult to have a normal romance. I loved him, but in my heart I knew I wanted to be free in my new life. It was especially difficult because I was letting go of my last big emotional tie to FSU and the life there I loved. Telling him I would like to stop wearing my ring and date others until he was out of school was only half honest. I wanted freedom, but the knowledge that he would still be *out there* for me later. He was far from happy about it, but accepted my decision. No question that Smathers had used every opportunity to discourage me from staying committed by reminding me that I had so many opportunities opening all around me.

The Senator was elated when he saw I was no longer wearing my engagement ring. But clever of him, he also said that he did not want me moping around the office, and that I could use his private office phone anytime I wanted to call Jim in Tallahassee. Umm, how thoughtful he could be when things went his way.

Now, Smathers made it a point to keep me near him whenever possible during working hours. It was my first experience in having anyone in such a powerful position pay so much attention to me. It was exhilarating to be with him so often. We would go over to the Capitol building using the private Senators' elevators and on the Trolley Car that went to the Capitol building. Later, he even secured "Floor" privileges for me, available only to his top aides. This ID allows the assistants to stand in the back of the Senate Chamber during discussions or arguments and votes important to his or her boss.

Sometimes we stepped into Lyndon Johnson's private office near the Floor entrance and cloakroom. As the Majority Leader of the Senate, LBJ wielded the most power on Capitol Hill. His immense personality and forceful manner augmented his elected position. The cloakroom is where the Senators relaxed, or quietly tried to pressure one another into voting for a bill he or she was supporting. The ever present Bobby Baker, Johnson's top aide, was always nearby watching out for LBJ's interest.

Smathers also began inviting me over to the Capitol where he filmed his weekly television program for home consumption in Florida. In August of '59, while having lunch with Senator Jack Kennedy following a broadcast they made together, he asked me to bring him some papers from his desk. In the months to come, I would better understand the behavior of these long time friends regarding women. George definitely wanted Jack Kennedy to meet me and the papers were simply an excuse. He would have also liked Kennedy to assume there was an intimate relationship between us, which there was not. . . . as yet.

I had a passing acquaintance with JFK. Our offices were very close in the original office building, but I hadn't had a real conversation with him before this. His extreme Bostonian accent and rather clipped way of speaking wasn't particularly attractive to me, but his huge smile and laughter were very contagious and appealing. He looked directly at me when he spoke. I later learned he had the most amazing memory for minutiae. He would mention a tie a man was wearing when he had last seen him, and then make a point of mentioning it again when next they met. Who could resist his talent for personalizing when it involved them?

When I watched Smathers and JFK walk down a hall together, I was amazed by how well turned out George was in his custom suits and overall appearance in comparison to Kennedy whose suit with pants always appearing too short. Because of his serious illnesses, JFK did not have the good physique George had as he glided through life with good health.

> *"Ninety percent of the politicians give*
> *the other ten percent a bad name."*
> —HENRY KISSINGER

Along the way, good and not such good doors kept opening for me whether on The Hill, or elsewhere. I was soon asked to be a Capitol Hill pinup for the Hill newspaper, "Roll Call" with my friend and co-worker, Mary Alice Martin. This was not a good yes choice for me. We were photographed in sweaters and skirts, not bikinis, and in my mind the picture should not have caused the repercussions it did. However, after publication, Senators started backing me up in elevators, or chasing me around desks.

There was one classic case. A senator from New Jersey literally used his two arms outstretched to pin me against the back of an otherwise empty elevator in the new NSOB, (no pun intended) while propositioning me. Thank heaven the door opened, two people stepped in, and he quickly assumed a Senatorial pose against another wall. This man ended up in a Federal Prison convicted of bribery. That put at least one Senate predator far from the women who in those days could not call a nonexistent harassment hotline for help. This avenue for women and then even for men did not yet exist in the work place.

On this same subject, but a year or so later, I was assigned a very long proposal to type. Senator Smathers had a private office in the Capitol building due to his position as number three in the Senate Leadership. It was so busy around my own desk in the front office, I was told to do this work in that quiet space in the Capitol.

The distinguished Senator from Tennessee, Estes Kefauver had a private office, which shared the bathroom in the same suite. He proved to be a rogue. Indeed this man, who had been a presidential candidate twice in the fifties and shared the losing ticket to be Adlai Stevenson's Vice President in 1956, turned out to be quite a challenge for me.

I say challenge because as I mentioned, in those days, a young woman had to fend for herself. This southern gentleman Senator was "delighted to make 'mah' acquaintance" when first we met in that bath hallway. However, he began spending a great deal of time in that suite and most of it seemed to be while sitting on the edge of my, or rather, Senator Smathers' desk. I was extremely uncomfortable around him from the beginning. Then one day, he quite literally began chasing me around that desk *and* the office.

It was Tom and Jerry time, a total cartoon, excepting that he was a person of great power, and I was a nameless young thing. I escaped and then asked Smathers for the key to lock the inner door. I would use a bathroom elsewhere in the Capitol from that day on!

> "Any man who wants to be President is
> either an egomaniac or crazy."
>
> —DWIGHT DAVID EISENHOWER

Unfortunately after assuming office, too many elected representatives developed the attitude that their seats became their entitled thrones on Capitol Hill. Their self-importance caused memory lapses, in that they are in Congress to serve the needs of the people and not the self-interested corporations, which in turn benefited their own power. I wish half of them had the morals and heart that Scotty Peek managed to keep intact and take with him when he finally retired from his duties on The Hill.

I witnessed the arrival of so many newly elected enthusiastic Congressmen or first term Senators. I think in their hearts they believed they could change things and introduce bills for the good of the people. It wouldn't take very long to observe how they melted into the naughty cauldron that is the Congressional Body.

It wasn't just the lobbyists from the major businesses operating and donating money in their districts who made clear what they expected of their votes. It was the established system itself. If you didn't play by the stringent rules of the hierarchy, you could never expect an appointment to one of the more important committees and certainly NOT a chairmanship. You played the ballgame by the Majority Leader's rules, or you could expect to sit on the bench! The Senate operated in the same manner.

I don't mean to imply that every Senator was unprincipled because many were very respectful, like our next door neighbor in the NSOB, Senator Proxmire of Wisconsin. Also I very much liked Senator Hubert Humphrey from Minnesota, who had a wonderful sense of humor and seemed to me such a good and decent man.

A solid and brilliant Congressman was John Brademas whom I met when he judged the Cherry Blossom Princess contest for Florida. He was recognized as quite a catch as an unmarried Congressman (D) and ranked in those days as one of the top ten bachelors in America. He was the first full blooded Greek elected to congress and represented the Indiana District that was home to Notre Dame. I was flattered when he asked me out for dinner. His intelligence was somewhere in the stratosphere and if he hadn't been so darn charming, I would have been too intimidated to talk to him.... a first for me! In fact he was the first Rhodes Scholar I had ever met.

The next time he asked me for dinner, it was to be shared with President Eisenhower at the Sheraton Park Hotel. A large banquet was planned to honor the Postmaster General. Because he hailed from Indiana, *all* of the Congressional representatives were invited to sit on the Dais. Hoagie Carmichael, another Hoosier, sang his most memorable songs as entertainment. The words to the music he wrote were beautiful and make today's rapper stuff even more unintelligible for me. For those of us over 55, "Stardust" strikes a lovely note from Hoagie.

Before that night arrived, I was surprised when out of the blue a Secret Service agent called me to ask what color my gown would be and several other questions regarding my clearance. There was always a private reception for the people sitting on the Dais. I would have the opportunity to meet this larger than life man I had read so much about as a great general before he became our thirty-fourth President.

I look back on the early months I spent in Washington, as quite fascinating and exciting. However, the Eisenhower years were quiet compared to what the 1960 Presidential election would bring in transforming Washington.

John and I dated for a couple of years, but of course I went out with other young men, and he certainly had no problem in securing dates with the most comely young women in the city, as well as any city he visited. Aside from his intelligence, he had the most wonderful smile and an edgy sense of humor. He was extremely popular.

He was also a wonderful speaker and in demand by many organizations because of this talent mixed with his superior intellect. One day I heard he had been invited to speak at the dedication of a new college in Florida. Smathers told me John was deliberating about whether or not to accept their invitation and then advised me that Brademas would be more enthusiastic about making the trip if I accompanied him.

At first I thought the Senator was joking. He knew this Congressman and I were dating, and this could put me in an awkward situation. George was confident that I was not having an intimate relationship with John, or any of the young men I was seeing socially. By this time, I confided in George about any and everything in my life. I ended up flying to Tampa, Florida with John and enjoyed the trip.

As always, he made a great speech and with his background as a Rhodes Scholar, he impressed upon these students the importance of getting as much education as possible in order to be successful in life.

He did not go unnoticed by the coeds during our time on this campus. They were quite flirtatious with him. I retired fairly early to my own room, so I don't know just how much socializing continued on his part.

"I always wanted to be somebody,
but now I realize I should have
been more specific."

—LILLY TOMLIN

During the time John and I were dating, LIFE magazine had chosen me as one of four young women they were planning for a feature. The article was to be titled, "How Nice To Be a Pretty Girl and Work in Washington." It would appear in a 1962 March issue. Arthur Rickerby was the official photographer assigned to this story, and I could not believe the hundreds of pictures he took of each of us while we led our daily lives.

My pages were headlined "A Girl on the Go in a Big 'Man Town.'" In 1962 there were actually eight men to each woman in the District. No wonder we found it pretty easy to be booked up as they printed about me. Included in the article was a large picture taken at night of John and me with a beautiful backdrop of the lit Capitol Dome rising majestically behind us.

When Arthur told me that I had been chosen to be on the cover of the LIFE issue, I was surprised. They had decided to photograph me on the balcony of the House of Representatives while President Kennedy was delivering a speech to the Joint Congressional Body. I dressed in a bright red wool suit and stood in the upper balcony while in the background JFK was giving his address. It was humorous to me that JFK would be in *my* photo background.

The original date scheduled for the article had to be changed, because a timelier event involving the space program was more important. Then they chose the edition of March 23rd. Because a large corporation bought a double truck (fold out cover) as well as the first inside page, I was very deftly booted from the cover. No complaints. I was quite happy to be included in the article.

John told me years later that when he was at the White House for a Congressional affair soon after the *LIFE* issue was published, JFK took him aside and said teasingly, "I see you're getting a lot of publicity these days."

John replied, "Anything for our party, sir."

"Well, Layte's a very pretty girl," added the President.

I'm sure John was a Congressman Jack Kennedy liked and respected more than many. He was also a Harvard man and even served on the Education and Labor Committee as had JFK. He also knew John was a very loyal supporter of his.

> *"Every life is a march from innocence,*
> *through temptation, to virtue or vice."*
>
> —LYMAN ABBOTT

There was one tall blonde gentleman with lovely blue eyes, who came into our offices whenever it was necessary for him to be on Capitol Hill, but he was not there to see Smathers, he was visiting me. When I first met him, Joe Tydings had to have been the best looking U. S. Attorney in the country and served the State of Maryland until 1964 when he was elected to the U. S. Senate.

I never understood why he developed a little crush on me that lasted so many years and in fact, long past a couple of his marriages and well into mine. We never had an intimate relationship, but did love to dance, dine and talk. He sent me the most beautiful love letter I ever received hand written on his U. S. Senate stationary. This brought out his propensity for wearing his heart on his sleeve, as well as his trust in my discretion at the time.

"It would be no more ridiculous for me to have lived in a former life, than it has for me to show up in this one.

—ELEANOR ROOSEVELT
(ON REINCARNATION)

Early in 1961, I heard about a supposedly extraordinary psychic from Hungary who lived in Georgetown and was becoming quite well known for her gift in this field. My cynicism about people who hung out their shingle for this line of work was strong, but my friends talked me into making an appointment with her. When I finally called, I gave only my initials and no other information whatsoever about myself.

It was a foggy evening with the early winter darkness closing in when I arrived at her townhouse. An elderly gentleman admitted me, and I was ushered into her parlor. The light was dim and the room had a mystical aura about it without any music to help create that mood. Without a word, I sat down across from her at a small square table covered in an old world floral silk fabric with fringe.

She was an older woman, somberly dressed and had pinned her graying hair back in a bun. Her long gathered skirt and sweater were as plain and dark as the gloomy room, but she fit my impression of the way Hungarian peasant women dressed.

I was surprised there was no crystal ball on the table. But what did I know about the different methods used by these practitioners? She smiled warmly at me and asked if she might hold my hands and look at the open palms. After a short length of silence she began by asking me three questions.

"Who is Jean"?

I replied, "Why"?

"She is especially worried about you right now." Madam replied.

Next she asked, "Who is Bob, he is also worried, but he can't seem to reach you?" I felt flushed, but said nothing.

Lastly she said, "I see a bent ring. Have you broken an engagement recently"?

Whoa! In that moment she had my total attention. Jean was my mother, and she really was expressing her concern about my overly busy life and lack of sleep in every letter she wrote. Bob was my former beau Bob Crenshaw who had been killed barely three years earlier. As he was in another dimension, I imagine it *was* difficult to communicate with me. The bent ring was the broken engagement with Jim. They all knew I was taking another turn in the road ahead of me, and they had reason to be concerned.

How could she possibly know about three of the most important people in my life? I tried to open my mind to her. She had now gained my respect for her seeming ability to reach into an energy field I had no idea existed at that time.

Here I sat, a young lady whose total travel experience at this point was back and forth between Florida and Pennsylvania on the east coast and as far west as Tallahassee, who was about to hear that her life would be filled with an extraordinary amount of travel on a global scale. That bit of news sounded extraordinarily good to me!

She also predicted that I would be married only once and bear one son. My life was to be a long, exciting one, and I would share it with powerful and famous people. She commented about many friends in my life by name. For example, I didn't think Emma was a common name, but we worked together. I felt at this point she was truly prescient. It would take me several decades to realize that in my case, she did indeed tap into the energy of the universe regarding my future. Everything has been *exactly* as she said it would be for me.

I'm bravely outing myself because most people think psychics are ridiculous, but then they didn't have a session as amazingly accurate with Madame from Budapest. I could never wrap my head around predicting the future when it hadn't happened yet. I accept the concept today after reading and seeking all the information I could digest on the energy out there and also that there are those who have the gift of tapping into it.

Stephen Hawking's "A Brief History of Time" for the layman was fascinating and, of course, over my head. But according to him, "in the great All There Is out there," the past, present and future are all happening at the same time. On this planet we live our lives by the calendar and clock, understanding only a three dimensional world.

We only have a five sensory brain to work with . . . yet we know animals have extrasensory perceptions and know when an earthquake is about to happen. Many years later I spent ten years reading books on quantum physics and mechanics and remain fascinated by the theories of what is possible for us. Since I've never been able to keep my own little life organized, it makes sense only to me that I would try to unravel the great mysteries of the universe. It's all about the particles . . . right, Dr. Planck?"

> *"Fantasy is a necessary ingredient*
> *in living; it's a way of looking at life*
> *through the wrong end of a telescope."*
>
> —PETER ZARLENGA

I was leading a double life now. One was public and the other very private, and I will get to the private one soon. One of my favorite escorts was General Godfrey McHugh who was the Air Force aide to President Kennedy in the White House. He had escorted Jackie to functions years earlier and was "a most perfect gentleman."

Every evening we spent together was at an interesting function. The National Symphony Concerts we attended were my introduction into the world of fine music and stimulated my senses carrying me into beautiful states of dreaming.

Godfrey hosted a dinner one night at the Private "F Street Club" in honor of former President Harry Truman. As I was Godfrey's date, I was seated near the ex-President, who by then was in his eighties. I have always treasured that experience because he had been a childhood hero of mine and seemed such a regular man to hold the highest office in the land. His values, decency and respect for the office and the people in this country makes the men who followed him almost qualify as outlaws, with the exception of perhaps President Reagan.

He was thrust into a situation where he alone had to make the final decision to drop the Atomic bombs over Hiroshima and Nagasaki. We read that in doing so, he probably saved more lives in the total war than were lost in the bombings, but at such a cost. His heart had to weigh heavily in his body every day following that tragedy. He bore no scars we could see, but surely was carrying them inside until he died.

The French Ambassador and Madame Hervé Alphand were very close friends of Godfrey's, and I accompanied him to a couple of marvelous dinner parties at their embassy. The "best" parties were determined by who the assigned Ambassador was to his country's embassy in Washington. While the Alphands served, the French Embassy earned that reputation.

One evening became totally crazy. Godfrey and I stayed on after all the other guests had gone. We drank even more champagne with our hosts. The four of us became quite silly drunks and ended up taking off our shoes and jumping up and down on the furniture while competing to see who could retain the most champagne in their flutes. It was totally ridiculous because of their station in life, but privately we are all simply homo sapiens doing our thing. Some of us easily let our silly side emerge when we are with like-minded friends. Of course publicly, the Alphands were the epitome of graciousness.

I must say that I never once saw or even heard of anyone who did drugs during my years in Washington. It was before that culture got a strangle hold on our society. Alcohol was most everyone's drug of choice and allowed you to make a fool of yourself legally. Another big occasion for me was the Maiden Return Voyage of the SS France from a Pier in New York City. The Alphands, Hugh and I flew up together and spent a glorious time partying through out the grand halls of her "Ladyship." We spent the night onboard and departed in time for the ship to be readied for the paying passengers who were sailing to France that day. I had my own stateroom, as Godfrey remained the perfect gentleman through out our friendship and only ever kissed me good night at my door. He never married so perhaps after squiring Jackie, no woman ever measured up to his dream mate.

Godfrey might have been the original reason I became addicted to Dom Perignon. Champagne remained my first spirit choice until a special friend uncorked a bottle of Chateau Lafite Rothchild Private Reserve for me. This brings to mind the song "Those Were the Days" by composer Gene Raskin. "Those were the days my friend. I thought they'd never end. . . . those were the days, those were the days."

> "I discovered I always have choices and
> sometimes it's only a choice of attitude."
> —JUDITH M. KNOWLTON

I suppose after the *LIFE* article and my Capitol Hill Pin Up pictures were circulated in Washington, I was one of the go to young women for the press in D. C. When they needed a publicity picture it was requested that I pose at one or another local event.

I have run across articles, or pictures to remind me, or most of these occasions would be completely forgotten.

In one, I look as though I have been planted in the middle of hundreds of azalea bushes for the opening of the Azalea Show at the Botanical Gardens. In another, I am presenting Vice President Nixon with a large bouquet of flowers, with Congressman Paul Rogers on behalf of the "Pom Pom" growers in Paul's Palm Beach, Florida district. And in another, I am pinning a flower on Speaker McCormick's suit lapel and aiming toward a few more Congressmen in line. 'Really important duties here!

I was selected as "Miss Emmy" for Washington. D. C. The television coverage then triangled between Los Angeles, D. C. and New York. I sewed my own formal to wear that night with an intricate corseted lining, which was a bigger deal than my duties on stage. What was I thinking to participate in such a mindless roll? The truth was I wasn't thinking. Life just happened to me. I let it.

I am selfishly grateful that I had a couple of years living in oblivion to what was an unpleasant reality outside my personal world. I was unaware that terrible events were soon to consume our society. It was not in me to march, or publicly show my anger over injustices. I was surrounded by politics, but I was not a political animal myself. In truth, I enjoyed being a girl and lived with my fifties values. I did not resent that I was then nothing more than an objectified female.

The second feminism wave for women's rights hit the main stream in 1963 with Betty Freidan's book, "The Feminine Mystic." I read it and agreed with all the arguments she made on behalf of women, but I wouldn't become an activist in this movement. My mother raised me to "be nice honey, or everyone won't like you." My God, how crippling is that for advice? An ill-tempered taxi driver could destroy my equilibrium for an entire day.

I marveled that a truly beautiful young female like Gloria Steinman marched at the head of every parade with the other brave women actually putting their reputations on the line for me and the young gals who would follow. I was and remain in awe of them.

Senator George Smathers

*"Will you walk into my parlor?" said
the Spider to the Fly." 'Tis the prettiest
parlor that ever you did spy. . . ."*

—MARY HOWITT

My boss on Capitol Hill was born with a silver spoon in his mouth as the saying goes. But many men who are do not accomplish much with their lives. Not so with George Armisted Smathers, who was New Jersey bred and Florida reared. He was intelligent, tall, good looking. He had that elegant personal style that is borne of your genes.

Descended from political royalty as he was, it was inherent for him to see his future in public service. His uncle was a U. S. Senator and his dad was a Federal Judge, so a hint of the red, white and blue carpet was certainly present in his future. In print he was often described as polished and dashing and referred to as Gorgeous George. So not much wonder that I was quite in awe of him. I was only twenty-three and undernourished when it came to sophistication, but I could recognize noblesse oblige in him.

I admit that I was used to men of many ages flirting with me, but his style was so suave, I can't pinpoint the actual day I realized he had a personal interest in me outside my typing ability and affability with people visiting his offices. He was very friendly and pleasant from the first day I met him, and it was such a smooth transition to more intimate conversations that I didn't find it at all uncomfortable.

One afternoon when he offered me a lift home, we stopped at a red light, and he pointed to a svelte young brunette standing on the corner and said, "That's Pamela Turnure, Senator Kennedy's favorite of the moment." Pam had classical good looks, but she wore very little make up and I thought she looked quite pale. She could be very glamorous, but she seemed to play down her beauty.

Whatever her background and schooling was, she looked very northeastern upper crust to me in her well-cut suit. It was the first time George had personally referred to Kennedy as a player. I had seen her several times in our office hallways, but admittedly was surprised by this personal reference. In his Senatorial days, Jack Kennedy drove around the city in a convertible with either blonde or brunette hair blowing in the wind on the other side of the front seat. He was not an international figure of note before his presidency so it created only local gossip.

On one occasion, I was invited to dine with Senator Smathers' whole family at their home. While his sons John and Bruce attended St. Albans School, I would type term papers for them at their father's request, and I think it was their idea to invite me.

At this point, there was nothing unseemly between George and myself, or I would not have accepted the invitation even though it would have been impolite.

Mrs. Smathers was extremely nice during the evening, and I was honored to be their guest. She was a well-educated and intelligent woman, but must have known after sixteen years or so of marriage that her husband was not exactly faithful. George later told me that she hated politics and their marriage finally had turned into a union of convenience. According to him, she agreed to keep up appearances until after his next election and then seek a divorce. That does not at all excuse the fact that in the near future, George and I would be morally very guilty. She was every bit a lady and deserved better.

> *"Money can't buy happiness, but it*
> *can buy a yacht big enough to*
> *pull upright beside it."*
>
> —DAVID LEE ROTH

In late 1959, George invited me to join him and several of his personal friends for a dinner party aboard a yacht, "The Natamor" which was usually docked on the Potomac River conveniently near Capitol Hill. Morris Forgash owned her and used this vessel for lobbying purposes with members of Congress. Mr. Forgash was the man who innovated the method of piggy backing trailer trucks on flat bed train cars for long distance travel. He became very wealthy. The boat was available to the legislators who could be most helpful to advance his business interests. Any time George wanted to borrow her for an occasion, it seems she was always available.

I arrived at seven P.M. and was helped aboard by Alex who had formerly been a proper English butler, but was now the steward on The Natamor. I was enchanted by him immediately and in the next few years would be totally spoiled by his attentive service to me each time I cruised on this lovely yacht.

Smathers had invited a few trusted staffers and personal friends aboard this night. It was a casual fun party on calm waters, and I think one of George's better ideas of courting me. I didn't envision the wildly amusing parties yet to come in my future. More than once I would have had too much Champagne and try to navigate my way down the circular stairwell to use a bathroom only to slide down on my bottom as we hit a wave. Alex never acknowledged that anything was amiss as a guest would, after a few drinks, take to the deck. He would calmly lift you up and steer you in the right direction. He was one busy fellow on the nights the winds stirred large frothy waves buffeting us about and making personal navigation quite difficult.

> *"Payola on Capitol Hill . . . shh . . .*
> *we never speak of it."*
> —ANONYMOUS COMMITTEE CHAIRMAN

Payola for some of us on the Senator's staff included more than boat rides. Mr. Forgash, who owned "The Natamor," had an assistant deliver two very large elegant boxes to our offices one afternoon. One was for Mary Alice Martin also in our front office and one for me.

When we opened them, I simply gasped, "My gosh Mary Alice do you believe this?"

She was gaping at a silky satin negligee and matching peignoir covered with incredible French ecru lace, as was I. Mine was a soft aqua and hers also pastel in a salmon shade. Every inch was hand stitched couture and boasted Paris labels from a chic shop on the Rue St. Honoré.

MA laughed and said, "Where in the world does he imagine we could wear these?"

I jibed, "Yes, he forgot to give us a mansion where we could swirl around. My God, Scarlet O'Hara would have killed for these."

We both tried to return them, but Mr. Forgash wouldn't hear of it. I don't know about Mary Alice, but mine remained in the box for years. I admit that a couple of times when I ran across it in a corner of my closet, I would put it on in front of the mirror and sing, "I feel pretty, oh so pretty, I feel pretty and witty and bright. And I pity any girl who isn't me tonight." . . . One of my favorite songs in "West Side Story."

Lobbyists work on charming the secretaries, as they are the gate keepers for powerful bosses.

> *"A kiss is a lovely trick, designed by nature, to stop words when speech becomes superfluous."*
>
> —INGRID BERGMAN

The day finally arrived when George made his first overt move. He suggested that we have dinner that evening at a condo one of his friend's owned, but rarely used. I accepted with trepidation, as I knew it was wrong, but I was quite smitten at this point. The evening of our assignation arrived. Leaving work I attempted to hail a taxi at the corner of our Senate office building. It was always difficult to grab a cab at that hour of the day, but as I did so, an elderly lady asked me if she could share it.

"Where are you going," she asked, and I must have turned a shade of red when I told her, "2500 Q Street in Georgetown."

"Wonderful, I'm going that way, and I can be dropped off first," she said.

Why did I feel compelled to tell her the *exact address*, instead of just saying Georgetown? The time had come for me to start fibbing—little white lies at least! Little Miss gotta tell the truth girl needs to toughen up. Obviously I was more immature than my chronological age compared to young women at the beginning of the twenty first century.

I can remember that the wind was stronger than usual early that evening and must be whispering to everyone that I was going to meet my boss for an illicit dinner, in a condo building that probably had Den of Iniquity carved on its' stone façade. It is incredible what guilt can do to your mind. What sort of situation was I getting myself into anyway?

As my friend Jenny said to me years too late, *"Treat your mind like a bad neighborhood. Never go in there alone for very long."*

When I arrived at 2500 Q Street, I saw that this complex was absolutely enormous.

This made me feel a little better. Surely no doorman could keep track of everyone entering and leaving. George had given me a key because I was to arrive first. When I entered the condo, I was impressed by the soft aqua glow emanating from the living room. Almost everything was in shades of sea aqua, which I loved. It expressed a quiet good taste and was surely created by a professional decorator.

George arrived within a few minutes with the New York strip steaks we would sear on the stovetop. The bar was well stocked, and I noticed several bottles of George's favorite scotch. After we mixed our drinks he asked me what I thought of the place. I told him I barely had time to shed my jacket by the time he came through the door, but would like to look around. When he showed me the bedroom it was also lovely and done in monochromatic salmon tones. This brunette said, "I've always thought blondes looked much better in salmon shades of pink than brunettes."

He laughed and we proceeded to have a couple of drinks and cook our dinner. In time, I would wonder if this man ever varied his menu. Every meal we shared consisted of New York strips, a baked potato and a salad. There was a wonderful little butcher shop in Georgetown. I began buying meat there and also picking up the groceries for our dinners.

He would always smile when I laid the change on the kitchen counter down to the last penny from the money he gave me for the purchases. Often he would give me a hundred dollar bill, just to test me I think. That was a lot of money then. I would never have considered keeping a penny, even years into our relationship. It was a little ritual I followed to assuage my guilt regarding the larger picture.

During our first private dinner, we must have talked for almost three hours, and he never mentioned taking our discussions into the bedroom. I don't know if he was afraid of being rebuffed after my blonde comment, or felt it was smarter to take more time with me. We never ran out of subjects to talk about and heaven knows there was plenty of Capitol Hill gossip for us. He understood my off beat sense of humor, and I made him laugh often. In turn he became my best friend, confidant, father figure, and protective shield on The Hill. The powerful male predators were plentiful there.

One evening after a dinner in Georgetown, he drove us over to Burning Tree, which was his favorite golf course in the country. It was located in Bethesda, Maryland and most of the golfing politicians played there. Twilight was approaching when we arrived, and he asked me to walk to the 17th hole with him.

The last thrust of light still flowed up from the western horizon, and in that glow we approached the flag. We stood framed by meticulously cared for greenery. He looked at me with an expression of unsuppressed pleasure. This is where George first kissed me, seriously kissed me. Then he held me in his arms for many minutes and I thought to myself, *Layte you have never felt this safe in your entire life.* The sun's glow was gone now, but not my own.

> *"The best date movies give you*
> *something to talk about. A movie that is*
> *a downer is a great way to find out more*
> *about someone."*
>
> —HENRY ADAMS

I am certain that more than a few staff members in the Senator's offices knew about our mutual attraction after a few months of my arrival. We would even play hooky once in awhile, and I would sneak out of the office so we could go to an afternoon movie.

The first one we saw was a shocker for this guileless gal from Florida. It was a film by Roger Vadim, "Les Liaisons Dangereuses," with French subtitles. For the mainstream movie going public in the 60's, I would say it was a bit over the top. I think this was the first film for gorgeous Catherine Deneuve who was having an off screen romance with Vadim. On the screen it was the ménage a trois from hell. Few movies ever depressed me more.

Skipping ahead to the 1970's for just a moment, I want to say that voyeurism has never been my thing. Three movies in '72 convinced me I would probably never be comfortable watching. It seemed as though "Deep Throat" was the big vice film simply everyone was talking about. It was scandalous enough that people would drive to another zip code to watch so neighbors would not see them in their local theater. I thought it was squalid.

At least "Behind the Green Door" had fashion glamor in it. The real kicker for me was "Last Tango in Paris" starring Marlon Brando. I was astounded as my clock must lack the toc. I was mesmerized however, by the way Director Bertolucci manipulated the mind games between Brando and Maria Schneider throughout their sexual encounters. The explicit intimacy left me feeling as if they had depicted every position in the Kama Sutra. Not that I did more than glance through that publication of course.

"I can resist anything but temptation."

—OSCAR WILDE

It is said that timing in life is so important and I agree. George and I went to Miami a few weeks later and stayed with one of George's closest friends, Bebe Rebozo. Colorful has many definitions, and it is a word that fit Bebe. He was totally delightful and comfortable to be with. He was not the tall, blue eyed handsome type like George, but once you knew him, his charming Latin style would sweep a lady off her feet. I should not have been surprised to learn that he started out as a steward for Pan American Airlines because he had that *personality thing* really going for him.

At this juncture, he was a successful banker and a very close friend of both Smathers and Vice President Richard Nixon. George had introduced him to Nixon for a deep sea fishing trip during Nixon's first visit to Key Biscayne in Miami. They remained friends for 44 years and traveled the world together. As Bebe was a bachelor, I introduced him to my beautiful friend and top model, Eugenia McLin. After they began dating, she joined him and the Nixon's for a trip to the Far East. I know he would have very much liked to marry Eugenia, but she preferred a friendship.

Bebe was a terrific cook, and being Cuban, his specialty was black beans with rice, pork, yucca and fried plantains. He also made potent Margaritas, which we all imbibed that evening from tall shapely glasses with the customary umbrellas. It's the tropical way of course and with the palm trees scattered around Bebe's man made beach behind his house facing Biscayne Bay, it was very appropriate. The umbrellas also helped me keep count of the number of drinks I was downing. George, of course, drank scotch.

This was the first night George and I would make love and sleep together. Knowing we were sharing a bedroom here, I can tell you I had one hell of a stack of umbrellas by the end of the dinner party. George seemed very happy the next morning. But I had one mean hangover and honestly couldn't describe our first time together if I wanted to do so. Since I hardly remembered even going to bed I can say it certainly relieved any apprehension I felt. There was no excuse for my immoral behavior and can only say that at this point I was totally enamored by him.

George had affairs before meeting me, including a European ballet dancer. At times I felt we were sharing a confessional of sorts. There seemed to be no area of his past he was reticent about telling me. Since he and Jack Kennedy had roamed many cities together long before I knew him, I was very intimidated that he was very sophisticated in the sexual arena. I needn't have been as he was a very conventional lover and always considerate of my body and my pleasure.

He wasn't shy, but I learned in the future he would not be the most exciting lover I encountered in my life. We would never have one of those movie moments where we ripped each other's clothes off and threw ourselves onto the stairs for sexual congress! 'Rather a pity actually.

Our relationship became so intertwined that the trust was implicit between us. It isn't that complicated looking back. I was his adoring young fan, fascinated with his charisma and power, and he was rather like a Peacock feeling as though he had the total attention of one of the prettier peahens on the hill, Capitol Hill that is.

1960 Democratic
National Convention

*"I'm not a member of any organized
political party, I'm a Democrat!"*

—WILL ROGERS

I was thrilled to be going to California with the Senator and his top aides, especially since I had never been west of Ohio. And I certainly had never attended a national political convention. We departed Washington in an F27, the "F" designating Fairchild (not fighter) that was on loan from the Davis brothers, AD and JE. They were close friends of Smathers and owned the Wynn-Dixie grocery chain.

The wings of this twin Rolls turbo-prop were connected above the fuselage, which gave me a clear panoramic view of the country below and my first personal sights of the west. This was the executive cabin designed with twenty luxury seats that swiveled and reclined for total comfort, (Of course terribly outdated compared to the designer personal jets today). Dressed casually in slacks, I gazed out the large window at the beauty of the land beneath me and day dreamed of one day exploring much more of the world.

We made a quick stop at a rather desolate airport in Lubbock, Texas to refuel and then flew to Las Vegas where we would overnight before continuing to LA. The Senator was welcomed by the owner of the Tropicana Hotel. It was the newest and most luxurious at that time. Compared to today (2013), Vegas was in its' teen years!

My first sight of this resort was the fountain shooting water 60 feet into the sky. The entrance was welcoming with luxuriously colored mosaic designs that guided us into a rich mahogany registration area. Smathers was given a lavish suite. We all had rooms nearby. Mirrors were everywhere reflecting little old ladies pulling the one armed bandits twenty-four hours a day. Almost everyone smoked in those days, and the air was rancid to me as a nonsmoker. I would practically gag in a crowded elevator with smoke wafting about in such a small space.

In 1943, Betty Grable married bandleader Harry James here, and famous celebrities have chosen Vegas to get married ever since. Elvis Presley married Pricilla there in 1967. It inspired thousands of ceremonies. There is a chapel in practically every hotel and in all nearby areas, 1,179 strong, at my last count.

This was a community for adult entertainment then and not geared to the family as it is today. Anyone gambling could drink themselves into a stupor for free. Cocktail waitresses dressed in sexy, tight, low-necked tops and short mini skirts and gaudy jewelry circled every table keeping the gamblers high to encourage their gambling activities.

Our only night there, we dined in an enormous tiered theatre restaurant and watched the most extravagant show on the strip, "The Folies Bergère." This entire production was imported from Paris, and I have never seen a nightclub act more dazzling anywhere in the world. It opened Christmas Eve in 1957, and its' final show was in March of 2009, so a raft of people must have shared my opinion.

The next morning as we were departing the hotel for the airport, I stopped at the last slot machine nearest the front door and dropped a single silver dollar into the one armed bandit. CLANG—BONG, BANG, buzzers started going off! I hit a $300 jackpot with that sweet coin. Large heavy silver currency was spilling out over me and onto the floor!

Actual sterling silver dollars were used to gamble in those days not chips. If only I could have looked into the future, I wouldn't have spent, or traded in all but seven of those coins. Recently I ran across them in the back of one of my jewelry drawers and for the heck of it, checked on the Internet to see what they might be worth. One of the Morgans from the 1800's is worth a thousand dollars today. The others, although worth much more than their face value, were not minted in the right city or year to be really valuable.

I departed with a very heavy bag provided by the casino and vowed that one day I would return. What happened *with me* in Vegas *didn't stay* in Vegas!

Continuing on to Los Angeles, we all wanted to fly up to view the Grand Canyon on the way, but I never expected that we would fly down into it. That sheer gigantic divide in the earth was mind boggling to see up close and personal. Today I believe it's against the law for a private craft to fly down through it, but a licensed National Park helicopter can be chartered.

Not much later we were looking down on the City of Angels and then the rooftops that sprawled on into the hills all the way to the very edge of the Pacific Ocean.

After driving into the city from the LA airport, we arrived at the Biltmore Hotel, which was to be the nerve center for some of the cloak room talks and secret maneuvering that inevitably accompanied political conventions. We checked into this rather sedate hotel with grey brown hallways and rooms decorated with no imagination regarding cheerfulness. I suppose I expected more of a tropical palm tree feel which embellished our southern Florida hotels.

We arrived a couple of days before the actual convention was to formally begin. There was much to do since Senator Smathers was nominated as Florida's "Favorite Son." A convention floor demonstration would be held in his honor. He had no legitimate chance to secure enough convention votes for the Presidential nomination, but he had Florida's votes to award his favorite candidate and the outside possibility of being named the vice presidential candidate on the ticket.

> *"Turn on to politics . . .*
> *or politics will turn on you."*
>
> —RALPH NADER

It was still not certain that Jack Kennedy would obtain the party's nomination by the time we arrived in LA. To his party's leaders he needed to prove he was capable of winning the presidency, as the first Catholic ever to run. Unlike today, not all states participated in primary voting run offs. In fact, if you wanted to vote in Florida, you could only do so as a registered Democrat. JFK won the seven primary states he entered, including a must win in West Virginia, an almost totally Protestant state. He was the youngest man at age forty-three, to ever campaign and win the presidency.

Would he have reached this pinnacle so early in his life without the money, power and political ambition of his father?—probably not. But he certainly had all of the personal attributes. He was an authentic war hero, had movie star looks, publicly and privately he displayed a genuine interest in people and had proven his mettle by managing to survive numerous surgeries on his broken body that might well have done in a lesser man. He had also served Massachusetts as Congressman and Senator for fourteen years.

He won on the first roll call of the states. But before that vote took place, his brother Bobby, who served as his hard hitting Campaign Manager, had his work cut out for him at this convention.

"If the world were a logical place,
men would ride side saddle."

—RITA MAE BROWN

When Kennedy and his huge entourage first arrived at the Biltmore, the entire block was paved with people cheering him. Departing the car, he immediately averted the path that had been cleared for him by a line of LA's finest and headed straight into the crowd. This was his style. His tan was golden and his smile was magical. He wanted to touch the people and let the people touch him. This pattern of behavior would continue to be a nightmare for the Secret Service who needed to bodily protect him. On July ninth, the convention delegates gathered in the Los Angeles Sports Arena. In 1960, only ten states participated in a Democratic Primary voting day and the Republicans held primaries in only six! So you can see that when the States' delegates arrived at the actual conventions, *these* were the assemblies that would determine the next candidate for their parties. 1960 is the last year in which there was real drama and anticipation at a Democratic Convention. In the following years, the candidates were selected beforehand through the primaries. There is no longer the same suspense or jockeying in back hallways to trade votes or promises, for backing a certain candidate.

When I first arrived at the Los Angeles Arena, the very air was electrifying, and the delegates themselves were highly charged. They were ebullient and excited to be an *important element* in this process of selecting the new President of the United States. The biggest battle for votes was between Senator Kennedy and the Senate Majority Leader, Lyndon Johnson. JFK entered this race with the majority of votes promised to him, but nothing was carved in stone. Bobby Kennedy and their strongest supporters had to work tirelessly to keep those votes in his column and not let the powerful and much more experienced Texan maneuver any promised votes.

My responsibilities at the convention were collecting the messages and mail from the lobby each morning and getting them to the senator, or the proper staff assistant. I also ran all the errands (a so called "gofer" on Hollywood sets) and helped as a liaison between the Senator and the Florida Delegation. Since my duties were light, I was able to stay in the background, but near Smathers during some interesting discussions between him and JFK or others.

In 1959, I was young and idealistic about almost everything and had never dreamed that not only would I be at a convention, but actually sit in smoke filled rooms, or be in private elevators and listen in on secret conversations between a president elect and my boss. I think I knew Lyndon Johnson would be offered the vice presidency before he knew for certain. This was the most controversial decision JFK had to make. He would be lambasted by the Democratic northern liberals, but realized there was no way he could win the South without Johnson.

Jack Kennedy would have enjoyed sharing the traveling and campaigning with his friend George Smathers on the ticket, but he needed Texas, and he needed Johnson to get that state. Bobby Kennedys' acrimonious attitude toward LBJ was known to Washington insiders, but this was Jack Kennedy's decision, and he was pragmatic enough to know it was the right one. None of the Kennedy family could stand Johnson. Johnson's feelings were the same toward this elite family with the exception of Jackie.

But Senator Kennedy's concern was not friendships. Johnson, who sat out the primaries, threw his hat in the ring upon arriving at this convention. Bobby Kennedy worked the floor to ensure JFK would not lose any of his pledged votes. Meanwhile Bobby Baker, the gregarious administrative assistant to Senate Majority Leader Johnson, was working equally hard behind the scenes with promises and commitments to secure enough votes to capture the nomination for LBJ. That was an uphill battle, and it certainly established even more rancor between RFK and the most powerful leader on Capitol Hill.

There was another problem for Bobby as well. He had made personal promises to the most liberal wing of the party. That most certainly did not include naming LBJ to the vice presidency.

On the morning following Kennedy's confirmation as the presidential candidate, JFK quietly visited Johnson in his suite. When Bobby learned of this, he was furious with his brother. It put him in an extremely awkward situation with the liberals to whom he felt they owed much of their success. It is believed that on his own, he later visited Johnson in his hotel room to explain that there was absolutely no way they could give him the second spot on the ticket. This caused quite a ruckus in the Johnson camp. Later in the day however, Jack Kennedy called LBJ and confirmed that he was indeed sticking to his promise to name him. He supposedly said that Bobby had been out of the loop that morning and didn't realize Jack himself had already made that promise.

The general public would not believe the conspiratorial huddles being held in every private spot imaginable by the insiders. That included two or more men stepping into a bathroom off a room where several more gathered. In public view, it appeared that every decision was *purring* along.

Before that final backroom drama unfolded, it was business as usual on the convention floor. Bedlam seemed to be taking place, rather than organized meetings. The state delegates were chanting or cheering in small groups and making all the noise possible, including reverting to a jig or two if only to get the TV camera's attention. Of course it was filmed in black and white without the computerized special effects of today. But, it was the first political convention ever televised and Americans loved it.

As Senator Smathers was Florida's Favorite Son, our delegation paraded through the aisles to celebrate his candidacy when our turn came. My family and friends back home saw me on TV waving my Smathers' banner while dancing down the aisle with the Florida delegates. His private life with me however was totally unknown to the public.

The final night's celebration for the youngest and certainly the most glamorous presidential candidate in our history went on for many hours after John Fitzgerald Kennedy finished his inspiring speech.

"For the harsh facts of the matter are that we stand on this frontier at a turning-point in history. We must prove all over again whether this nation— or any nation so conceived—can long endure—whether our society—with its freedom of choice, its breadth of opportunity, its range of alternatives— can compete with the single-minded advance of the Communist system. Can a nation organized and governed such as ours endure? That is the real question. Have we the nerve and the will? Can we carry through in an age where we will witness not only new breakthroughs in weapons of destruction—but also a race for mastery of the sky and the rain, the ocean and the tides, the far side of space and the inside of men's minds? Are we up to the task—are we equal to the challenge? Are we willing to match the Russian sacrifice of the present for the future—or must we sacrifice our future in order to enjoy the

present? That is the question of the New Frontier. That is the choice our nation must make—a choice that lies not merely between two men or two parties, but between the public interest and private comfort—between national greatness and national decline—between the fresh air of progress and the stale, dank atmosphere of "normalcy"—between determined dedication and creeping mediocrity. All mankind waits upon our decision. A whole world looks to see what we will do. We cannot fail their trust, we cannot fail to try." . . . It is amazing when I read back over these words how much it relates to the situation we are facing today by adding Al Qaeda, the Middle East, North Korea and Iran.

> *"If you ever injected truth into politics*
> *you would have no politics."*
>
> —WILL ROGERS

The convention had barely ended when Jack Kennedy's father departed. He began work at once behind closed doors in lining up support for his son and calling in all the favors he had earned. This Patriarch, former Ambassador Joseph P. Kennedy had made many enemies along the political path he chose and he was wise to work behind the main stage during the campaign.

When he was young, he was smart to put himself at President Franklin Roosevelt's beck and call. FDR appointed him as Chairman of the Federal Security and Exchange Commission and more importantly, as our first Roman Catholic Ambassador to Great Britain. It was said that this appointment actually served to move him out of the U. S. for a while!

His dreams were heavy with his own Presidential ambitions, but he became a staunch isolationist, which distanced him from President Franklin Roosevelt and our Nation's political outlook at that time. We could hardly stand by idly if Germany invaded England. Finally under pressure from Sir Winston Churchill and other conservatives, he was forced to resign. Ambassador Kennedy was also tainted because of all the rumors saying he made his fortune by bootlegging alcohol during the prohibition.

His personal history made it very important that in 1960 he indeed needed to work behind the scenes, but there he wielded great power and did not fail to use all of it. Mayor Daley was in his camp and even today it is strongly rumored that many of the Chicago ballet boxes from the 1960 election have never been located. Or one might say, "expunged from the Chicago River."

There were many people who would have labeled Joe "One tough son of a bitch" who didn't give a damn what anyone else thought of his position on anything. In my thoughts, Bobby Kennedy had a lot of his father in him. He was a black or white kind of guy. There was little grey on the color chart for him. You might need heaven's help if you made a real enemy of him. He seemed so intensely serious and the time would come when even I would experience a little of his ire. However, his loyalty to those who were in his camp was unquestioned, and he could be deeply emotional when a hardship befell anyone for whom he cared.

Jack was cut from a different bolt of cloth. There was nothing ambiguous about him, but he had a gentler touch with people with whom he might disagree. Most of all, it was his humor that set him apart. He was able to separate himself from the seriousness of life and enjoy the hell out of the moment. In truth, as gregarious as everyone saw him, he was very happy within an intimate group, or could at times be satiated snuggled up with a good book. He was a voracious reader, and his brain was a trap in retaining voluminous amounts of factual information. A course he took years earlier raised his reading capacity to 1,200 words per minute. This ability would serve him well as the campaigning began and he needed to digest hundreds of pages of information and facts for his speeches.

> *"Bullfighting is the only art in which*
> *the artist is in danger of death and in*
> *which the degree of brilliance in the*
> *performance is left to the fighter's honor."*
>
> —ERNEST HEMINGWAY

Following the '60 Convention, a couple of the Senator's assistants and I joined him for a few days of pleasure. We drove down to La Jolla for the night. I don't believe I had ever seen an entire town so meticulously landscaped. Every square foot looked as though it had been manicured by talented gardeners. But what struck me was the juxtaposition of very exotic palm trees lining streets that featured rock gardens with desert cactus plants. This was something I had never seen in Florida although it certainly had very sandy soil as well. Obviously cactus plants hated humidity as much as I did.

We stayed at a hotel right on the ocean, and at dinner that night, the restaurant seemed to be entrenched in the Pacific. The ocean waves appeared to be breaking over the panes of glass next to our table. It was fascinating—rather like being in a storm, watching and hearing the undulating water, but not feeling the wetness.

The next day we drove down to Tijuana, and I saw my first bullfight. I HATED it! Words fail me when it comes to the terrible treatment of animals by the human race.

There were no video, or electronic games in earlier days, so Romans fed Christians to the lions for entertainment. And in 1133 in Spain, bullfighting was created to entertain King Alfonso VIII. But watching the destruction of an innocent animal in the "civilized" world, totally escaped my capacity to understand. We were with a U. S. Senator in Mexico and we were seated in the first row of the arena as honored guests. The Matador walked over and bowed to us and then the fun viewing of this spectacle began.

The bulls bred for fighting are usually from the same bloodline and must be four years or older. They need to weigh between 500 and 800 kilos (1,102 to 1,765 pounds) and *never* have faced a man on foot before entering the ring.

A most magnificent bull charged into the sunny open ring, disoriented from being held in a dark holding pen. When the Picadors riding blindfolded horses began plunging their darts adorned with bright colorful ribbons into the bull's neck to weaken him, my stomach began churning.

At first I was enthralled by the first few graceful passes by the Matador, until my senses caught up to my brain, and I saw that the front of the bull was already covered in his own blood and he seemed dazed. My God, *this* is what a civilized culture serves up as entertainment? When the kill took place very near us and the blood splattered toward us, I absolutely fled for fear I would vomit right there. How could it be an honor for anyone to receive an ear from this poor animal? Once outside, my heart was still pounding and I found it an effort to breathe.

When George and the others joined me after the bullfight, I was told I still looked quite pale. Well of course I did. The Mexicans around me were quite tan! I was so eager to return to *my* country where this insidious amusement was against the law.

1960 Presidential Campaign

*"If we do not lay ourselves out in the
service of mankind whom should we serve?"*

—JOHN ADAMS

The entire Kennedy family campaigned in 1960. His sisters, Bobby and Ted's wives all traveled and did more than was asked of them. As it was with any endeavor undertaken by any one of them, it was a joint effort carried out by *all* of them. There was one exception this time. Jacqueline Kennedy was pregnant and unable to travel.

Officially, Senator Smathers was announced as the Democrat who would work the South and Senator "Scoop" Jackson of Oregon, the North and West. I made trips on private planes and acted as stewardess on board the flights with Senators and others, who would be making speeches on behalf of JFK and the Democratic party in any given state.

There were schedules and speeches to be typed, but most of all I enjoyed working the crowds whenever possible. I mixed in with the people and made reassuring comments that their devotion to this vital young candidate was not misplaced. The volunteers everywhere can make or break a (campaign stop) and those in Kennedy's camp were beyond ebullient. Their enthusiasm helped drown out the Nixonites around the country.

In the beginning, Kennedy's speech making was a little ragged. He then studied Churchill's style and took advice from many speech therapists to deliver his speeches with the proper cadence. He was a quick learner however and could finally feel comfortable while communicating with even the folks in the farmland. Let's face it, this was not a world he knew from growing up, far cry as it was from the elite eastern schools and society life he experienced in America and England. His capability of devouring so many words per minute, enabled him to race through his briefing materials for three or more speeches a day.

Kennedy would have garnered many more votes, if his wife could have campaigned with him. Jacqueline had had two miscarriages and who could fault her for being afraid of exerting herself with too much travel since she was again pregnant.

These were the first campaign debates in history that would be televised. It caused the undoing of Vice President Nixon's chances of winning the hearts and votes of the people when they saw the movie star quality of Senator John Kennedy at his lectern. Nixon came over as somber and uncomfortable while perspiring constantly under the heavy lighting. JFK's sense of humor and great smile were the perfect condiments to his grasp of the issues and also the agenda he hoped to carry to fruition for the American people.

As a televised event, it was a very primitive presentation in grainy black and white, but Jack Kennedy provided all the color needed to reach into the loneliest Iowa farmhouse and make that family feel comfortable with him. Richard Nixon's insecurity when viewed alongside the Kennedy worldliness, power and money was dramatic! Television seemed to only exaggerate his discomfort. JFK was complacent in front of a camera, and the actor Peter Lawford, his brother in law, helped advise him about makeup to lessen the effect of the hot lighting necessary in the studio. He also offered other suggestions on what worked well in front of the camera. By contrast, Mr. Nixon was visibly stressed and perspiration was streaming down his face.

Before the second television debate, Kenneth Galbraith who had been helping prepare Kennedy, said JFK stated, "When I first began this campaign, I just wanted to beat Nixon. *Now I want to save the country from him.*"

It was, as are all political campaigns, a rough road for both candidates. Jack Kennedy at age forty-three emerged the victor. It was one of the closest elections in history. Over 68 million people voted, and the difference was only 113,000. A few days later when Republican election officials dug deeper into the Texas and Illinois results, they found deception.

Fannin County in Texas had only 4,895 voters who registered, but 6,138 votes were counted and three quarters were for Kennedy. And in Illinois, one precinct of Angelia had only 86 people voting, but somehow Kennedy ended up with 147 votes and Nixon garnered 24. Many people felt that would definitely be termed ballot stuffing. It was said that Mayor Daley (the Senior) could bring the dead back to vote.

Nixon's advisors pressed him hard to ask for a recount, but he refused as he felt it would damage the country. He may have been bitter, but not enough to hurt the nation. You never read about that anywhere as Watergate cast a huge shadow over anything good he did when he finally became president. There is much to be said for having people skills if you want to be a good politician and leader.

A new era was now manifesting in Washington, and the city would not be the same again.

> "Wise married women don't trouble
> themselves about infidelity in their husbands."
>
> —SAMUEL JOHNSON

Shortly following JFK's success in winning the presidential election, he called George and invited us for dinner at his N St. house in Georgetown. He was the President Elect and had not moved into the White House as yet. His wife was out of town and when we arrived I met a prominent married woman who was his dinner guest for the evening. Jackie, though not yet the official first lady, was already being hailed as the Queen of Washington. She was so young, yet sophisticated and strikingly beautiful that until I understood Jack Kennedy better, I simply could not understand why he kept seeking out women who seemed to me quite inferior to her. By 1960 however, many Washingtonian socialites already knew him either biblically, or by his sexual resume. I was comparatively new to this life and naïve enough to be easily surprised by the audaciousness of powerful, famous men on such a wide scale.

This was my first visit to the Kennedy's home, and I was certain I would be dazzled with the interior decoration by this stylish woman. I was disillusioned to say the least when we entered the living room. It was absolutely dreary to me. Had we entered the house of seventy-six year old Alice Longworth Roosevelt by mistake?

I certainly had no design pedigree, and I came to understand that those who do, find it very important that their furniture and carpets have a proper ancestry. I am sure that each and every piece of mahogany, cherry, oak, maple or whatever hardwood piece in that house came with papers. I found it terribly dull in appearance for such a vibrant young couple.

As Jackie was so enthralled by French design, I would have expected to see beautiful couches and chairs upholstered in fine fabrics with elegant braiding and fringe. Ah, not so. She preferred the simple English slipcover look. The entire place was so totally colorless, that I couldn't even appreciate their fine art because it was also dark in appearance and heavy tone. I readily concede that I knew absolutely nothing about proper interior design and decoration at that young age.

Assuredly I did not let the decor ruin my evening. Not everyone enjoyed private little dinner parties there with Jack Kennedy as the host. The conversation was invigorating. Jack and George were very comfortable while in each other's company. There was much laughter and camaraderie.

I was just as comfortable and audacious sparring verbally with JFK every time he articulated any subject in an off color manner. If I had met him after he was already President, I'm sure I would have been more intimidated. But from our first hello, he displayed the informal saucy side of himself. He was young and fun—definitely not exemplifying the President Eisenhower stature.

George told me after we left that he enjoyed himself that evening so much more than usual because when Jackie invited couples over for dinner, it was more exhausting than enjoyable for him. She loved playing word games using history question/answer sessions in competition. She was at the time, taking courses in U. S. History at Georgetown University. The men had worked with their intellects all day. After a scotch or two, the last thing they felt like doing was competing in a brain game.

Jackie Kennedy and Rosemary Smathers had a mutual dislike for politics. They were both raised as cultured young ladies, and politics was not a genteel profession in their world. I learned that after George became immersed in politics, Rosemary's choice for enjoying herself was a nice cruise with some good books to read. Later when I learned more about Mrs. Kennedy, I realized that she must have had a complicated point of view regarding the political mountain top. When I reminded myself she was only thirty-one years old when she became First Lady, I was in awe of how she handled herself publicly. She also held her head high in spite of the indignations she suffered by the infidelities of her husband.

Rarely in those days were women themselves serving in Washington's major positions of power. We had only two ladies in the U. S. Senate in 1960, so it could still be called a "good old boys club." Jack Kennedy liked women for sure, but it was out of the question that he would have considered any one of them, no matter how qualified, as candidates for important positions in his administration. He was his father's son on this matter.

1961 Inauguration

*"Now I believe I can hear the
philosophers protesting that it can only
be misery to live in folly, illusion and
deception, but it isn't—it's human."*

—ERASMUS

While we were in Los Angeles at the convention, Smathers and his aide Scotty Peek met a young California gal named Barbara Anderson. They convinced her to quit her secretarial job in LA, move to Miami and work in the Senator's law firm there. Over the years, she and I became best friends. Over the Christmas holidays in 1960, I flew down to visit her, and we went to a few parties together. One evening, I met Miami bachelor John Renuart at a gathering and he went into a big dissertation about how great it was that Kennedy had been elected. John was a very strong Catholic and I could understand his enthusiasm.

When he heard that Barbara and I were invited to attend the Inaugural activities, he was beside himself with envy. Since I had not yet made a date for the events and he was an attractive, seemingly fun bachelor, I invited him to join us without giving it a second thought. I told him he had only the problem of finding a hotel room in a city that would be quite booked up that week in January. He handled that problem.

After returning to Washington, I was working at my desk one afternoon when I answered the phone. It was Jack Kennedy on the line. He asked me if I could get hold of Bud Luckey right away and requested that we both come to his private office because he wanted to talk with us.

Bud worked on one of Senator Smather's committees and was popular, living the good life of bachelorhood on The Hill. Everyone who knew him thought he was a very bright appealing fellow with a sense of humor that put everyone around him in a congenial mood. I called him immediately and told him we had been summoned to President Elect Kennedy's office because he had something to discuss with us.

Bud asked, "What in the world could he want to see us together about?"

I said quickly, "I haven't the slightest idea, but please come right away so we can get ourselves over to his office."

Twenty minutes later we knocked on the Senator's private office door as he had suggested, and he unlocked it. This was a first for me and a total mystery visit. Even before JFK became the busiest man in the country, he always got right to the point. Directing his words first to Bud, he said that he had invited an old flame of his from Europe to the Inauguration and wanted to be sure that she had a great time while in Washington. He asked Bud to be her escort for all the events. Of course, Bud agreed to this favor.

"Layte, Smathers told me you've invited a young man from Miami as your escort. Do you think you can get another amusing couple to join you? A party of six would make it more enjoyable for everyone."

I replied to JFK, "My friend Barbara and her date also from Miami are every bit as entertaining as I am at my best. Plus she's smart and beautiful. We all ready planned to go to the events together so it's no problem at all."

"Perfect," said the president elect. "I'll see to it that you have good seats for all the functions and have an aide take care of all the arrangements."

It was a short exchange, quickly settled and we left.

"Well Buddo" I said, "this is going to be a more interesting week than I realized!"

Social Life in and Outside of Washington

*"It has been my experience that folks
who have no vices have very few virtues."*

—Abraham Lincoln

During the summer of 1961, Kennedy invited George and me over for dinner in the family dining room at the White House. I found no notation in my diary about any other woman being there, so he must have simply wanted to kick back and talk politics with George. I was bored and sleepy after dinner and wine, so I asked JFK if I might take a nap elsewhere since they weren't ready to call it a night. He said, "No problem, you can nap in Lincoln's bedroom. Everyone seems to enjoy that."

Leaving George in the family living room, he walked me down the hall to the bedroom and found a lightweight throw for me so I could just lie on top of the spread. I think I was asleep within three minutes after first saying to myself, "Layte, you are sleeping in Lincoln's Bed—how big a kicker is that?" Thinking back, it was quite a privilege that I had that opportunity. I slept until George awakened me so we could leave.

Some people don't know the history of this room, but Lincoln didn't actually sleep there, as it was his working office originally. In one history of the White House I read, it said he signed the Emancipation Proclamation in this room. It was turned into a bedroom after his death and has undergone many incarnations over the years, but always with his heavily carved Victorian bed and furniture. In fact, many people who have slept there over the years swear the room is haunted by Lincoln's spirit. Some of the White House staff refused to go into it. President Reagan's dog would bark in the doorway, but never enter. I have no ghost story to report, but perhaps the ghost doesn't wander about in that room until after midnight and like Cinderella, I had left by then.

> *"Grandma's my name . . .*
> *and spoilin's my game."*
> —ANONYMOUS

That summer my grandmother came up to Washington for a visit. I took her to all the tourist sights. Being in her late sixties, she even walked down the steps of the Washington Monument. It was the last time I ever did it, as once committed, there are 558 steps until you reach the bottom, or top, if you happen to have a portable oxygen tank on you.

I thought on a whim, it would be a special treat for her if I could arrange to take her to see the White House and possibly introduce her to the president. I called and told Mrs. Lincoln, the president's secretary that I would love to bring my grandmother over and asked if the president might call me at his convenience. A couple of hours later, JFK called back and I asked him if it would be possible sometime during the week.

He was delighted, or so he said. If we could come in about an hour, he would also arrange for the WH photographer to take our pictures. How neat is that I thought.

I went into the kitchen and announced my surprise for her. Now to be clear, my grandmother was never one to compromise and was very opinionated about everything. She said in a curt voice, "I absolutely do NOT want my picture taken with that president! I *never* liked the Kennedys, none of them. I never considered them respectable. Surely you know that!"

"Actually Grandma, I knew you didn't vote for him, but I didn't know you felt *that* adamant about the entire family." Now I was left with the chore of calling JFK back to tell him my grandmother didn't like him, hadn't voted for him, and certainly didn't want her picture taken with him! In total honesty, I related her exact words and received the reaction I half expected from him. That is, after he finally stopped laughing.

"Now I know exactly where *you* get your spunk."

Washington was more to me than my life on Capitol Hill. The city was teeming with bright interesting young people serving in different roles during my years there. Young men were spending two or three years in one of the Military Branches. ROTC was a given when we were in college so this was the natural evolvement. Many went on to secure law degrees, or their masters in business. Indeed, most of those I knew became very successful. I'm describing here the men on the other side of the coin I kept flipping while living my unorthodox life. These were the men I *should* have taken more seriously.

I would have had to include serial dater in any new resumé of mine. My girlfriends and I were awash in dating material. I wasn't in the ambitious category, or spending time in an effort to forge a real career on Capitol Hill. I simply fancied being a social butterfly, enjoying my life as it unfolded daily. My world was crazy fast and I wasn't able to slow down long enough to think about my future, much less *plan* for it.

I couldn't kick my love of football habit, so I dated Jim Steffers who played end for the Redskins team. It made the games in D. C. more fun for me.

Florida Congressman, Paul Rogers had two brothers. My mother dated his oldest brother Dwight and I dated the youngest, Doyle. He was a wonderful dancer, and that was always a huge plus for me. We went to several dances in Washington and Palm Beach, and he introduced me to the elegant Everglades Club there. Thank Heaven many of my male escorts traveled in and out of Washington, which allowed me to shuffle my time with each. I didn't sleep with a single one, and yet I had proposals of marriage from several.

As young women we weren't the *players* they are today, nor did I ever think of being the *aggressor*. So the men were more apt to marry us to have a sexual relationship. I definitely wasn't shy, but *not* a flirt. Plus, I was actually sewing most of my dresses and even formals for events. I don't know how I found time to sleep, much less use part of that precious unconscious time to have sex!

New York and Broadway

One winter, Beverly and I decided to go to New York City. We visited our sorority sister Barbara (Hendrix) Egan, who worked in a hospital on Staten Island. We didn't have the warm coats, boots, gloves, or hats, any thinking person would don for a freezing ride on the ferry to the canyons raging with frosty winds in the Big City. I still have a mental picture of us bracing against that wind while *walking backwards*, runny noses and tears almost turning to icicles on our cheeks.

> *"Life is a cabaret old chum. . . . come taste*
> *the wine. . . . come hear the band. . . .*
> *Start celebrating . . ."*
>
> —Cabaret, the Musical

"Beverly, I keep bumping into people because I can't see where I'm heading—behind me!"

"And you think I can? My nose must be frost bitten by now!"

"The wind has to be 40 mph roaring through these tall buildings. I would beg for a buffalo fur from any of those Indians who sold this darn island to us. No wonder they accepted only twenty-four dollars for it—they probably wanted to move south!"

Barbara was better prepared since she lived there, but was also freezing. We were Florida girls after all, and I dispute those who don't agree our blood is thinner in the south.

I would not have dreamed then that New York over my lifetime would become my *heart city*. Joking today, I say I could be lowered out of a chopper in many areas of the city when I reach my 80's, and I would feel right at home. I figure by the time I'm 80, the traffic will have come to a total and complete standstill, and a helicopter may be about the only way to get into the center of that city.

But in 1959, the bus or walking was all we could afford. Scotty managed to get us theatre tickets to *West Side Story* and "Camelot," both with their original casts. Chita Rivera, Carol Lawrence, with Larry Kert and Julie Andrews, Richard Burton with Robert Goulet all sang music from Steven Sondheim and Leonard Bernstein, Fredrick Loewe and Moss Hart. Broadway was a magical visit to music heaven for me, and these are two of my most revered productions of all time.

I would soon learn that the song "Something's Coming," from West Side Story was a psychic reading for me in musical phrases. I've lived in NYC three different times since that first visit and have seen all the *BIG* ones on Broadway, but nothing on a stage ever thrilled me as much as that first introduction to the Great White Way.

The Cherry Blossom Festival staged in Washington every spring celebrates the blooming of 3,000 Cherry Trees. In 1912, Tokyo gifted them to our country, and they were planted around the Tidal Basin in front of the

Jefferson Memorial. It is serenely resplendent with a powder pink glow there in early April. It draws tourists from all over the world as the buds unfurl. Each state sponsored a beauty contest to select their Princess to represent them in the parade and festivities for that week.

> *"Do not dream in the past, do not*
> *dream of the future, concentrate the*
> *mind on the present moment."*
>
> —BUDDHA

In April of 1960, I was one of the candidates representing my state of Florida at a dinner dance. Among the judges were Betty Beale, Society Editor of the Washington Post and a very engaging young bachelor Congressman from Indiana, John Brademas.

The festival ripened into a delicious week for me. Computers were just coming of age and were almost room sized. The one the Festival used was named "Transit Univac Machine." The event organizers sifted our personal information into the computer along with that of the eligible young military men from the Washington area who had been selected and approved as escorts. The machine then decided who would escort each young lady according to what we had *in common*.

All the princesses were lined up one side of a huge hall and the gentlemen were lined against the other. I'm sure the conversations on the male side were much the same as ours. In clusters, we were discussing who the hotties were, especially the tall Air Force Lieutenant, who turned out to be Jerry J. Jenkinson from Iowa.

An official of the festival began pairing up each State Princess with her escort. I never figured out what the computer mind thought Army Lieutenant Irving Levine and I had in common, but pair us up it did. We were all in our twenties, but I was the eldest of the gals and Irving was numerically the oldest of the officers, so this must have determined our doublet. I was very disappointed not to get Jerry for the week, but Irving was a good sport and an above average dancer.

Senator Smathers was to escort me on the runway where the State Princesses were first introduced at a fashion luncheon. No one noticed me I'm sure. He looked so stunning every woman in the room was *"aggah"* over him. I laughed out loud and told him to stop grinning and enjoying it so darn much.

"This is my event George!"

Lt. Levine escorted me through the formal activities, but it turned into musical chairs the rest of the time with everyone socializing with their preferred choice. I hung out mainly with the Marines and of course, Jerry in his Air Force blues. Today the festival is probably a grander affair for the young ladies, but in 1960, the collective lot of us made it a totally hedonistic week. Our fare was sumptuous with good champagne and fine wines, and we played dress up at least twice a day for official celebrations.

I managed to contract a case of total laryngitis. Not even a whisper crossed my lips for almost two days. I've never been accused of brevity, and I know my best friends would have loved to witness that streak of quiet in me. With the word "laryngitis" inked on my left palm to flash, my southern smile carried me through. The actual Queen of the Festival is chosen by spinning a huge wheel with the fifty states marking the circle. There are enough politics happening in Washington without adding this little contest to the load.

> *"He is simply a shiver—looking*
> *for a spine to run up."*
>
> —PAUL KEATING

Following the Cherry Blossom Festival, Jerry and I began dating. Of all the men I'd known, in all the clubs I've been, on all the dance floors I've been twirled and dipped—no one could dance like him. I could have followed his 6'4" frame anywhere. He was the best lead I'd ever had dancing the tango, rumba, samba and even the waltz. Being an Adonis on top of that brought other challenges. It was downright embarrassing how many officer's wives at Bolling Air Force Club would cut in on *me* in mid-dance with all the style and class of trollops.

Several times he said to me, "Layte, I have to go to this Colonel, or that General's house for a party. Please go with me and don't leave my side for a minute because the wife is really becoming a problem for me at social functions." Regarding Jerry, we are talking ridiculously good looking here. His crystal blue eyes and blond hair topped off his perfect physique. This young man had to walk a narrow line, especially after he was appointed as a White House aide for formal functions.

One evening at a Major General's house, I became embroiled in a political discussion with another guest, When I looked for Jerry, he was nowhere in the main party rooms. I went into the kitchen and sure enough, the general's wife had him pinned against the refrigerator. I *rescued* him by playing the extremely jealous girlfriend, shocked by the sheer nerve of our hostess.

Guiding me into the living room, he said, "That's it! We're leaving!"

We could commiserate over this dilemma because we both had to contend with unwanted attention from the mighty and powerful in this city. Incongruously, the only thing he lacked, was a swelled ego. We talked about marriage, but I knew in my heart that career military life would not be for me.

I was hooked on the power people and I knew it. In my case the expression, "Power is an aphrodisiac" was too true. Once I got a taste of being in the smoke filled rooms, I craved hearing discussions that would create the headlines a day or so later.

> *"There are 204 bones in the human*
> *body. No need for dismay, however, the*
> *two bones of the middle ear have never*
> *been broken skiing!"*
>
> —BARBARA LIPSTADT

Jerry and I had had a really sweet uncomplicated relationship that didn't reach real intimacy, only tenderness. It would have been hard to find a more solid values man with whom to share my life and this alone should have strongly alerted me that my thinking and decision making were totally botched. Our relationship became vague, but a few years later when I lived in NYC, and George was no longer my vice, we began dating again.

Jerry and I stayed in touch until several years later when he was deployed to Vietnam. I never saw Jerry again, but prayed for him as the death toll there was frightening. I saw a mutual friend of ours many months later and asked about him. He told me that Jerry's jet was shot down over North Vietnam. I was devastated to think that not only Bob Crenshaw, but also this special person, had been taken so young in life.

Later I looked, but didn't find his name on the Vietnam Wall in Washington. So by a miracle, I pray that he is a happy grandfather back in Iowa, or anywhere else in this country he loved so much.

The winter of 1961 was my first introduction to skiing. My girlfriend Eugenia McLin chided me into it. She was modeling in NYC at this time, although she worked all over the world, including Coco Channel's collections in Paris. I joined her and her boyfriend of the moment driving up to Hunter Mountain in upper New York State.

Skiing for a beginner has to be the most awkward damn sport ever invented. It is especially so for a water skier who has been taught to lean back on her skis and then to unlearn that in order to lean forward on her snow skis. I was never a good athlete, but I've never made such a complete fool of myself in any other sport. Nothing is more cumbersome than those two *really* long boards attached to heavy clumpy boots that do nothing but go in the opposite direction from that which you are aiming. Snow plowing to stop is so embarrassing, especially when you fall forward on your face. Just layering up to go outside is so tedious compared to throwing on a bathing suit for a nice swim. And without fail, after you've layered fourteen pieces on your body, you need to go to the bathroom.

Of course, I sprained my leg that day. It was planned as my final run anyway . . . just *not in this manner.* Late afternoon shadows on the trails should have told me not to take that last run since it's harder to see the snowy bumps.

Actually, a sprain was not a worse case scenario, as near the top I had passed a girl laying on snow that had turned red from the blood flowing down her broken leg and onto the snow beside her. Not *only* broken, but the bone was sticking out of her flesh! I'm sure the shock and fear of the same fate caused my fall a few minutes later.

After I married and spent many winters at ski houses in Vermont or Utah and Colorado, I at least got the hang of it and actually loved being on the mountain peaks. But in the beginning, it was shear terror for me. No real skier would grant Hunter the time of day, as it is such a dinky hill in comparison to the Rockies or Wasatch ranges, but for me that first day, it was awesomely high.

That joyful afternoon at Hunter Mountain sent me home with crutches. My diary entry that night was, "Layte you wild and crazy girl . . . don't *ever* go skiing again without lessons!"

By this time, I was living alone at the Capitol Hill Apartments building. Beverly had married that major looker in a Naval uniform, Nick Jones. She and her Navy Doctor had a charming wedding in a small Virginia Church, and I became her Maid of Honor, instead of her roommate.

I was now in a quandary, alone and getting around on crutches. Just getting to the couch from my kitchen swaying on those sticks with a Pepsi in one hand was such a challenge. I ate several meals at my kitchen counter for a couple of weeks and was so grateful when George would come over to cook and serve me dinner. He was most pleased to see me living on my own of course, as it was easier for us to be together.

European Trip

Several times a gentleman named Matty Mathews came to our office to meet with the Senator. As he operated a charter airline business and as George served on the Aviation Committee, he would come to lobby about a particular bill. On one occasion he asked if I would be interested in going to Europe for free if there were any empty seats on one of his charters. Needless to say I answered with a resounding positive. Good to his word, one day in 1961, he called and said there were a couple of extra seats on a charter flight to Belgium the following week. He suggested that I invite a friend and he would make arrangements to include us on that charter manifest.

> *"I never travel without my diary.*
> *One should always have something*
> *sensational to read on the train."*
>
> —OSCAR WILDE

George was not thrilled about my taking two weeks off at that particular time, but he knew I was itching to cross the Atlantic so he gave me permission. My salary on the Hill was thankfully more than my pay at the Pentagon. $6,400 a year went further then, so I could afford a "Eurail" train pass for $120. 00 to tour Europe. It was a First Class ticket and good for a month, all over Western Europe.

I called my sorority sister Jeani Kitchens that very night. Jeani had moved to New York City after college. She had come from a well to do family and had toured Europe once already but I knew she was eager to go back.

I reached her late after she returned home from a Broadway play. "Really? . . . that's fantastic since I haven't found a job here yet anyway, I'd love to go," Jeani said very enthusiastically.

Jeani was a tall, beautiful brunette and in fact, looked so much like Jackie Kennedy that Life Magazine featured her with several other Jackie look a likes in one of their issues. She was also a *very* strict Catholic girl. When we boarded our flight, she was mortified that every person on that plane was a Jehovah Witness except the two of us.

I never scoped out the details of that charter as I was just too busy leading my life, but I thought this development would add to our fun. And, they did spend much of the flight trying to convert us, so when we landed in Brussels, Jeani fled the baggage claim area shoving me toward the exit.

We could not avoid running into some of our fellow passengers now and then during our travels, but we exchanged rapid pleasantries and moved on quickly.

We checked into a splendid hotel in Brussels and had a stellar view of Tivoli Gardens from our twenty third-floor window. An hour later we were enjoying the first of those delicious little open-faced sandwiches usually served on tartines, for which Belgium is famous. A day and a half later after touring the gardens and light sightseeing, we were ready to embrace the first leg of our train travel.

We arranged our trips so that some of our overnights could be spent on the train and we could save on our hotel costs. We realized very quickly after paying our first bill, that we would not be checking into another three star hotel on this trip!

European rail travel was very comfortable and all the first class cars had individual compartments with two couches, seating three or four people facing one another. On many legs of our trip we were lucky enough to find empty spaces and could spread out to the point of washing our panties and brassieres and hanging them from the luggage rack under our bags to dry out by morning. We slept pretty well stretched out on those horsehair fabric bench couches . . . having changed into our fresh lingerie of course.

Naturally there were segments when we had to sit with others. It provided some very animated conversations, because our companions could not speak English any more than Jeani and I could speak their mother tongue. Hands were used charade style, and we became as talented as any Italian, using this method to communicate.

During daytime travel, we would lower the wide window half way and let the fresh country air swirl around our compartment. We purchased good local wines, tasty cheese and bread of the region, which served as our feasts aboard. This was such a glorious way to taste and feel Europe.

Germany

When we reached Germany, Baden-Baden was quiet and boring. Their famed bath springs did nothing to regenerate us, young as we were . . . how would we even know? The elder Europeans however swore by their powers.

"Anyone who has never made a mistake
has never tried anything new."

—GERMAN PHYSICIST ALBERT EINSTEIN

Heidelberg proved to be much more exciting. We went into a Rathskeller the first night and met a couple of very attractive young German men. Considering how cautious we had always lived, I am amazed looking back that we were brave enough to go off alone with each of these fellows. I don't remember what Jeani's "date" did for a living, but mine turned out to be a race car driver who even drove in the Daytona 500. In his broken English he explained that he wanted to drive me up to see the Castle on top of Heidelberg Mountain. "Wunderbar," said I, until I realized that I had to climb over the door to get into my seat. There were no door handles, as that would cut down on the aerodynamics of the car. We screeched away, leaving my stomach at the curb.

My God, what a ride that was. He had to be completely mad, or certainly not concerned about dying in his twenties, because if I thought the ride up the mountain was frightening, it was nothing compared to the sheer terror I felt on the way down. One spiral after another interspersed with hairpin turns. For a second, my mind flickered a picture with a small headline in my hometown newspaper, making my death sound rather glamorous. "She was killed, as the International Racer's car careened off the mountain road just below Heidelberg Castle."

I would have worried more about Jeani that evening, as this was the first time we had been more than 30 feet from one another on the trip, but I was so worried about myself returning alive, I barely gave her safety a thought. Our Guardian Angels worked overtime that night. We both ended up at the hotel in very good condition (if you don't count the stress factor) and the guys certainly weren't overbearing Nazi types.

Everywhere we went, it was fun listening to the local people calling out "Jackie-Jackie" to my companion. She would just smile her usual, and we'd continue ahead. We had nicknamed her "smiley" at the sorority house in college and it fit her.

These were before the days that young ladies wore blue jeans anywhere and packing was much more complicated, for me at least. Jeani was cool and confident, so she confined her clothing to one bag that she could move about easily. I, on the other hand, took tons of fancy clothes. Jeani maintains I even packed a peau de soie dress. Well, I didn't take a silk dress (I don't think), but I did take an iron to press anything I wore before I would leave our hotel room, much to her chagrin. I had a large heavy suitcase, which meant I always needed a porter to help me. Plus, I had a weighty carry on case. My perfectionism was crippling on many fronts.

I picked up a paperback copy of a mindless romantic novel named "Angelique" along the way and became so engrossed in this literary twit, Jeani considered throwing it out a window at one point. We were on a cable car riding up to Mount Blanc, which rendered a spectacular view of the Austrian countryside, and I had my nose and eyes buried in Angelique's adventure. I came to my senses along the way and never turned the pages of another silly romantic novel. Barbara Cartland became wealthy without me, but that suggests there are millions of women lacking enough romance in their own lives.

Italy

When we boarded the train to Venice, we had no idea what was to befall us. It began normally enough as we washed our "undies" and hung them on the luggage rack, then stretched out for a night's sleep. Within a couple of hours our train came to a sudden halt, and there was great commotion outside our window. Before we knew it, armed guards entered our chamber and ordered us off the train.

> "The Creator made Italy from the
> designs of Michael Angelo."
>
> —MARK TWAIN

We didn't understand their words, but we did get the gist of it because of the rifles they were pointing at us. We grabbed our still wet underwear off the bars and in my case, began dragging our baggage down the aisle. Out of pity, one of the young soldiers helped me along the tracks, a good twenty-five yards, to the station. Pity, that fellow who invented luggage with wheels hadn't come along yet.

Thus began one of the stranger ordeals I've experienced. All of the passengers were rounded up and steered into one large, coldly lit waiting room of the train station in Bolzano, Italy. We seemed to be the only Americans and could not find anyone who could communicate to us in English what was happening.

The other passengers didn't seem overly distraught, so we didn't panic, but it was more than uncomfortable sitting straight up on hard high backed oak benches with terribly harsh florescent lighting above us. After a time, some people actually fell asleep in this dreadful atmosphere and started snoring very loudly.

One of our fellow passengers was a large German Shepard who kept walking around this room nudging awake those who were making the most noise. I wanted to hug him in appreciation, but I was too busy enjoying the startled faces that appeared following a major tongue licking. It wasn't a particularly pleasant way to come out of a dead sleep.

On top of this, and with my timing in life rearing its head again, I went down to the bathroom only to discover that I was beginning my monthly blessing. Great, just great! There was not even any toilet paper, or should I say wax like paper that was the European bathroom product then. Never did a telephone book serve my purposes more than the one I found that night.

Now, having returned to the waiting room with a roll of telephone pages in my crotch, I said to Jeani, "I have had it with this. Wait here, I'm going to get us out and into a hotel." I walked to the front entrance slowly and carefully because of the paper between my legs and pushed open the door.

"I am an American," I pronounced loudly and my friend and I are going to a hotel!"

That announcement was met by two soldiers and crossed rifles with bayonets. Bayonets! My God, what were we in the middle of here anyway? Eventually, we learned we were caught up in the Tyrol Border dispute and the Austrians and Italians were taking this whole thing quite seriously.

That was a very long night and by morning we were almost catatonic. We learned that our First Class Tickets meant nothing at this point. When finally the first two trains were allowed to pass through Bolzano from Austria, they were filled to the point where people were hanging on the handrails from their places on the steps between the cars.

We were becoming quite discouraged, when at last a train with a little spare room stopped at the terminal. We managed with much shoving, to board ourselves and were actually quite happy to be amongst the Italians with their chickens and piglets in tow. In no way am I exaggerating this when I say, I believe the animal count was equal to the human quota aboard. The engine noise drowned out the clucking and oinking, so it wasn't a problem unless one cared to discuss the aroma.

We were as debilitated as the City of Venice itself, when we finally disembarked the train. I had always read such romantic descriptions of this place in cultural history and indeed, it is most unusual. But, perhaps due to my exhausted condition, I found myself disappointed. We probably should have taken a proper tour, but that wasn't our style. We enjoyed roaming on our own, seeing quaint cafes and glass blowing studios suggested by friends.

Jeani and I walked almost everywhere since there wasn't a car on the island, which certainly gives you better oxygen to breathe. We did take a couple of gondola rides to observe the ornate palaces from the water. How strange to see the waves lapping against the very walls of homes. For me, palace or not, it would be like living in a flood zone my entire life and not pleasant for longer than our visit would last. A big draw for the visitors was the pigeon population in the Piazza San Marco, considered the center of activity for foreigners. The *very* friendly pigeons would sit happily on your arm or head *if* you kept feeding them. This was long before city officials began quietly extinguishing these birds because they carry many diseases and reproduce rapidly due to all the extra nourishment they receive.

The pigeons are a small problem now compared to the rising water levels and the sinking of this historic community. No one knows how much time is left for comfortable survival there. It is sad, but factual reality according to many scientists.

Over 100,000 actual *residents* lived in the municipality of Venice when we were there, but the citizen population has been dropping dramatically since the flood in 1966. Less than 60,000 people deal with over two million tourists a year now.

To remember that this Republic was a world maritime power until Napoleon conquered it in 1779, reminds me how many nations fell while others were rising. Our American Republic was born in that very decade.

Florence was next on our agenda, and I cannot say I look back on my first visit there with fondness. We arrived in the afternoon and checked into a rather shoddy hotel. The faster our money departed our wallets, the cheaper the hotels we selected. We had no bathroom in our room here, but could choose to go up ten steps to one, or down ten steps to another just outside our door.

We dressed for dinner and thanked the concierge for suggesting we dine outside the city at a former castle, now a restaurant in its' new incarnation. I remember the ambience as being so like the stone castles described in books. The seafood was delicious.

After we went to bed and unfortunately, this night of all nights, we had only a double to share, my stomach really started to rumble. Then the cramps began, and suddenly I grabbed my robe and raced down the steps to the hall bathroom. I just barely made it before expelling what I assumed must be my entire dinner. Oh I wish! The smell was terrible and when I opened the door, I hoped the cleaning man working on the steps just below would not notice.

I was back in bed barely fifteen minutes when I bolted out and down the stairs again for an encore. It was embarrassing having to pass the cleaning man who had worked his way slowly upward while polishing the stone so intently.

Please no. Again in twenty minutes, I was out the door and this time took the ten steps *up*, in quite a weakened state. Looking back, perhaps it would have been faster going down, but at any rate, after closing the door, I didn't quite make it to the commode. In the midst of the worst diarrhea, or food poisoning I would have in my life, I found it impossible to look at this poor cleaning man who would face "repairing" after me. Somehow Jeani who managed to get most of a night's sleep having eaten the same food as I, couldn't understand my degenerated state by morning.

"Layte, get dressed, the sunshine will do you good and you *must* see the jewelry creations on the Ponte Vecchio Bridge at the very least."

Never have I been less interested in jewelry, or anything else for that matter. I practically crawled over the bridge and then leaned against every store front that we passed, barely breathing. She realized then how weak and dehydrated I was and that I needed to return to the hotel for a nap if I was to survive. I slept through a thirteen hour "nap."

Before we departed Florence, I managed to view the magnificent art in the Uffizi Gallery and appreciated the intricacy of the baptistery doors designed by Lorenzo Ghiberti. The twenty-eight Gothic panels of gilded bronze took him twenty years to complete, but they were still magnificent after seven centuries of wear. I questioned if these artists stopped creating long enough for meals? I thought as a tourist, it would probably take months to see a fraction of the inspiring art and architecture in this exquisite city.

We saved the best for last, and that was David. In those days, Michelangelo's famous sculpture depicting the man who slayed Goliath, stood outside the Galleria Dell' Academia, but I read it has since been moved inside for protection. Now *there* is the figure of a man you can only describe as perfect. I was so enamored, my purchasing of a fifteen inch plaster replica of David was a necessity. Ah, finally the *perfect* man for me! He was wrapped in lightweight paper with no such thing as bubble wrap for protection. The problem was that each time I had to go into my purse, I had to ask Jeani (the devout Catholic) to hold David. She began with "Uhh, David," who became "Damn David" and evolved into

"This *Gosh Damn* David!" So traveling with my new amour became an irritation for her, as well as myself. I was just too afraid of the fragile plaster breaking if I put him down anywhere.

When we checked out of our hotel, I would have belted the concierge for the great dining suggestion of the Castle, if only he had been on duty. And for sure, I left a very large tip for the cleaning man. I only hope it reached his hands.

The rest of our travels through Italy were great fun and devoid of negative incidents.

France

We had a few days to enjoy Paris before rejoining our compatriots for the flight back to Washington. But, much to the chagrin of Senator Smathers, the charter was delayed for almost a week, which greatly extended my holiday from the office. We, however, enjoyed every minute in the City of Light and renamed it the City of Great Cuisine. We ate soufflés and croissants until there was a question of fitting comfortably in our seats on the way home.

> *"You can't escape the past in Paris, and
> yet what's so wonderful about it is that the
> past and present intermingle so intangibly
> that it doesn't seem to burden."*
>
> —ALLEN GINSBERG

The Louvre Museum would certainly be heralded as the best home for art in Paris and I was overwhelmed by the sheer quantity of this collection and the enormity of many of the paintings. They were humongous. I couldn't imagine an artist completing any one of them in a lifetime much less painting several.

Of course we loved the Mona Lisa and made the ritual walk from side to side to see if her eyes actually would follow us. They actually did. This was long before she was encased in glass and velvet ropes holding the viewers at a distance.

But, I must say that after all those life size depictions of dead horses lying beneath slain warriors and the naked cherubs flitting all over the canvases, I was caught breathless upon arriving at the top of the grand stairway in the Musée del'Orangerie des Tuileries. We reached this smaller museum by walking the entire length of the Tuileries gravel pathways.

Suddenly after all the dark and haunting art we had viewed over the recent past, my eyes feasted on the color palettes of the Impressionist Artists. I jested later that viewing for the first time that panoramic collection, was the equal of an orgasm for me. I was only required to take a single course in "Art Appreciation" in college, so I must credit this experience and my gallery visits yet to come on Pan American travels, as causing me to fall passionately in love with art.

Finally our charter flight arrived to return us to our own capitol city. The Jehovah Witnesses were also satiated and tired themselves, so they accepted that Jeani would remain a good Catholic girl and that it would be years before I found my path.

Florida's Presidential Dinner and Air Force One

It was billed as "Florida's Presidential Dinner" in March of 1962, when President Kennedy flew down to Miami to honor his friend Senator George Smathers at the Fontainebleau Hotel on Miami Beach. All of the elected Democrats in the state would sit at the dais and the big Democratic spenders were to fill the lavish banquet room. I had flown down a few days earlier with staff members to help organize the event. It was quite a sumptuous affair as political dinners go and private parties were scheduled for the entire weekend.

"Flying on Air Force One is one hell of a ride. One President—one parachute—no problem—who would jump alone."

—ANONYMOUS

Several big supporters docked their huge yachts in the Intercoastal Waterway across the street from the elegant hotel. Eugene McGrath, a Smathers friend from Panama, had reserved the space directly in front of the hotel and made his luxurious sailing vessel available for some heavy duty entertaining. I was invited to a couple of the parties on board and met several movie stars and entertainers who became more politically active once Jack Kennedy began campaigning.

The dinner was a big success and when it was time to return to Washington, JFK invited me to fly back aboard Air Force One. This was the same Boeing 707 with the tail Number 26000 which would become one of the most well recognized in history within two years. Because of movie portrayals of presidential travels, many people know just how luxurious these jets are. I would imagine the 747's they use today are especially grand. Even in 1962, the craft was equipped with more than two million dollars of high-tech hardware. This was before computers, but the best of every up-to-date communication was aboard. There were five daily newspapers and fifteen magazines subscribed for AF1. It had monogrammed sheets and pillows for Kennedy and his wife, and the meals were served on fine china. The Presidential Seals were everywhere. JFK seriously loved "his" airplane!

There were so many different quarters, because the President needed a private office away from invited guests, be they politicians or friends, the Secret Service or the press pool. The pool rotated and was selected from a much larger White House Press Corps assigned by communication corporations from all over the world. Pan American Press Charters transported the bulk of the Corps during any Presidential travel. On this, my first flight aboard the "Angel" as the Secret Service had coded her, I sat with my friend Congressman Paul Rogers, the Representative of Palm Beach County. We were airborne for a very short time before landing in West Palm Beach to pick up Bobby Kennedy, who had been visiting the ailing family patriarch Joseph Kennedy at his home there.

After Bobby visited in the President's private office with his brother and George who was spending this airtime with his friend, Bobby began roaming around to greet those aboard. When he came to where Paul and I were chatting, he leaned over to shake hands with Paul who then introduced us. After turning his steely blues on me without any sign of a smile, Bobby said, "We've already met several times."

Happiness in seeing me on board was not in his voice, which included a chilly distrust. I never saw the President or George during the flight, but when we deplaned at Andrews Air Force Base and headed for George's car to go into the city, he asked, "What in the world did you say to Bobby when he went back to the main cabin?"

"I told him politely that it was nice to see him again and that was all! Why, what did he say when he returned to the compartment?"

His first words to the President were, "Why is Layte on board?" George relayed. "Jack looked up and told him that you had spent time working on the dinner, and he invited you to ride back up with us. But the best part of it was when Jack told him without a smile that it was *his* airplane and he would invite whomever he chose to fly on it!"

Then he added, "When you are President, Bobby, *you* can decide the passenger manifest list!"

George was not Bobby's biggest fan, and we both started laughing at Jack's response. But since I spent so much time traveling and socializing with the press, Bobby thought his brother used bad judgment inviting me to share their space. I was beginning to feel that everyone in D. C. assumed I was sleeping with JFK, even his brother.

The following week I had an invitation to lunch at the White House down under restaurant where staff and some of the press would have their meals. Hugh Sidey and Peter Lisagor (*Chicago Tribune*) asked me to join them. I always thought they had humor down to a fine science and I leapt at the opportunity.

As luck would have it, when I was walking down a hall to leave, I had to walk past the First Lady coming from the opposite direction. Well, her expression was absolutely the "if looks could kill" kind. Oh yes, a chill descended, but I simply smiled and kept walking.

Aboard the Honey Fitz

In April of 1962, an absolutely perfect spring day arrived and the President called George to invite us for dinner that evening aboard the Honey Fitz. The official Presidential yacht was "The Sequoia," however JFK much preferred the HF, which he named after his maternal grandfather. He chose to use this vessel, one of many that served at the pleasure of the President, for personal social and family entertaining.

> *"A pleasant dalliance . . . that was all . . .*
> *unless of course disclosed."*
>
> —Anonymous

George and I arrived at the dock simultaneously with JFK who emerged from a large black limousine accompanied by three young women. Fiddle and Faddle have been written about in many books. Pricilla and Jill (their real names) were assistants in the White House who could neither type nor take shorthand. They were nicknamed by the press and "Fiddle" worked near President Kennedy's private secretary and "Faddle" worked in the press offices for Pierre Sallinger, the Press Secretary.

It became pretty common inside knowledge that they were playmates of Jack Kennedy and always available whether in the White House for a swim, or at many of the hotels during presidential travels. I had never met the third young lady before.

Almost wherever the President goes, the rituals of respect are carried out for this high office. However, I was astonished and embarrassed when the six of us were *piped* aboard, considering the personal circumstances of these two married men. Not the slightest bit embarrassed, JFK gave a proud salute to the young men in the Navy blue and white.

Once we were all gathered on the after deck, Kennedy introduced me to Mimi Beardsley, 19, who was the new intern working at the White House. Drinks were served before the crew finished casting off the ropes, which was probably a good thing since Jack's mood had turned sour from earlier in the day. I realized he was uptight when I saw him tapping his teeth now and then, an agitated habit he had. As we sat in the soft breezes from the Potomac, it soon became apparent why he was angry.

He had met earlier in the day with steel executive Howard Blount and obtained from him a solid promise that the industry would *absolutely not* raise steel prices. Hours later he learned from a journalist that Blount announced to the press that they *were in fact, raising the price.* JFK had been working for months to keep the prices status quo. With great frustration he said to George, "They kicked us right in the balls!"

A torrent of swear words then flowed from him. He couldn't believe how Blough, eye ball to eye ball, could lie so flagrantly. This would be a battering to the economy as so many industries used our steel for manufacturing. No wonder he was so ticked. Fortunately for those of us on board, after a few drinks, he worked that out of his system, for the evening anyway.

An hour or so later, we heard a couple of horns being exchanged with an oncoming yacht. JFK said, "Oh, that's "The Sequoia" approaching and I promised to give a wave. Ladies, would you please step into the cabin until they pass us?"

Quite obviously four attractive young women could not be seen enjoying dinner with the very married President and his friend, the Senator from Florida. But, I had my own reasons for wanting to be out of view from the other boat. A young man I had known since college and who had previously proposed marriage to me was hosting the businessmen on that yacht.

Joe Kruse was serving on the President's Committee for Equal Employment Opportunity and that was one reason for his organizing this cruise. He would have been more than a little shocked seeing me present on the "Honey Fitz" this night.

In fact, Joe called me the next day at my office and told me about passing the President's Yacht and how excited his guests were with that surprise greeting. He also told me that George Smathers was on board. Joe and I have been lifelong friends in what I feel has been a heartfelt relationship.

The previous evening could have been totally delightful for me except when Jack turned to George after we disembarked and quietly said right in front of me, "I would trade a lot for one weekend with Layte."

I was so unnerved that he would show such disrespect. I wasn't some stuffed rag doll George dragged around for over four years. I turned on my heels and after giving JFK a disgusted look, headed for the parking lot. I tossed a fit in the car and told George I was even happier now that my plans to leave Washington and begin working for Pan American Airlines out of New York were nearly organized.

I think Jack is always fun and exciting to spend time with, who wouldn't? But, I will watch my back with him in the future.

Pan American Airlines
1962–1970

*"Airplane travel is nature's way of making
you look like your passport photo."*

—AL GORE

Smathers knew I had a travel bug following my European trip with my Theta sister Jeani. He understood that I wanted to take a year off to see the world, preferably with Pan American Airlines out of New York. I was almost twenty-six, the cut off age for acceptance with the company.

As George was on the Aviation Committee in the U. S. Senate, it would not be any problem to wave matters for me if necessary. He was a personal friend of Juan Trippe, the founder and President of Pan Am. I felt it was the best airline for me as their routes were almost entirely international. My mother was stricken by my decision as she had flight fright. I convinced her it was the best option other than my joining the armed forces. She certainly understood that. Comparatively speaking, PAA was a good choice.

That summer, Joe Kruse offered to drive me to NYC with everything we could fit in my Chevrolet Corvair Convertible. Wow, I had really upgraded from my tin Ford Falcon. The back seat was stacked, and I remember driving part of the way with the top down to enjoy the late June breezes.

I still had my apartment near Capitol Hill, but would spend that July in Pan Am training with the new recruits in Queens, NY. That made it an easy commute to Idlewild Airport, where the stewardess classrooms were located near the Pan Am hangars. After helping me settle in, Joe went back to Washington with planned visits for us to go to the theatre in New York City

He graduated from the University of Florida, but my senior year lived at the Phi Delta Theta Fraternity house while earning his Masters Degree from FSU. He asked me out when we first met, but because I was dating only Jim Magee who lived right down the hall in the Phi Delt house, I did not date him, or anyone else. We would have a coke together, or talk on the phone once in a while as friends.

Jim Magee and I had broken up long before Joe moved to Washington for his good job with the administration, and we dated more often. He was so comfortable to be with and we laughed endlessly.

The day came when he wanted me to take catechism lessons because he was a very pious Catholic. By that I mean he was the kind of man who went to church *every* morning of the week. He could not marry out of his faith. He arranged for one of the top Priests at Georgetown University to teach me, and I truly tried to process this dogma that was so different from my Methodist upbringing. I suppose that made sense since I was baptized German Lutheran, but preferred going to the Episcopalian Church during college and quite honestly was as squeamish committing to one religion as committing to one man. I knew Joe was much too religious not to have a good Catholic wife who believed as he did.

I have always found it very difficult to be a person deeply bound by the rules of one church. And after reading "A World Lit Only By Fire," the *history* of the Catholic Church is frightening to me. It isn't fair for me to single this church out when I consider all the horrendous warring mankind has inflicted on itself in the name of religion for centuries. Some of the people I love most in the world are good Catholics, but I have had to follow my own path.

The community service all churches do are commendable and a blessing to everyone who finds comfort within those walls. I'm one hundred percent in favor of anyone's personal choices. In this world, I would say, "Whatever gets you through the night" in this area should be respected by all those who love you.

Joe and I remained friends through out our lives and marriages and have talked to one another for advice during very difficult periods. Who says the Gators and Seminoles don't like each other?

"How do you get a French waiter's
attention? Start ordering in German."

—JIM CRUM

Today stewardesses don't work any harder than we did, but it's no longer considered as a glamorous profession for a woman. In the sixties, Pan American was regarded as the finest airline in the world and thousands of young women competed for the jobs when ever they heard, or read, about hiring in their city. The executives in charge of flight personal would interview women all over the world. The European gals were most thrilled to be hired and have the opportunity to base in New York City, or Miami. Pan Am hired Hawaiian, or far eastern girls to handle most of the San Francisco based flights along with the American bred women.

International air travel was not nearly as common as it is today, and passengers dressed quite properly for their trips abroad. It was quite normal to see gloves on ladies and even hats. Recently I was departing Miami for a trip, and I could not believe how slovenly some people, both young and adult, were turned out. One guy was sporting a t-shirt shouting out in large letters, "FUCK YOU." 'How charming! It was, especially so for the young children in the waiting area who were able to read. I try so hard not to judge people, but it's the disrespect people show one another that is so depressing these days.

PAA was a global airline, and it was necessary for every stewardess, or steward to speak a second language. It became problematic for me as I had studied only Latin and was a poor student in that language. But I plunged right in and studied with a tutor, as well as spending many hours every week with earphones and French tape recordings. My tutor did his best, but knew I had no ear for foreign languages. One day he absolutely threw his hands in the air and exclaimed, "*Layeete.* you *seemply* do not hear me enunciate and I can do no more for you. I theenk the only way you weel retain any vocabulaire is to learn it on the peellow. I suggest you take a French lover as soon as posseeble." Well, it was "bon au revoir et la bonne chance" to me!

I spent much more time with the earphones and tapes from that day forward, as my life was much too complicated already to add a French lover to the mix. The powers that be were not thrilled with my progress, but I did in fact learn enough by the time I became a purser, to make the in flight announcements and personally comfort the passengers.

I flew to Paris so often that I picked up enough vocabulary to order in restaurants, and of course, do my shopping. "Est combien celà" or "how much is that?"—is a phrase I used many many times a day while in Parisian shops. In fact, you *had* to ask the sales girl several times in order to get her attention, as she would be spending most of her time primping in a mirror. I never purposefully singled French women out for criticism, but they begged for it! They were so egotistical and self-absorbed compared to the American women I knew.

In Queens, NY, I roomed with a couple of extremely nice young women, and since I had my "hot" convertible, it was also an easy commute to our classrooms at Idlewild airport everyday. Training began July 2nd and took four weeks. Though some of it was important and quite informative, much of it was comical.

I really got a kick out of the exercise for delivering a baby in case a premature birth occurred on a flight. Our instructor turned a stool sideways on the floor. As we took turns reaching into the rungs on the legs, he explained how we should proceed. Hello?

This was our "hands on" training to deliver a child? I think a good film on that procedure would have been a bit more informative. I chose to hope that the money they saved on this stuff was being spent on the best maintenance for the aircraft fleet.

The most important part of our training was for emergency situations and the security of our passengers. We used an actual aircraft and jumped on the slide chutes then herded people immediately away from the airplane in case of an explosion. They even took us over to a very calm little lake where we exited the mockup craft and then inflated rubber rafts to pull one another to safety. I don't know how well that exercise would have translated to the North Atlantic choppy frozen seas in the unlikely event that we even survived the crash.

Big surprise here, my favorite days were spent while learning about wines. PAA certainly served the best, such as the 1959 Chateau Haut Brion. They were mainly French, and complimented the excellent French meals, which were catered by Maxim's of Paris. In First Class every thing was served from a cart.

We were required to have inoculations against diseases in dozens of countries, and when I next saw George in Washington, I looked like a heroin addict from all the needle bruises. They also drew a lot of blood, and that was something else we had to do for our on going health regime. After awhile I kidded the nurses that they would get nothing but red wine out of my veins, perhaps mixed with some champagne bubbles. It was wonderful living in that time before AIDS became epidemic and no one worried about getting some horrid report from the company doctor.

We were measured for our uniforms by the last week in training. We wore skirt suits when I started, and shapely legs were taken into consideration during hiring. Pan Am chose only the more attractive women. If you gained too much weight in their opinion, you were advised to lose pounds "or else." Our uniforms were form fitting, and you had to button all the way up. I immediately started wearing brassiere minimizers because I looked more buxom in this suit style which didn't please me.

One rule they had, I thought was terrible. Every gal had to cut her hair just below the ears. Naturally they didn't want hair so long it would flip over your shoulder and into the food when you leaned over a seat, but what would be neater than pulling it back into a neat bun or pony tail? I knew one gal who had hair even finer than mine and looked beautiful wearing it in a bun. It was a huge job for her to keep the shorter "bob" in tact, and it wasn't flattering to her at all. I think flight supervisors were more controlling of us than MGM was of their contract actors.

I saw more than one young woman pulled off flight when her unapproved nail polish color was spotted in the briefing room. Flight service would then quickly call another stewardess from the pool to report immediately. Oh, I forgot the white gloves which we were required to wear whenever reporting for a flight, or disembarking the plane. Pan Am had more rules for me than my mother and Florida State put together!

Scheduling could make or break your social life and for the six months while you were on probation, you had last choice of any route. Monthly flight schedules were doled out strictly by seniority. God forbid you missed showing up for a flight briefing. You went immediately into the pool standby group. This meant you had to be half packed and near a phone every minute. If you had to go to the grocery store, you had to call in and get permission. Cell phones would have been heaven sent in those days.

Gratefully, I found a new apartment in NYC, and my commuting life would be much easier, though I would still be going to Washington often. It was one block off Fifth Avenue on the corner of Fifty-fifth Street and Sixth Avenue. The building was brand new, and I even got the first two months rent-free. Good grief, talk about a fantasy in today's world. The rent was only $285.00 a month!

Well this meant that financially, I needed a roommate to make ends meet. Especially since my shopping habit had now expanded to include the market bazaars around the world. I had just shared fun flights with Kelly Tangen from Minnesota and she was looking for an apartment to share. I called her in early January because I thought it would be a good fit. She had a very outgoing personality with a neat freak gene like myself. I could never live with someone who was not clean and neat.

Living with another person who flew long international routes meant that I would have time alone, and I've always liked having only myself for company. That must be inbred as an only child. Artistically temperamental people I've met feel as I do about this. Later in my life, I would be very selfish with my time, but for now I was too busy attempting to explore this world filled with such amazing people and cultures.

In the first year of a flying career, you vary your schedule as much as possible because of all the cities you wanted to visit. I was astonished at how many seasoned flight attendants just stayed in their rooms the entire layover, reading books and ordering in room service. I felt I would never reach that point with such fine restaurants and art museums in any city we visited and of course, the shopping excursions.

Paris

After months of exploring, I had definite impressions on which cities were my favorites. I flew to those as often as possible. Even today, there is no way I could limit my favorite city to just one, as they each offer something unique and special all their own. New York however, will always be my heart city—that's a given. The gateway cities (as we labeled them on the line because they were turnarounds, or one layover before flying further east), all offered culture that was interesting to me, but I have to admit, because of the art scene and restaurants, Paris would have to be my favorite gateway.

"We'll always have Paris."

—HUMPHREY BOGART

Fortunately, my vocabulary in French grew slightly, so I enjoyed ordering my meals and all the shopping my meager salary would allow. Happily they gave anyone with an American passport 15% to 30% off retail prices. One accessory most all Pan Am girls owned was the Hermes silk scarf. We collected them in fact, as they were practically affordable then. Today the vintage silk go for as much as $500. As for French women, it was practically a rule of law that they had one casually draped around the neck or shoulder, or at least loosely looped around her purse strap.

The Montmartre was definitely one of my favorite areas, as it was an artist's district located on the highest hill, where you can grandly view the city. The bistros frame the square where dozens of the most famous artists in history worked and played. "Lapin Agile" is the café Picasso had his infamous shouting matches with Modigliani. Renoir, and Vincent van Gogh mixed with the intellectuals at the beginning of the Twentieth century on those quaint streets. I bought some very weird art from sidewalk vendors before my taste developed almost by osmosis due to my exposure to some of the best art museums and galleries in the world. Later in my flying career, I had an interesting trip to Paris due to some famous friends coinciding with my trips. I was flying with Birgitta Lind from Sweden and while we were shopping one afternoon, we ran into a suave gentleman with a most stylish umbrella upon which he was leaning.

"Hi Ruby," I greeted him. After the perfunctory kiss on each cheek, I asked him why he was simply standing on the sidewalk.

"I'm waiting for Odile (his wife, whom I also knew) who is upstairs at the hairdressers," he replied. Frenchmen are *much* more apt to do this sort of waiting than American men!

I introduced him to Birgitta, and he then invited us to his home in the Bois de Bologne for a party he was having the next night for a famous French movie star. I thanked him but declined. We would have both needed to call in sick, both with the same flu. Surely we would have gone into the pool upon our return to NYC. When we finished talking, and Birgitta and I continued down the avenue, she asked, "What a gorgeous man. What did you say his name was?"

When I told her it was Porfirio Rubirosa, she shrieked at me, "No, I can't believe we turned down an invitation from the most famous playboy in the world! I will never have another opportunity like that."

Ruby was world renown because of the famously beautiful and wealthy women he had squired or married. I've never understood why a movie hasn't been made of his complicated, fascinating life. He married five or six times, and his rich wives gifted him with Polo Ponies, airplanes, estates and money upon their divorces!

> *"I'm colored, Jewish and Puerto Rican. When I*
> *move into a neighborhood I wipe it out."*
>
> —SAMMY DAVIS, JR.

Birgitta and I were flying together all month. One of our subsequent flights also took us to Paris over the weekend that Sammy Davis was opening at the Olympic Theatre. Sammy and I were friends at this point, and I was invited to the opening. Because of this, I had bid for this trip in particular. They had an interesting arrangement at the Olympic, in that the opening act began the same night as the preceding act was closing its' engagement. In this case, Johnny Hallyday the extremely popular French singer in Europe, was ending his show.

I took Birgitta with me to the theatre after dinner around nine or ten o'clock. That meant we would hang around back stage for a couple of hours before Sammy went on stage at midnight. This was not a new experience for me, but I think Birgitta was rather fascinated. Here is this delicate young Swedish beauty mixed in with mostly black, on the road show people. Shirley and George were two of Sammy's great friends, as well as his keepers of the faith. Shirley kept him as organized as was possible with an over the top talent like him, and George played the piano. I genuinely enjoyed them.

Before long we were included in a card game and laughter was everywhere. It's always hyper on an opening night and this was no exception. Just before the time Mr. Davis was to begin, one of his assistants showed us to our seats in the front row center. As always Sammy put on the most incredible one man act, with energy only he possessed.

He danced, he sang, he played instruments and even thumped a tune on a chair he held in mid air. He received a thunderous standing ovation for his performance and earned it. Birgitta and I were dressing for our flight back to New York about three hours later. I'm not sure the passengers received the energetic service they deserved from us that day aboard Pan Am.

Rome

Is there anyone who spent time in Rome who didn't LOVE it? I can't imagine. The Italian men made the plainest young women feel pretty, or at the very least, desirable. You dated them and let yourself feel adored, but you *never ever* married an Italian man! They are *so incapable* of fidelity—words which may have been written in stone not long after the Ten Commandments.

"Everyone soon or late comes 'round by Rome."
—ROBERT BROWNING

I cried when my gorgeous modeling friend, Eugenia McLin told me she was marrying one Fabrizio de Toledo. Eugenia spent one year at FSU before becoming a very successful model in New York, where she met Fabrizio.

Frustrated I said, "I don't care if he IS from a fine old titled Italian family and you will qualify as a Countess ... AND he is good looking, brilliant and attending MIT. He is a control freak and will make your life miserable. Okay, so you CAN go to Italy and select precious stones from the family jewel vault and have your own designs set with them. He is soooo wrong for you." However, she did indeed marry him ... and he WAS!

Now moving away from the male specimens in this gloriously historic city, one could go straight to heaven from most of the tables in most of the restaurants there—with a full tummy and a smile on the face, if not a little cheese sauce on the chin. We use to go to the original Alfredo's and Alfredo himself would come to our table of beautiful females to mix our pasta with his personally created Alfredo sauce! He always left one portion in the bottom of the large wooden bowl and presented it to the lady of his choice that evening. Yes, once I even got the bowl. It made my day. There is always extra cheese sauce on the bottom!

Rome was especially fun for me because my friend Nancy Larson was living just off the Via Veneto. We had originally met on the LBJ Presidential charters when she was working at the White House. We were instant friends as she had flown with TWA before going to Washington and I had done the opposite. At this time however, she had been assigned a position at the American Embassy and had met so many interesting people through her job.

Very near her apartment was a place called Davey's Dive where all the cool Americans hung out. We often went there after dinner. It was more a saloon than a good food restaurant, and you never knew whom you might see. Elizabeth Taylor and Richard Burton might well be in the room with Richard holding court or even my early favorite, Clint Eastwood.

Clint was making his spaghetti westerns in Italy then as Hollywood had shunned him—hard as that is to believe today. I shot darts with him, because that was the big game at Davey's. He wasn't the big deal he later became and was just one of the simply gorgeous, sexy, cool, hunky guys around town then. This is a nice example of the good old days.

One of my close friends from the Pan Am days is Barbara Klenk, who still lives in NYC. She came from a fine Connecticut family and was very refined compared to me (diamond in the naive, I liked to think of myself). That was the era of the popular TV series "Hogan's Heros." There was a character called Colonel Klenk, a name some in the airline used for her.

Often when I call her now I just say, "Klenk, it's me." She was small in stature, but huge in personality, and I think in the company, people either loved her, or really didn't care for her. There were few people in between. She was straight up and in your face when she wasn't happy about something, but she had a powerful sense of humor I loved. We bid together often because we had such a great relationship. She had flown for years before I came along, but from the beginning she accepted me as okay to share her time.

The continuation flight from Paris to Rome, which originated in New York, never had more than a few people on it because it didn't depart Paris until almost midnight. Who would choose that hour to travel if they could avoid it? I can tell this story now, as Pan Am is defunct. We always finished up the First Class bottles of delicious French wines that were left over. And, per chance there wasn't a bottle left open, we would just have to uncork another for this short continuation of the trip.

We drank these smooth wines in those darn paper cups because with even the few passengers on board, it would have been unseemly for them to see their stewardesses enjoying red beverages in stemmed wine glasses. I promised myself that when I quit flying, I would never drink any liquid out of a vessel other than a beauteous stemmed cut crystal glass. I have pretty much stuck to that promise whenever possible.

London

Our round the world route leaving for London on flight # One for our first layover, was a 14 day trip. We had a turnaround after staying in Hong Kong two days before taking flight # Two back to New York. A crew from San Francisco worked it from from Hong Kong back to the west coast. I'm pretty sure the cost in the sixties was one thousand two hundred dollars in the tourist section to circle the globe. You could stay in any of our stop over cities you chose along the way. That would be quite a deal today.

"When it's three o'clock in New York,
it's still 1938 in London."

—BETTE MIDLER

London has to be on my favorites list because if nothing else, I could converse freely with the British. I also had a girlfriend who lived there and I often stayed at her flat instead of the hotel. I loved her expressions, which translated quite differently in our language. The first time she said to me, "He's going to bang me up," I asked quickly, "What?" and she explained, "He's phoning me." The British usually said "telly" for TV or television and at a restaurant they would queue up for the bog while we wait in line for the bathroom, not the water closet. . . . but you knew that.

I also loved going to the theatre there. I do believe the longest running play anywhere had to be, "The Mouse that Roared." I myself must have seen it five times during my eight years of flying. I didn't find the restaurants as inviting as in Paris, and I'm sure they are quite sick of that comparison by tourists. The pubs were great though.

Shopping was not my favorite pursuit in London, but one always strolled around Harrod's Department Store because it was so diversified and more of a happening than the usual retail places. I felt it was their Bloomingdale's, that is, the original store in NYC on Lexington. My favorite activity was in the Mayfair Section at the White Elephant Club. They were happy to have pretty Pan Am girls there any evening because it was an additional attraction along with the gambling. I never drank enough wine or cocktails to lose much money, and the dealers would let us win when possible because it kept the guys at the tables longer, and they were the spenders. I did pick up some talent playing Black Jack, however, by watching and listening. *And*, I met and talked with Sean Connery here. A bonus!

Beirut

Tempest Beirut, though it was beyond the gateway cities was as special as they come. It was known as the Paris of the Middle East. Our crews stayed at The Phonecia Hotel which was a totally white marble palace, staged against the deep blue Mediterranean Sea. I genuinely loved every visit I made there and never once missed a trip to the gold market. It was probably the best in the world then. We carried pictures of the latest designs from Van Cleef, Tiffany or Cartier, and they would copy them exactly. The amazing part was that the gold merchants charged nothing for the workmanship. They simply weighed the gold (14k or 18k, your choice) and charged you for the grams used. They did the same for the karat weight of the gems. I have jewelry to this day from that market. I should have bought MORE.

On the drive into Beirut from the airport, our route always took us past a huge territory of cardboard housing, tents and an awful odor that diffused onto the highway. This, I quickly learned was the Palestinian refugee camp. It was extremely depressing. I could see small children playing in the squalid standing water after a rain, or without warm clothing in the cooler months. It was another chapter unfolding in the history books being written about the never ending battle between the Arabs and the Jews.

*"It was once considered the
Paris of the Middle East."*

—Lyn Mathews

Whenever someone in America would say, "Life just isn't fair" over some trivial thing, my mind would jump first to that refugee camp, followed with the primitive style of living by so many people I saw first hand in my travels around the world.

Later in my flying career, I dated a handsome Lebanese air force pilot on these trips, as did every other Pan Am girl who was his type. Some of them fell quite in love with Philippe, and I assume they had deeper relationships than I had.

He knew I had worked for a U. S. Senator and his dream was to live in Washington. He was extremely polite and never pushed himself on me. Once, many miles out of the city with him, visiting ruins near Balbek, I thought to myself, he could rape me, or do anything else, and I had put myself in this scary position. But, thank heaven, he turned out to be trustworthy. I heard Philippe al Fata was shot down while fighting in the Six Day War with Israel, if so his dream of living in Washington died with him.

Calcutta and Rangoon

The world's weather affected the airlines as much then as it does now. We could never be absolutely certain we would end up where our luggage and crew tags marked our final stop for the night.

My Guardian Angel traveled with me throughout my flying career though all of my friends were not so lucky. Most of us knew at least one crew member when Flight 103 went down over Lockerbie, even though 1988 was long past my flying years. Once, I was on board a flight bound ultimately for New Delhi, but we lost an engine going into Calcutta, one of our stops en route. That turned into a neat four days for me as I had never been there and the only pilot who ever made my heart beat a little faster was also on this flight.

We didn't often fly with the San Francisco based cockpit crews because the turn around city was Hong Kong. But now and then, they would fly on to Bangkok or New Delhi with the NYC based cabin crews. Marty Seaholm lived in Seattle and commuted to San Fran for his flights. We explored the city together until another engine could be brought in from Hong Kong for us. This was the first time I had seen a Boeing fly in with five engines, as they ferried our replacement engine as their fifth "pod."

A passenger piled his cases on the scale at an airline counter in New York and said to the ticket agent: "I'm flying to Hong Kong. I want the large case to go to Calcutta and the two smaller ones to go to Rangoon. "I'm sorry, sir, but we can't possibly do that," said the ticket agent. "Why not, you did it the last time!" the passenger replied.

—ANONYMOUS TRAVELER

Meanwhile, Calcutta offered a departure from our usual layovers. Our hotel was in the middle of the city on a very busy street. Though I had known that cattle are sacred in India, it was made clearer to me as I stepped outside the hotel and literally walked within inches of a huge cow *with* horns. I stood as a statue until he meandered past us. No one in the market places we walked that day would even lightly slap one of those bovines on the rump to hurry it along. They moseyed around at their own pace as though they were equal partners with the human species. They, however, would depart from us socially when it was time to drop enormous plops of dung.

After one such event, Marty and I were near enough that it dampened my desire to ogle more wares, so we walked back to the hotel.

We were briefed by the airport station manager upon arrival that we needed to be extremely careful not to ingest *any* of the local water, or risk severe diarrhea. So, at the hotel, I brushed my teeth once again and rinsed with warm coca cola (which became a dreaded ritual after several days). I put on my bathing suit, sundress, and grabbed my sunglasses. We were going to spend the afternoon at the British Country Club.

On the street again we boarded a rickshaw with its one man engine or rickshawalla to deliver us to our destination. It was actually quite a lovely club, and we ordered sodas and drinks "neat," all the while thinking, "My God, ice cubes are made with *what* water?" No wonder the English carried on this Colonial habit for generations, even in Britain. "I'll have a whiskey neat, please." I'll say it again, "Wine is the answer."

The real trick was actually swimming in the pool without daring to touch your tongue to your lips, which were wet with *that* water. I don't know how we managed, but I don't believe anyone on our crew suffered dysentery. Thanks to Marty's company, that engine loss provided special memories for me.

On another trip, a sketchy landing decision was made by our Captain during a slight *monsoon* in Rangoon. He felt the winds were not yet so bad and that he could make it safely, or he wouldn't have taken it on. Every pilot I ever flew with was very disciplined, and I always felt confident that we had the best in the world. Our touch down was okay BUT something ahead required the crew to engage those brakes with sledge hammer force. Everyone not buckled in tightly were forced forward in their seats.

In first class, we had one of those clowns in the front row aisle who unbuckled the second we hit the runway. Without the bulkhead to stop him, he came sailing right at me in the jump seat. This was not a Don Knotts type. He was a BIG guy, who with a few more meals could become a sumo wrestler. I quickly leaned as far to the right as I could and somehow he was able to bend his body so as not to hit the cockpit door with his head. He did deplane with large bruises, but no broken bones that we could determine. My guess is that he never unbuckled again until a plane's engines were silenced!

Iran

Tehran was another city I found fascinating and, of course, very different from the Iran we know today, as ruled under the Mullahs. It was very westernized under the Shah, and young people especially latched on to every American trend from clothing designs to music. Being a Pan American hostess was almost like being a movie star there, especially for the tall blondes. We stayed at the Hilton Hotel built high above the city with a backdrop of the beautiful Alborz Chainal Mountains. If your room was on the north side, that was your view, but just as spectacular was the south side in offering you a panoramic scene of the city.

The smarter gals saved their money for the shopping here because Persian carpets were a very good investment. The Persians were among the first of the Ancient Civilizations 2,500 years ago to loom these pieces of art. The process of dying their wool, cotton and silk was very secretive and passed down through generations. Even Alexander the Great coveted and collected them. I found it somewhat crazy, but the merchants would lay these gorgeous creations out on the sidewalks (which were very wide) so that the pedestrians would walk over them all day long.

I came to understand that a new carpet obviously possessed NO history, and the idea was to have one that had served generations of your family before you. This could also mean that you descended from a higher lineage. The more thread bare the better! Florida girl that I was, I liked the ones that weren't "dirtied and aged" first, so those I bought still look almost new after years of *indoor* use.

Many of us in the crew enjoyed going to the "American Club," the night spot that drew much of the local American community and the wealthy young (or not so young) Iranian men who very much wanted to meet Pan American stewardesses. Kelly, my roommate in NYC, had met several Iranians previously and according to a letter I wrote to my mother in March of 1963, we had quite a time there.

> *"The world's first global superpower in human history. It's no wonder with their history reaching back to 7 centuries BC, they are offended by a usurper like America."*
>
> —ANONYMOUS

These are snippets from that letter. *"We arrived in Tehran about midnight from Beirut, where Kelly's friend Manu met us at the airport and introduced us to two very attractive young Persian men, Iradj Firoug and Prince Marmoude who is the younger brother of the Shah. They took us to a* darling (youth speaking here) *cabaret in the foothills where we ate our fill of caviar and drank great champagne. Our bosses at Pan Am would have had a fit to see us still in our uniforms at this point.*

We had dressed them up by sticking flowers in all our jacket buttonholes and a couple in our hair. Towards dawn everyone enthusiastically decided to drive over to Iradj's ranch for horse back riding. After borrowing strange looking pants, we rode these exquisite Arabian animals while the sun rose over the mountains. It wasn't a sunrise I will easily forget."

Without a speck of sleep, we barely arrived back at the airport in time for our 7:30 A.M. shuttle flight to Istanbul. Kelly was in the galley and whipped up some bananas flambé to the passenger's delight—for breakfast and we all had fun in the front cabin.

My letter continued; *"I slept the entire day in Istanbul before returning to Tehran where we again went out with our newest Iranian friends. The Prince is more physically attractive than his brother, but not blessed with as much intellect. He isn't affected by being a 'your Royal Highness' type and is fun. We went to a beautiful hotel bar that Iradj owns. He seems to be very wealthy, as his ranch was more like a grand mansion with a library of leather bound books from floor to ceiling. This is another country that seems to have almost no middle class. You are either very rich, or a servant."*

Tehran was usually a two night layover without the Istanbul shuttle when we worked the round the world flights, One or Two. The turn-around point as I mentioned earlier was in Hong Kong for the crews. It was rough physically because of the late night arrivals and middle of the night departures however.

My favorite specialty food comes from Iran. The Caspian Sea has always yielded the delicious large grey globule Beluga Iranian caviar, and I missed that as much as almost anything else when I stopped flying. We bought it from a fellow right at the airport for the price of $7.50 per half kilo, or $14.00 for a full kilo. It goes for hundreds of dollars now, so I can only daydream of the days I spread it over my English muffins for breakfast, or filled a crispy baked potato skin and then put sour cream on top.

In those years while the Shah ruled Iran, there was no oversight by the Religious Mullahs and the society was very westernized. The young people especially loved all things American, from fashion to films and television programs. For those more structured by the Muslim faith however, veiled women were often seen in public. I felt quite comfortable alone in that city, as our two countries were "friends." But as in all of history, alliances shift from year to year between countries. The Shah became totalitarian. Students began demonstrations against him and stirred the population into the revolution that caused him to abandon his throne of thirty-eight years, in January of 1969.

He sought refuge in Egypt, Morocco and even America for cancer treatment, but returned to Egypt where he died in July 1980. President Anwar Sadat honored this Shahanshah with a State Funeral in Egypt.

Karachi

Another stop on our far eastern travels was Karachi, and those were the days I would go exploring on my own, walking through tiny rough streets in neighborhoods so distant that I carried the name of my hotel and the address along with questions in Farsi in my purse.

Since Karachi was in the South, many of the family's activities could be carried on outside their primitive houses. The children played with simple sticks or balls, anything they could chase or throw to one another.

The women would be pounding their dough as thin as possible to create their Chapati bread, which I found pleasant if crisp, but still fairly tasteless. I loved sampling local breads all over the world. Hey, if they made good bread and wine, that country got four stars from me.

> *"We think in generalities,*
> *but we live in the details."*
>
> —ALFRED NORTH WHITEHEAD

It was a good time to explore the cultures of the Middle and Far East as an American. Today it would be a suicide wish to wander around alone over there. I wanted to educate myself by witnessing the local people and the way in which they lived. In the out regions, they were as fascinated by me as I was with them. They were always extremely courteous and friendly to my very American self.

There were beautiful sandy beaches near Karachi, and one activity many of us enjoyed was fishing with "Capt'n Charlie." He was very popular, and you had to call as soon as you hit town and hope he wasn't booked. His boat was a hand hewn wooden sailing vessel about thirty feet long with a pretty decent size beam. We would meet him at the harbor where he would explain his rules. When the winds were strong, he would show the first timers how the dagger boards (long lengths of lumber) were used to help balance the boat after we were underway.

This was *my* thing for sure. When the vessel leaned either to the starboard or port, the dagger was pushed out from the opposite side about seven feet. You would then move your weight to the end and sit while holding on. The hull was shallow, so you were not riding very high over the waves and this meant your legs were often in the splash.

Sometimes a high wave would absolutely soak you. It was like riding in space, so exhilarating and I absolutely loved it.

One particular voyage with Charlie is memorable because of the four stewardesses I took with me. They were new and each was from a different country. They all loved riding the dagger board and when we reached the narrow peninsula of sand that stands between Karachi and the open Arabian Sea, we rode on the dromedary camels. Sure it was touristy, but how many people were able to experience this so freely along this stretch of beach?

Everyone seems to refer to both the two hump and one hump animals as camels, but actually the one hump animal is a dromedary. When you ride the saddle on top of that one it feels as though you are floating wildly up there. Whereas on a horse, you can feel the muscles of the animal with your legs, which gives you a more secure fit. I never fell, but it was hardly a graceful ride—simply a bouncy uneven loping affair. They are also nicer than purported, certainly those who are accustomed to being ridden by strangers. And, I might have done harm if I had long sexy eyelashes like theirs.

Sailing back, Capt'n Charlie anchored as always and showed the girls how to fish for crabs, which he would cook and serve as our afternoon meal. Our fishing poles were actually nothing more than a long cord to which he attached a little piece of fish as bait. I was squeamish the first time I brought a crab up, but *nothing* compared to these gals. I could not believe the squealing, along with hysterical phrases in four different languages. I didn't understand a single word of their Chinese, Swedish, Italian or Icelandic. They were terrified whenever a crab appeared on the end of the string as it broke the water's surface. Each gal reverted to her mother tongue. Charlie and his mate had to "boat" the crabs, but I must say after they were cooked, everyone devoured them with enthusiasm. He had his recipe for his bounty of the sea down pat.

Bangkok

Everyone flying with Pan Am whom I knew, loved the layovers in Bangkok. Most of us acquired a taste for their delicious spicy foods, although I always ordered mine lightly spiced. I was sucking on ice cubes during my first meal there and learned that I couldn't even handle what they labeled medium spicy.

We stayed at The Princess Hotel right in the middle of the city and it was a ritual when you awakened in the morning to head down to the hotel spa. We spent many hours getting our hair done, followed by a massage, a manicure and pedicure, all of which cost under $10. After my first stress releasing appointment, I was sun bathing by the pool when a seasoned stewardess came up to me and said, "I hear you gave the girls a $10 tip."

I confirmed that I had, because with such a low charge for all that pampering, I would have felt too guilty leaving anything less.

"Well, she said curtly, don't do it again or you'll spoil it for the rest of us!"

Despite a few brittle babes, most of the young women with whom I flew were extremely responsible and thoughtful. One errand we always shared in Bangkok was going over to Jim Thompson's Thai Silk Shop. The bright hues and mixes of orange and pink or aqua and lime green in his prints were breathtaking. I had difficulty buying bathing suits for my size 6 bottom and double D top. This was a perfect place for me to have my suits custom made. Another bonus was being able to order a sundress and hair scarf to match from the same fabric. The price then was so affordable that, after I used them 5 or 6 times, I could just discard the suits. The pool water was hard on those, but the dresses lasted for years.

Jim Thompson is a legend in Thailand and for good reason. His liberal politics caused a rift with his very Republican family and he ended up with the OSS during World War Two.

> *"Do the right thing. It will gratify some people and astonish the rest."*
> —MARK TWAIN

The OSS was the forerunner of the newly formed CIA in 1947. Soon after V-J Day, he was assigned to run their offices in Bangkok and his love affair with all things Thai began. The cottage industry of weaving silk was dying out, and he revitalized it into a world renowned business when he founded the Thai Silk Company.

He provided colorfast dyes, and standardized looms as well as technical assistance to the Thai women who then were able to work at home. He made millionaires of many of them by giving them shares of stock in his company, which made a profit the very first year. Since the seventies, the work has been done in huge factories in order to fill the large orders for the bolts of silk worldwide.

One Easter day in 1967, he went out into the foothills to hike and never was seen again. His mysterious disappearance only added to the folklore in Thailand. For years, articles have been written around the world about his life. We were the lucky ones who were able to meet him in person and listen to his fascinating stories. He created a stunning home Thai style and filled it with his superb Buddhist and secular art from many countries in the East.

I knew a few of the girls who were invited to see it but my trips there were never good timing for an invitation. If I ever return, I definitely want to see it. Outside the Grand Palace, it is the second most popular attraction for tourists.

Of all the cities I have traveled with Pan American, I think Thailand and the Thai people were the most courteous and sweetest of any people with whom I spent time. Today, I have dinners or lunch at several of the wonderful Thai Restaurants in Miami, not only for the food, but to talk with the Thai waiters and waitresses. They tell me that Chiang Mai meaning New City, which is north of Bangkok, is cleaner and very popular with American tourists today.

Hong Kong

If a psychiatrist had asked me to say the first thing that popped into my mind in response to a word he would say—it would have gone like this: "Hong Kong"—"Shopping."

> *"Whoever said money can't buy*
> *happiness, simply didn't know*
> *where to go shopping."*
>
> —Bo Derek

This is a city where we waited to sleep until after everything we needed to buy or have custom made was finished. Whoa, what a place this was for finding bargains and getting great custom work for anything, once the Pan Am old timers told you exactly where to shop. We ordered everything from silk lampshades to golf shoes. We spent precious little time on anything else, but showing the workmen pictures of what we wanted and giving them our personal specifications. *That* was fun. It would usually take until your next trip to pick up your order, but it worked for us.

Hong Kong bustled in much the same manner as New York City and I enjoyed the pace very much. I also enjoyed the bargaining and was getting fairly good at it after all my practice in the Lebanese and Turkish bazaars. It was, I think, the most manic of cities. Simply everyone was rushing, rushing, rushing!

Famous Jet Setters

You never knew who would make your flight interesting when you boarded your aircraft in any city. Some flights were nothing but enjoyable and others more like the Chinese torture drip.

Phyllis Diller and one of her later husbands (pretty young as I remember) sat in First Class one afternoon when I only had a couple of other passengers seated there. It had to be the funniest four or five hours I ever spent working. She had a few drinks, and it became a regular sit down comedy routine. At one point she pulled out her travel jewelry case to show me how many times she had been engaged, or married.

I expected to see six or eight rings, but no, she had every diamond from the individual rings all set in one enormous ring. The gems were different shapes, but all size large. She convinced me to put it on and I needed Jackie-O sunglasses to look straight at it. Then out came a couple more sparklers and my hands looked like Marilyn Monroe's in "Gentlemen Prefer Blondes," minus the long pink satin gloves.

This is not much of a story compared to a friend of mine who related getting into Elizabeth Taylor's jewelry case with her in a First Class lounge during the middle of the night. While, I might add, her little doggies were pee peeing all over the carpet. More than one stewardess complained about their doggie act. Surely they were trained, but perhaps the long flights were just too much for their little bladders.

On one of my flights to Rome, I was delighted to see Emilio Gucci sitting in one of my First Class seats. It was well known that if you were lucky enough to have him on board, you were sure to get his personal card with a note awarding you with the shoes of your choice in his store. I picked up a beautiful pair in his Gucci Flagship shop after checking into my hotel in Rome.

> *"Celebrity is the chastisement of merit*
> *and the punishment of talent."*
>
> —EMILY DICKINSON

Charles Lindburgh served on the Pan Am Board of Directors, but he chose to sit in the first row behind the First Class bulkhead. Three seats were always reserved for him so that he could stretch out and sleep. I, as well as every stewardess who had him on board, treated him with great respect. He rarely ate and talked very little.

We had every famous person or movie star you can name on board at one time or another. It was always interesting to see how they treated the lowly working crew. I have to say that most of them were absolutely super nice and some were down right fun.

Gina Lollobrigida and Marcello Marciano were two of my favorites. The Italians just seem to add spice to life wherever they are. These were the days before hijackings and the Captain would usually invite a beautiful actress like Sophia Loren into the cockpit, so he could have his picture taken with her.

Certainly the most distinguished personage I ever shared a Pan Am fuselage with was the Shah of Iran. This is where you will ask yourself, why would the Shahanshah, His Imperial Majesty of the Iranian Monarchy, not be flying on one of his own private jets? I began to realize, empirically speaking, one experience that many world leaders from Presidents to Dictators shared in common was that of having a Pan American stewardess as a lover or mistress.

Mohammed Reza Pahlavi was provided a private cabin between cabins, where his beautiful blonde German friend served him and his bodyguards. Since his friend was also mine, she felt comfortable having me as the Purser on this flight. We were given all sorts of etiquette rules and as I welcomed him aboard, I lowered my head to the point where my hat fell forward into my hands. Very cool of me! When you entered his cabin you had to back out as you never turn your back on the King of Kings!

When we arrived in Frankfurt, our German stewardess departed the flight shortly after the Shah. She told me they were flying to St. Moritz aboard his plane for a ski vacation at his Chalet there. He was gracious however, in giving me a gold coin ring with his face on it.

The rest of us in the crew flew on to London, which was our layover destination. My closest guess regarding this particular incident is that the Shah was curious as to her actual job on flights. I was just a witness and not psychic enough to understand why a leader of his stature would fly on a commercial Pan Am flight. He was infamous for his insatiable appetite for women, and he loved blondes in particular. Fara Diba and his children had come to the bottom of the ramp to see him off and I learned that she was well aware of his philandering. It couldn't be easy to be the wife of a totalitarian Man-King.

Military Charters

Then there were the bloody hard work trips, when I flew the Military Charters out of Maguire AFB in New Jersey to Germany. Every single seat was filled and so many were entire military families. Some couples had five and six children, especially the Army flights into Mildenhall, England. Well, it only cost twenty dollars in co-pay to have a baby then—so why not. They could buy all their diapers in the commissary. If you could stand not being able to make many personal decisions throughout your life, it wasn't a bad career choice. For those born without the opportunity for a good education, it was perhaps the best choice, as you could gain a skill and good training.

Some of our stewardesses volunteered to live in the Far East and work the R&R flights for the guys and gals coming out of Vietnam. They sure needed those breaks and a little rest and recreation. Bangkok and Hong

Kong were favorite destinations for many. I was still based in New York, but flew many legs in the far East, when we had quite a few servicemen on board. We had large First Class sections and not very many passengers seated there on those flights, so I made a ritual of "special upgrades."

> *"A young man who does not have what it takes*
> *to perform military service is not likely to have*
> *what it takes to make a living."*
> —JOHN F. KENNEDY

Before takeoff after everyone was boarded, I would go into the tourist section which was usually quite full, and choose four or five guys, always the privates or noncoms. With a very business like attitude, I would request to see each one's ticket, and they quickly foraged through all their paperwork as though I were some General in front of them. As I examined their respective boarding passes, I would say with authority, "There has been a mistake here, please gather your things and follow me."

Concern and anxiety accompanied them up the aisle until I closed the partition and said, "Okay guys, take a comfortable seat because your party is starting right now. I'll be back with your champagne, "These were always the most unlikely fellows to ever sit in First Class. I decided Pan Am could afford a little extra wine for the war effort. These men had earned it. I loved doing this, and they got a big kick out of knowing that plenty of their superior officers were crunched in the back of the bus.

The Pool: Standby Flights

Certainly not all of our flights could be described as delightful. The one many of us dreaded was the Puerto Rican one-day turnarounds. They departed JFK very early in the morning, which meant getting up around 4 am, which for me has always been walking zombie time. The flights were always full to the max with many mothers holding infants, and that made the human count out number the seat allotment. They also carried on board tons of crazy looking bags of "who knew what" in every description of shape and color. Then to add to the joy, we could count on a number of them getting airsick. In fact, it became labeled the "Vomit Comet." Being on stand by for a month would guarantee you a couple of these stinkers.

"Sometimes you find the most amazing thing, in the most unexpected places."

—SAMBO MUHAMMAD

Stand by months were times when you could totally forget about planning anything in your personal life for any particular day or evening. You were at the mercy of scheduling. I was always as sweet as I could possibly be over the phone with them. There was much begging going on from many of us when we got the call that would dash our hopes of attending something important to us the same evening. Dating was a helter skelter affair to say the least. I mainly stayed home with TV dinners then.

"On call" could mean being in the Bahamas or Bermuda and forty-eight hours later, being ice bitten in Alaska. There was no covered ramp from aircraft into the arrivals building then. We threw our scarves across our faces and walked the 100 or so feet into the building. It only took a couple of minutes, but by then the moisture in your nostrils was frozen, your throat was sore from the few breaths you had taken and your eyes stung. I had never experienced 35 degrees below zero before and that wasn't counting the wind chill factor. Later in my life, Vermont skiing in icy winds would help me better acclimate to the cold.

Humor on Board

When you fly for an international carrier (Pan American was the first), you are going to experience first time passengers and different cultures that would cause a little private giggling amongst the crew. It was not malicious, but it reminded us that many in this world will die before they ever experience a flight on an airplane. We met some for whom it certainly was a first.

One particular afternoon I remember looking out the window at the Pakistani desert below as a long caravan all in black, excepting the camels, edged slowly forward. Further on I saw an encampment with large black tents in miniature from my lookout 35,000 feet above. I thought to myself, here am I in the twentieth century world of jets and skyscrapers and these Bedouins are living as their forefathers lived thousands of years ago. Travel was a gift to help me understand and learn reverence for all those who share this beautiful planet with me simultaneously, yet in very different dimensions of time.

In the Far East, we often noticed passengers both male and female, remove their shoes the minute they were seated. They often walked down the aisle in their footwear with awkwardness, especially the women trying to navigate in high heels. Many would assume the lotus position in their seats, which I found an extraordinary feat in a tourist sized space.

*"The scientific theory I like best is that
the rings of Saturn are composed entirely
of lost airline luggage."*

—MARK RUSSELL

I was in the tourist galley cooking during one flight when I glanced around the corner and saw an Indian man standing on his tippy toes in order to pee into the water fountain. Now this called for a little diplomacy on my part as I tapped him on the shoulder and motioned for him to put himself back inside his zipper and follow me. I showed him the lavatory and how to work all of the handles and buttons. Then I taped off the water fountain. This would not be the last time I would repeat that ritual.

Many women breast fed their babies aboard with no concern for privacy, which was not a custom in America in public places. They were quite relaxed with this custom. I became fairly comfortable with seeing it after a couple of years. In Pakistan, I was fascinated by the local cleaning men when they boarded during our short stops to brush and clean all the carpeted flooring. They would waddle through the entire cabin in a very low squatting position that if I tried, it would have left me crippled after a few rows. They had my total admiration for their great dexterity.

Then there was the glorious morning when Kelly and I were making that quick flight between Istanbul and Beirut. We were required to cook and serve one hundred and thirty three trays of breakfasts. I was in the galley and Kelly with another stewardess were in the aisle asking passengers to set up their tray tables so they could zip through with all of the hot food trays and pour the coffee in less than an hour and a half.

Large tin foil shallow containers of stirred raw eggs had been loaded by commissary along with equal amounts of sausages which the galley girl (after attaining altitude and the leveling off of the aircraft) was required to cook, spoon onto the plates, add sausage, then set on the trays for distribution. Each tin contained enough eggs for twelve passengers, which made it pretty heavy and almost full to the top. Well, as I lifted one container out of a very hot oven shelf to stir it and move it to the other side, the metal tray buckled!

This mental picture will NEVER leave me. People were lined up to go to the bathrooms not two feet from where I screamed out in pain as the scalding hot eggs slid down over my legs and onto the floor. I was cata-tonic as Kelly rushed into the galley and threw the curtain divider across the galley opening. Almost numb from the burning sensation on my legs, I said, "My God Kelly, what will we do? This is twelve servings lost."

Not missing a beat, she grabbed the container and said, "Scoop 'em up!"

Well, scoop we did, off the dirty floor and off my legs. She thought when we mixed them in with another batch, the damage would simply appear as though they had all ready been peppered. That had to be the worst of my galley experiences in the years I flew. There were no perma-nent scars on my legs, but I felt guilt about the "unclean" eggs we served a couple dozen people.

Challenges

As in many businesses, there was back stabbing and even blackmail for personal gain among some in Pan American. I flew with one male purser when I was fairly new, who always seemed to bid on the Bermuda turnarounds. On one such flight, I walked back to the galley and asked another attendant where the small milk cartons were, as I needed three for some children. The purser overheard me and in a mean voice asked me why I needed THREE. When I told him they were for children and I would probably need more than that, as there were other children I hadn't reached yet.

> *"Some cause happiness wherever they go;*
> *others, whenever they go."*
>
> —OSCAR WILDE

"You're not ASKING them if they want milk are you?"

"Why yes, I always do on flights," I commented.

"Well, not on my flights!" he lectured. "Don't ask anyone else."

I learned from another stewardess that he tried never to give out milk as he had a deal with a ground worker in Bermuda to whom he sold the crates of milk. It seems he was a deals kind of guy and worked other schemes to Pan Am's disadvantage.

I asked her how he got away with this year after year and she told me that as an old-timer, he kept a little Black Book on the Pan American Executives and none of them would dare say anything against him.

"What do you mean, little Black Book for what?"

She told me that many of the top executives would take girlfriends free on flights and this purser kept the dates and flight numbers, along with the lady's name from the manifest. Ah yes, men centuries later remain the hunters and the gatherers, while the mate stays home and keeps the hearth warm.

Gift to Parents

After several years of flying, I took my parents on a wonderful trip. Once a year we could take family members anywhere in the world for only ten percent of the total price.

As an around the world tourist ticket cost $1,200.00 normally, it cost only $120 for each of them. They came up to New York, and we left on Flight #1, for the overnight to London. I was a Purser by then and it was a courtesy we extended one another when there was room in First Class, that we upgrade each other's families.

"Seize the moment. Remember all
those women on the Titanic who
waved off the desert cart?"

—IRMA BOMBECK

Well, as an alcoholic, Gig was in heaven with a big comfy seat and lovely young ladies serving him spirits as fast as he could drink them. I should have clamped down because I didn't want the trip ruined for mother. After we helped him off the flight at Heathrow, he went into the men's room immediately to throw up, I made sure this would not become a ritual on our following flights.

I loved sharing all the wonderful sights, sounds and delicious restaurants I had been describing to them for years. We stayed in all the good hotels that Pan Am crews stayed and went in and out of the cities on the crew bus. Mother loved shopping in the bazaars and was amazed at what a negotiator I had become while purchasing items. In Lebanon, I made them ride camels and still have those silly pictures of Mother awkwardly hanging on for dear life.

It was the first time I felt I could do something meaningful for them both. I certainly wasn't hurrying to marry and give them grandchildren!

Cabinet Room Lecture to JFK

I was now living full time in New York City while flying, but often flew down to D. C. between flights to see George. One late summer afternoon when I was there, George and I were sitting in the comfort of the aft deck on "The Natamor" yacht having a drink and gossiping about things on The Hill.

I asked him if he'd seen Jack lately and he said, "No, in fact I haven't. It's only 6:30, let's call him and see if he's free to take a break and join us for a drink." Mrs. Kennedy spent much of the summer at their Hyannisport home, so JFK had even more *free* time then. I was not feeling as threatened as the last time we were together.

We weren't planning on leaving the dock, so it wouldn't have been difficult for him to pop in a car and come over. By that, I mean it would require only a bullet proof limousine with a few secret service men in tow and *not* the dozens or hundreds of personnel usually involved every time the President scheduled ahead to do anything.

> *"There is no human problem which*
> *could not be solved if people would only*
> *do as I advise."*
>
> —GORE VIDAL

When George reached him with the invite, he said, "I'd like to, but I have a few things left to do in the office. I'd love to see you and Layte though, so why don't you come over *here* and we'll have a drink together?"

When we arrived at the west gate of the White House, an assistant said that the President had asked him to show us into the Cabinet Room and he would meet us there. From the west gate entrance, that room is very conveniently located right off the garden patio.

I rarely wrote what I was wearing in my diary, but such unimportant things like that pop into your head sometimes. I was dressed in the *only* yellow outfit I owned, a lightweight pure mohair long sleeved sweater over a white shirt with yellow sharkskin pants and sneakers. When Jack entered the room donning a big smile, he said, "Layte, what a great color on you and so snappy for yachting!" He so often said complimentary things and would then go off on another subject immediately.

He called an aide to bring in the drinks we ordered and then we launched into light conversation. I look back at my irreverence with some embarrassment because I plopped my fanny down on top of the Cabinet conference table and propped my (very clean) white sneakers on a chair in front of me. George and Jack sat in chairs on either side of me. Perhaps subconsciously I enjoyed sitting higher than the two of them.

Before long I found myself lecturing JFK on being more discreet in his private life. The more amused he became, the more serious I grew. I told him that so many people I talked with knew he was being very risqué socially, and he was putting his presidency at risk!

He didn't pursue this with a single comment, but instead asked me if the stewardesses talked about him and what they were saying. Yes, I'm totally aware that one would think here that this is ridiculous babble. Others who knew him well, know it was quite predictable he would ask me a question like that.

I told him they all talked about him as though he was a movie star, and he was quite delighted hearing that and kept pushing me to relate other comments I heard and from whom. I couldn't believe how little fear he had in being exposed as such a womanizer.

Finally I said with a concerned voice, "Jack, it's only a matter of time before the press will pick up on your constant extracurricular activities and they *will* expose you."

His lack of concern was astonishing to me. Thinking back, I believe he felt himself on a plain above exposure. And after all, Chappaquiddick, which I always refer to as "Pandora's Box," had not yet been opened. Twenty-four hour a day news coverage on Cable Channels had not yet arrived either.

In truth, many in the press were absolutely captivated by his charm and physical comfort in their presence. Some who might have realized what his private life was about would quite possibly have been protective of him. He commanded that sort of personal shield. They of course were never privy to the behavior the Secret Service witnessed on a daily basis.

On another occasion, George and I joined JFK at The White House for a swim. I wasn't really surprised to see his younger staff women there to entertain The Man. Jack again swam dans le nudité. I always looked away when he entered or exited the pool. I amazed myself with my cool but managed to have fun in a one-piece bathing suit! The indoor pool was warm and quite pleasant as Ambassador Kennedy had commissioned a mural of St. Croix Harbor to adorn the walls. It wasn't sufficient to convince me I was swimming in the Virgin Islands, as one would have found nothing virginal around this president at play.

Lisbon

My years with Pan American were such a gift to me in this life and widened my eyes to so many cultures around the world. I'm afraid I was quite a challenge for Jim Kilites however, who was the boss of Flight Service personnel. I think he fired me at least three times. I would request time off to work on my Public Relations assignments from Bill Fugazy (then President of the Diner's Club) through the proper channels.

Jim would deny my request, and I would then call Senator Smathers in Washington and he would call the President, or a Veep at Pan Am and my request would be approved after I had already gone on my way. Meanwhile, Kilites would have put a *"you're fired for missing your assigned flight"* pink slip in my box. But later, I would be reinstated because the "okay" had filtered down to Jim.

One evening I showed up for a flight check in to Lisbon and was called up to Jim's office. He gave me quite a lecture and told me I had better not pull out for another one of my PR assignments again any time soon! I hadn't felt well all afternoon and I got sicker by the minute as he was scolding me. But I knew I HAD to somehow work this flight and not push his tolerance further.

> *"Reality is the leading cause of stress*
> *among those in touch with it."*
>
> —LILLY TOMLIN

I managed to help board the passengers, but after take off, I became so weak I almost fainted in the aisle. As there were very few passengers in First Class, one of the girls helped me lay down in the last row and covered me with several blankets. I was suffering chills and the sweats alternately. Toward the end of the flight, she must have told the Captain that she was quite worried by my condition, and he came back to talk with me. He became alarmed as well and asked me when I started feeling sick. I told him that afternoon, but I was afraid to cancel out of my flight because Jim Kilites was angry with me. After the flight deplaned the passengers, a hospital van pulled up to the front steps and they carried me to the vehicle.

I learned when I was alert enough to care, that I had been in a Catholic Hospital in downtown Lisbon for a few days. They thought I had Spinal Meningitis and wanted me to sign permission for them to give me a spinal tap. This is a moment when you would wish you were in a good American hospital and not in Portugal.

But, once again my timing was not so terrific. I gave them permission in hopes that I would not be paralyzed during the procedure. They tapped me, but it didn't prove to be the meningitis and only left me with terrible headaches at the base of my brain. After medications and a prescription for migraine (only worse) headaches, they sent me to our hotel until Pan Am could *deadhead* me to New York, (Again, no pun intended).

Poor Jim Kilites, he couldn't catch a break. The Captain on my flight over had called him upon return and gave him holy hell for making me fly when I was so sick. *He assumed other flight attendants* took their flights no matter how ill they were as well.

China Trip with
Senator Smathers

*"The rewards of the journey far outweigh
the risk of leaving the harbor."*

—ANONYMOUS

Considering the hundreds of television channels and reporters hiding or not, behind every tree in most cities today, a well known United States Senator could not possibly carry on an open affair such as we had in the early sixties. But in Europe and Asia, George felt a higher comfort level as far as privacy was concerned.

I had not been flying long with Pan American when George arranged with one of the top Vice Presidents of the company for us to make a trip to the Far East together. It was certainly comfortable first class travel and we stayed over in Paris, Beirut, Bangkok and Hong Kong. As for the Pan Am in-house gossips, I was not intimidated being George's in flight companion as everyone seemed to know my personal life by now.

The first evening in Paris, we went to a party at the American Embassy just across the street from the exclusive Hotel de Crillon on the Place de la Concorde. Though I had worked flights to and from Paris, I had not been inside this exquisite dwelling inhabited at that time by Ambassador Charles Bohlen.

I was overwhelmed by the French décor and extremely high ceilings over European marble floors and walls. American art was displayed to showcase our most famous artists and remind the French that art is not their exclusive domain. It was not a formal party, but most certainly the guests were very chic in their couture outfits and bijouterie. I was wearing a diamond broach that George had given me and quite a lovely opera length strand of Mikimoto pearls he bought for me during a previous visit to Hawaii.

Except for a gold watch (which later I quite accidentally sent sliding down my apartment trash bin with the kitchen refuse) and taking me to a furrier he knew in New York City for a jacket, I accepted nothing of real value except for these birthday gifts from him.

The second night in Paris, we were invited to a party at the home of Baron Guy de Rothschild. Theirs is one of the most interesting family histories in France. This home in Paris was their main residence and there are not enough adjectives for me to describe how ravishingly glamorous it was. I have loved art and design my entire life, and this would be the epitome for my eyes to devour. Every piece of their art, or collection of inlaid wood, or marble furniture were museum quality and worthy of display in the Louvre Museum. The pedigrees were impeccable of course.

Just a walk through house tour would have satisfied me, but I became engrossed by the ultra sophistication of the guests. They radiated self-confidence, and the women were so elegant in their flawless couture. They presented a glittering, polished exterior but it looked like hard work to me. Their frozen smiles framed their perfect sparkling teeth, which seemed to be competing with their jewelry! The only time I ever saw that many *huge jewels* in one place was at the Petroleum Club in Midland, Texas many years later. Style being what it is to the French, I suppose that's the only comparison I could make between Texas and Paris.

The champagne was French, of course, and the superb red wine was from the Rothschild's private stock of Chateau Lafite Rothchild. It was the first time I ever tasted it, but thankfully, not the last. Yes definitely, the wealthy and titled are very different in the way they live compared with most folks. I've never been jealous, as everyone's life has its own set of challenges, but it *was* fun to witness that level of society in their element.

The following morning it was "bon au revoir." George and I were off to our next destination in Lebanon.

Beirut

We flew into Beirut from Paris and stayed at the Phoenicia Hotel, which was where Pan American housed us on layovers. I loved this hotel. Everything in the entry foyer was white marble with large round columns scattered throughout. Arab men in traditional floor length garments offered tea from huge silver trays to arriving guests, a gracious welcome indeed. I took George to Le Cave, which I was told was the very first actual discothèque in the world and where I had been many times. I knew he would enjoy seeing it, even though I also knew he wouldn't disco dance with me.

> *" I have the simplest tastes. I am always*
> *satisfied with the best."*
>
> —OSCAR WILD

One day we were driven the 85 km to Baalbeck, which like so many areas in the Middle East, has documented history dating back over 5,000 years. During the Roman era, a complex of stone temples was built, parts of which have lasted all these millennia The Temple of Bacchus originally had forty-two majestic Corinthian Columns and nineteen of the intricate structures still remained upright. It is considered to be the most well preserved Roman temple in the world and was well worth the 55 mile drive.

Beirut was one of my favorite cities, and it was emotionally painful to me years later when I saw on television American warships shelling it from offshore. I thought of the friends I had made there in my favorite neighborhood cafes and shops in the gold market.

Bangkok

Our next stop was Bangkok, which was another of my very favorite cities. The PAA girls especially loved going there because we were so pampered. On this trip I would be pampered in a different way. We stayed in a multi star hotel and dined in the highly rated restaurants. Did I say George was born with a silver spoon in his mouth? I think knowing what his life was like for the 93 years he lived it, that spoon was platinum.

Today I hear that Bangkok traffic, filled with old inefficient American cars, makes it hard to breathe in a city smothered in exhaust fumes. George and I did what most tourists do when first visiting Bangkok. We took a tour of the klong and life as the Thais live it along the river edges within view. It was the soul of the city. Commerce and the inhabitants' everyday life chores permeate in and aside its core. Throughout each day, boats carrying enterprising salesmen and women would pull along side other boats with their wares, making it a floating marketplace.

*"If you look anything like your passport
photo, you are too ill to travel"*
—WILL KOMEN

Shacks and hovels were about all we saw in those days after leaving the inner city river way. Thai people have always been extremely industrious, and even the children were busy with their crafts after playtime. There was one scene I will never forget. A mother, dad and two young children were standing knee deep at the edge of the klong. As the father was shaving, the mother was washing clothes and the little girl was brushing her teeth while the little boy was peeing in the water right next to her!

If you could survive childhood in those polluted waters, you built up an immune system strong enough to reach a very old age!

Of all the countries I visited in my life, no society of people were as sweet and soft in their mannerisms as the Thais. They seemed to honestly like Americans, and if that was only for show, then they also qualified as great actors.

Hong Kong

It was now time to do Hong Kong. Of course at that time, interior China was closed to Americans, but there was plenty to see and do in this bustling city. We checked into the Mandarin Hotel, which was newly opened as the flagship for their luxurious international hotel chain.

George had a nice suite on a top floor, and I had a room a couple of floors down. His windows provided us sweeping panoramic views of much of the city. It was so terribly crowded with people that having run out of ground space to build, they simply put together shacks on the rooftops of many of the buildings. It resembled a refugee camp from above, but wasn't noticeable from the street level.

"What's love got to do with it?"
—TINA TURNER

One evening I remember us taking a sampan which was one of those little boats used for ferrying everything from tourists to fish from one area to another in the harbor. Our destination was a large vessel that had been suggested to us as a great dining spot. Indeed, it was unusual, as the wooden ship was quite old and ornate in design. The atmosphere provided an expectation of seeing Errol Flynn swing by pirates on a rope. The evening sky was flawless and contained a huge round, very iridescent pearlized moon. That night remained a clearer picture in my mind than most from our trip and for good reason.

This was our first night and though I officially had my own room as usual, where I would dress and shower, I spent little other time in it. In this Hong Kong hotel, I found it curious that there was a Chinese man sitting near the elevator on every floor, because I didn't see that much need for security. After returning from the floating restaurant, we went to George's room for the night. About two in the morning, the phone rang and George mumbled several things into the receiver, "Oh, I see," and "Yes, I understand, no problem."

He turned toward me and out of my sound sleep I also heard him say, "It seems you have to leave and sleep in your own room."

"WHAT? You must be kidding!"

"No" George said, "they have us registered in different names, in different rooms, and it appears that you are not allowed to sleep all night in mine." As you had to submit your passport to even register for a room while traveling, it would have been difficult to register anywhere as Mr. and Mrs. Jones.

I was extremely surprised, and sputtered, "Well, you'll walk me down won't you?"

Caught up as I was in my embarrassment over this whole turn of events, I didn't realize how mad I would be later when he said, "Well, it's silly for both of us to have to get dressed and you'll be perfectly safe."

Well, *that was obvious*, as they seemed to know exactly what bed in the hotel I was in at that very moment and would certainly see to it that I would find my own *registered* bed! Now I knew why those *security* men sat beside the elevator doors on each floor. Hong Kong was still under British rule, but how strange was this? Why this Victorian moral set of rules? I knew Queen Victoria had died ages ago!

This was the first time I had experienced George being anything other than a perfect gentleman and considerate of me in every way. So what indecorous curmudgeon behavior was this? I dressed and departed his suite en haste. Summoning any shred of dignity I had left, I headed down the hallway.

At breakfast the next morning in his room where I was allowed to return by the hotel authorities, I was rather curt.

"I hope *you* had a good night's sleep. I certainly didn't, wallowing around in my bed with only embarrassment and guilt for company! I could use a tall Bloody Mary to start my day. It will help me forget how selfish you were last night."

I heard a quiet "uh huh" from George as he walked over to mix us a couple of Bloody Marys.

Thank heaven we ran into Barbara Storer a few hours later. Her father had been Mayor of Miami and an old family friend of George's, so she had known Smathers since her childhood. She was now a stunning blonde with a perfect figure. Since she was a National Airlines stewardess and we hit it off immediately when he introduced us. She loved Marilyn Monroe's look and to this day has kept her style much in the same vein. Years later she married Ellis Rubin, the prominent Miami lawyer and wrote a society column in Miami for years. We are still best friends in the land of sunshine.

Being with her made our visit so much more fun. We explored the New Territories and Kowloon. The ferry between the islands was quite an experience, jam packed to overflowing with humans, bicycles and a varied assortment of small animals. They use the expression press the flesh in politics, but that expression would mean something else entirely on these ferry boats.

George planned to remain in Hong Kong to attend a conference, but I left after a few days to return whence I came.

I stayed over in Beirut to break up the trip on the way home and that is when I first met the local lothario I mentioned earlier, Phillipe al Fata. He walked over to the pool where I was reading.

"Hello, my name is Phillipe and I've seen you at the Phoenicia before today. Don't you fly for Pan American?"

"Yes, I do in fact but I am on holiday now. My name is Layte Bowden."

His eyes surveyed me quietly, then he asked quite politely, "May I order some lunch for us?"

"Yes, that would be nice. I'm hungry and I always enjoy eating beside the pool."

Phillipe was extremely good looking whether you wished to think of him as Lebanese, or any another nationality. His hair was jet and his blue eyes were piercing, but friendly. He was in the Lebanese Air Force, but yearned to be assigned as an aide to his Embassy in Washington.

In fact, he was consumed by the idea of living in Washington, and I think that had much to do with his pursuing the American stewardesses he made a point of meeting in Beirut. That evening he took me to his Officers' Club where I devoured the most delicious Middle Eastern cuisine. He made no overt move, but asked if he could see me the next time I came to Beirut. "Not a problem," avowed I.

The trip with George had been more glamorous than most of my Pan Am travels, and it was truly good being alone together instead of in the midst of his faithful entourage. We most definitely found a high comfort level being with one another, and he was thoughtful to want to share some of my Pan Am world.

Back in New York, I resumed my job flying around the planet. It was most certainly a good job at that time, if you could survive the time changes and lack of sleep.

JFK White House
Press Charters

*"A lie can travel half way around the world
while the truth is still tying its' shoes."*

—MARK TWAIN

I had been flying with Pan American a couple of months and still on the required six month probation for new hires, when George and I went to the White House for lunch. My life still centered around Washington and my free time was often four days at a time, which made it easy to commute. One afternoon in June, we joined the President and their long time social friend Bill Thompson at the White House. We had lunch upstairs in the family dining room for one of our gossipy get togethers that distracted and relaxed JFK for a short break in the middle of a workday.

He loved hearing stories about what happened behind the public screen on Capitol Hill, and certainly my recounting (again) the details of some Senator backing me up in an elevator, or chasing me around a desk when I worked there. I told him a young woman needed track shoes, to work on Capitol Hill to avoid sexual harassment.

Then he began talking enthusiastically about a big Berlin trip being scheduled with a stay in his homeland of Ireland included, which would give him the opportunity to visit with distant relatives again. I told him

I was happy for him, but would probably *bail* on that, as it was a rather long trip, but I was really excited about the Hawaiian trip before that as I had never been to those islands.

He gave me a curious look and said, "Why would you want to skip the European trip? I'm going to give an important speech at the Berlin Wall, and I think it's going to be pretty exciting!"

Ouch, I really didn't want to tell him my reason because it would sound so totally trite. But he just wouldn't give it up. He kept prodding me for an answer, so I had to tell him the truth.

"Okay, the Chief Purser on the Press Charters really resents that I was automatically assigned to his crew when I joined Pan Am. He's flown them for years, and he hand picks his own crew, and he makes my life miserable when we are on board since I'm so new."

Without my saying another word, JFK picked up the phone and called Pierre Salinger in the Press Office. In his clipped Bostonian style of speaking he said, "Pierre, come up to my dining room now, please." Then he turned to me and asked the Purser's name.

Reluctantly I said, "Danny O'Keefe."

"O'Keefe? That sounds like a good Irish name to me, but you're part of my campaign family and he isn't. So, we'll have to change this."

After more talk, Pierre arrived. The President said, "Pierre, call whomever you need to speak with at Pan American and tell them you are requesting a crew change on the White House Press Charters, and you want Layte Bowden as the chief purser."

Immediately I said, "You can't do that! Danny's been flying eighteen years and is quite senior with the company."

At this, JFK looked over at Smathers and laughed. He said "George, remind Layte that I'm President of the United States and that I can probably get this done."

"Well, I can't be the Chief Purser because I'm still a stewardess on probation or a *probationist* as Danny calls me. But my roommate in New York just checked out as a new Purser and we can assign her, I guess."

Jack said, "Done. Pierre, this week call Layte and ask her who she has selected for the new crew and have them assigned." With that said, this subject was closed!

It would be weeks before this announcement would become official, and there is no gossip that traveled faster around the globe in any company than at Pan American Airlines. The minute the word would go out on this, they would be discussing it in Hong Kong and Fiji. And, we didn't even have cell phones. My PAA file had a big "PI" stamped on it from the beginning, but now I think they would translate it from "Political Influence" to "Sleeping with the President." Wrong. But I won't go into that here.

"When everything seems to be going against you, remember
that the airplane takes off against the wind, not with it."

—HENRY FORD

Flying with Pan Am would become much more exciting for me when this change took place. I gave Pierre my list with Kelly Tangen as Chief Purser, an attractive blonde Norwegian, Keri Mette Steiner the second Purser and four of my favorite friends in Pan Am, as stewardesses with me. In the next few years, several of the girls would quit to marry, or leave for other reasons, but I pretty much directed the show regarding these enviable flight crew positions.

In the very beginning of my flying career, however, it was a different story. As soon as I graduated from stewardess training, I was called into the supervisor's office and advised that Danny had been notified from on high that I was to be assigned to the White House Charters. These were highly coveted positions within the company, and Danny O'Keefe was the chief purser with his wife as the second purser in charge.

Danny might have had a sense of humor, but I certainly never witnessed it. He was furious that this "probationist" had been assigned to his team, like it or not.

He took great satisfaction with his position of authority in deciding who would and who would not qualify to accompany Air Force One on Presidential excursions. I thought he was quite arrogant about it. I didn't blame him for preferring more experienced girls on board for these services. I was not yet aware of all the little extra duties you only learn though experience and these charters were all First Class seating and service. Danny showed his displeasure at every opportunity by just lambasting me. I was actually frightened of him, which is exactly what he wanted.

My naiveté was extreme when it came to what a "little person" he was in the larger scheme of things. He quickly learned you don't cross an order when it is born of a White House request. All I can say is that the press guys were thrilled when the time came to have seven beautiful, humorous and qualified young women at their beck and call in their traveling home with wings. Many in the press told me it had been more rigid and absent of humor when Danny was in charge. They worked very hard on board before and after important trips when the President made ground breaking speeches. But, there were many hours when it was great for them to feel as though they now had this private club in the sky where informality was encouraged.

The men, and a few women, sat in clusters relating to what area of the media they served. There were never assigned seats, but over time they narrowed down their spaces. The print journalists like Hugh Sidey, Peter Lisagor, and Chuck Bailey sat together near the front of the cabin. The broadcast group including Dan Rather, Doug Kiker and Robert Pierpont sat near them. Toward the rear of the cabin were most of the photographers whose work took place mainly on the ground. They were freer to play cards and hack around on board. The writers or intellectuals as they referred to themselves enjoyed calling the back of the cabin the animal section. As far as I could tell, they all respected one another's efforts in covering the activities of the President, so no offense was taken.

When we made the big international tours, stringers would join our flights in order to cover the news event for their own country's newspapers or television channels. They might make only one leg of the trip but every news outlet wanted their own man on the scene. Of all the stringers we had on board, Alister Cooke was my favorite. He was such a proper English gentleman and reported for the BBC. He had actually become an American Citizen and served as a foreign correspondent for the Manchester Guardian as well. Most Americans remember him as the host of CBS's "Omnibus." He was definitely on my top ten favorites list in the press group.

Once in awhile, the girls and I would decorate the cabin and wear something extra over our uniforms to match the theme. One of our most popular was entitled the "Solar Flight." We hung silver foil stars, moons and half-moons from the overhead racks and each of us wore a wide satin sash (beauty queen style) with the names of planets printed on them. I was "Mother Earth" and the other stewardesses each chose a planet to represent. It was silly, but they loved our efforts to keep them entertained in flight.

Before working on the campaign and then flying the presidential charters, I had no idea just what was entailed whenever a president attended a simple luncheon in another state outside Washington. It was like moving a small town to an event. Aside from the president's personal jet and the press jet, a cargo plane flew ahead with the presidential limousine and any other large equipment the Secret Service felt was vital for his security away from the White House. The advance team's work could take weeks in order to map out every fine detail for the president to spend a night or two in another city. It was and is a big deal to move our leader from one place to another safely.

Kennedy Western Charter

*"Weapons are an important factor
in war, but not the decisive one; it is
man and not materials that counts."*

—MAO TSE-TUNG

I have already related the details in the "Introduction." El Paso was our first overnight on this interesting tour in the west. The consequences of my tussle with JFK is explained further in a future chapter.

We departed El Paso and flew to China Lake in California for an ordnance demonstration set up for the president. I had absolutely no idea what that really meant, but it turned into an extraordinary experience. The Navy had prepared a faux fleet of ships on the desert floor representing an enemy presence that was quite realistic, I felt as though I was looking out to sea. In another area there were tanks and transport trucks.

We watched Vanguard missile chasers and Skyhawk jets exhibit a thrilling demonstration, destroying the entire fleet. The roaring sounds of jets and speed of the weapons alone made my heart pound, even before the missiles found their targets and filled the sky with cumulus white clouds. One strike sent up a mushroom shaped cloud mimicking an atom bomb strike. It was certainly smaller in scale and of course contained no nuclear contamination, but was an amazing sight non the less.

Few civilians see something this dynamic in their lives, and I knew that I was very fortunate to be in the viewing stand that day with the press. The president sat on a raised platform nearby with the hierarchy of the military, where he was briefed on classified information regarding details of our latest weaponry.

I'm sure I wasn't the only person who felt as though he or she was living under a huge rain cloud at some period in their life. But it had not rained on the China Lake Desert for a couple of *years*, and I said to a few of the crew en route, "Finally, I will enjoy a day of sunshine!" I had been flying all over the world as usual for the past month and *everywhere* I went, it RAINED. Well, my timing surfaced again when inconceivably, it rained later that afternoon in the desert after years of blazing sunny days.

> *"Many of us pursue pleasure with such*
> *breathless haste that we hurry past it."*
>
> —Søren Kierkegaard

Next on the presidential agenda was an overnight on the USS Kitty Hawk, where he would personally witness the carrier's task force weapons demonstration on a real ocean. The carrier was just off the California coast. It was decided that none of the females in the press, and certainly not the seven stewardesses would be allowed on board. The crew had been at sea for quite some time, and we would be a distraction!

Friday, we went to Point Mugu in California for a second weapons demonstration. That night, there was a $1,000 a plate dinner, which the president attended in LA. It was a posh affair where only a few of the White House press members were invited.

Most of the press and staff attended a buffet at our Hilton Hotel's poolside. After a glass of wine, I accepted the invitation to join New York Times' Tom Wicker and Hugh Sidey for dinner at Chasen's. At that time it was one of the most popular spots in Beverly Hills for Hollywood stars and an international clientele.

Chasen's literally began as a shack that served great chili. Movie stars began stopping by, and in the forties, it had evolved into "the" place to eat in Beverly Hills. Its' patrons included all of the Hollywood big names, and even Queen Elizabeth and a Pope enjoyed their edibles. Ronald Reagan ate there so often, a booth was named after him, and it now resides in The Regan Presidential Library.

Their pasta dishes transported you to Italy through their aroma as well as the chef's talent in serving them up perfectly al dente. The sizzling steaks were scrumptious too. Pierre Salinger, General Clifton, several other White House aids and one of my crew joined us after dinner. We all headed for the Peppermint Lounge, a well-known night spot. Somehow we became involved ringside judging a twist dance contest, which the men enjoyed much more than my girlfriend and I. With minimum energy left, we went over to the "Pink Pussy Cat" for a nightcap. Knowing Jack Kennedy, I'm sure he would have *much* preferred being there with us than at the fundraiser.

> *"Hawaii is a unique state. It is a small*
> *state. It is a state that is by itself . . . It is*
> *a—it is different from the other 49 states.*
> *Well, all states are different, but it's got a*
> *particularly unique situation."*
> —VICE PRESIDENT DAN QUAYLE

Saturday was free time and many of us hung out at the hotel pool after sleeping late. At seven that evening, the crew vans took us to the airport to fly to Honolulu. I was so enthusiastic to see at last these celebrated islands. On board, we served champagne and a steak dinner to the press and there was a huge in flight party. If not for the roar of the four jet engines, everyone on board would have felt as though they were at a social dinner party. I didn't see a single journalist "working" on the flight. They were also looking forward to the Pacific's tropical gift to us.

A full moon over Diamond Head awaited us on Oahu Island. "Wow" is all you can say the first time you see this. Since Alaska had become our forty-ninth state in January of 1959, how could we find more diversified beauty to round out our nation than this island state?

After landing and checking into the hotel, we quickly abandoned our flight uniforms, donned our bathing suits and went swimming in the cool Pacific water at two A.M.

We sunned on glorious Waikiki Beach during our stay at the Hawaiian Village, which had several swimming pools. Godfrey McHugh, Kennedy's Air Force Military Aide, secured a large catamaran sailing boat and a crowd of us went on a most exhilarating sail. There were strong winds and our double pontoon boat passed the classic sailing vessels as though they were dragging their anchors. An evening beach barbeque and tropical rum drinks kept us well nourished.

Our five day journey came to an end, and we faced an almost thirteen hour flight from Hawaii to Washington D. C. Everyone was in a super mood and the press demanded that we, the stewardesses, wear island styled muumuus, flower lays and sandals as our uniforms on the way home. No one seemed willing to let go of the wonderful free spirited island atmosphere.

Before take off, dozens of pictures were taken of us, much to the consternation of Pan Am Flight Service in NYC, when pictures in our tropical uniforms were printed in newspapers around America. If we thought it was a party on the flight out, this one going home was totally over the top!

Half way through the flight, some of the girls pulled large T-shirts that the press brought us as souvenirs from the Kitty Hawk over their muumuus. The shirts were autographed by dozens of the Navy crew, including the Captain. I recorded on film silly pictures of our fashion mix, including a couple of the gals holding big cigars as though they there smoking them. They sat on the laps of some of the press for more pictures. Danny O'Keefe, the former purser of these flights, would have been speechless by all the fun we had without the decorum he demanded. With a flight of this length, we certainly had plenty of leisure time, while giving our special passengers great meal services and attention to their in-flight needs as well.

These press charters were unlike any other flights Pan American flew and turned my years of flying into more a privilege than work.

> *"Sex in America is an obsession. In other*
> *parts of the world it's a fact."*
>
> —MARLENE DIETRICH

Shortly after I returned to New York City following this western charter (and the situation that occurred in El Paso), Kennedy called me at my apartment. He wanted to know if Hawaii had lived up to my expectations.

"It was spectacular and I can't wait to go back again for a longer visit."

After a little small talk, he referred to El Paso and asked, "Layte, why is it such a big deal just to have sex?

I answered him sincerely. "I really don't consider myself a toy for anyone and I know that's what women are to you."

I didn't say George had told me that Jack maintained he couldn't do without sex for more than a few days, or he actually got terrible headaches. I wanted to say; "I don't want to be put in that Bayer bottle with all the other aspirins."

I was extremely cheeky with him because I knew he enjoyed that in me. His sense of self and humor emboldened me to say; "You know Jack, your reputation is that you are a bit like a rabbit—you know, quick and often. You don't take the time to be a romantic lover."

He *actually* laughed, sounding unoffended. I decided he was probably self effacing with many of the women he was interested in bedding.

Politician that he was, however, he suggested a plan. He said an official presidential visit to Australia was in the planning stages for the next year and it would last a week or longer.

"I'll devote all my spare time to you," he said, trying to sound sincere.

"Wow, a whole week? That's more time than Marilyn Monroe got!"

I envisioned a grin on his face, as he must have assumed he made a diplomatic score.

Sparring with him was marvelous fun for me. He was very quick witted and I found that sexy in a man. I didn't find it sexy that he had slept with almost every attractive woman he had ever met, simply to fulfill his insatiable need. His disrespect for the female gender, albeit always charming, did not escape me.

Our Flying "L's" Powder Puff Football Game cheerleadeers, 1953
left–right: Kellar, Halsey, Casteel, West, Huegele

Eight Belles Lauderdale High School Reunion, 2008
back row: Babs Walker, Jeanne DeShields, Norma Davis, Layte Bowden
Front row: Barb Burkhardt, Sally Erickson, Patting Murphy, Lyn Mathews

ATO Frat House with Ham Bisbee and Jimmy Christo. Florida State Homecoming Queen, 1956

1956 Seminole Homecoming Queen with my court.
left–right: Linda Jones, Paula Parsons, Anne Monroe, Liz Armes

Jim Magee, 1958

Kappa Alpha Theta Sorority
Dance with Bob Crenshaw, 1957

Theta Sorority Sisters Reunion, 2006
left–right: Layte, Caryl J. Cullom, Barb Hendrix, Nella K. Schomburger, Beverly Perkins Jones

Senator George A. Smathers, (D-FL)

1960 Presidential Campaign

Selected to represent
Florida in the Cherry
Blossom Festival.
Layte Bowden,
Congressman John
Brademas, Betty Beale

National Cherry Blossom Festival 1960
Washington, D. C.

FLORIDA

1960 Cherry Blossom
Festival, Washington, D. C.

Senator's office.
left–right: Layte Bowden,
Scotty Peek, Loretta Lewis

Capitol Hill Pinups: Layte Bowden and Mary
Alice Martin

"Miss Emmy 1961" Layte Bowden

Joe Kruse 1970's

JFK at the Cape 1962

Vice President Lyndon
Johnson's office. Layte
Bowden, Senator Smathers,
Vice President Johnson

Ft. Lauderdale
Airport, 1964.
President Johnson
meeting parents Jean
and Gig Bowden,
friend Nancy Larson
in sunglasses

Inflight White House Press Charter Honolulu to Washington D.C.
Peter Lisagor, *Chicago Tribune (left)* and Hugh Sidey, *TIME* magazine *(right)*

LBJ Captain of Air Force One Col. Jim Cross 3rd from right
with Pan Am girls Kelly Tangen, Layte & Angela C. Anstatt
Power. Pan Am Captain Doug Moody 2nd from right

London nightclub with Senator Joseph Tydings, 1964.

East River NYC on friend's yacht with actor Peter Lawford.

Aid to LBJ, Colonel Haywood Smith.
pictured earlier as Major

East River NYC on yacht with entertainer
Sammy Davis, Jr.

LA during filming of movie "Billie"

Austrailia with Kelly Tangen, CBS' Dan Rather, 1966

Viet Nam war zone with PAA crew and Hero Buck Coffman

Capitol Hill with President Nixon and Congressman
Paul Rogers (FL)

Aboard the Queen Mary during her
final cruise with actor Robert Stack,
1967

Final Cruise of the
Queen Mary with singer
Vic Damone, 1967

Jamaica with Smith Barney CEO Hugh Knowlton,
1970

Best friends for life Jenny Felfe
Goldman and Angela Anstatt Power

Barbara Storer, Society Editor, Miami Florida

Garden Wedding in Ridgewood, NJ,
Mr. & Mrs. Dopp, 1971

Paul Dopp, sailing off the coast of Portugal

Kennedy Berlin Charter
June 23–July 2, 1963

"Ich bin ein Berliner"

—PRESIDENT JOHN F. KENNEDY

From the moment the Presidential plane touched down in Bonn, Germany, hoards of people turned out to greet John Kennedy. He gave a short speech upon arrival, then we all joined in the motorcade north to Cologne. It was unusual that I would end up in the same vehicle as Kenny O'Donnell, a top aide to JFK. However, on this beautiful day we watched the enthusiasm of the Germans, stretching the full length of our commute on both sides of the road. Most of them were waving little American flags and screaming "Empfang, empfang" to cheer us in the motorcade.

Kenny looked out at formally beautiful cathedrals and buildings, so many not rebuilt since the Second World War and said, "This is *very weird* for me, considering I bombed the hell out of this city during the war. I could never have pictured this day in my mind." Our group took a quick look around the city of Cologne, while the president spoke with various dignitaries, then returned to Bonn for an overnight.

After three days following speeches that held the German people enthralled with every word our bright, stimulating leader spoke in west sector cities, we arrived at Berlin's Tegel Airport. The anticipation of the West Berliners in having this vigorous young president visit, turned the city into a mad frenzy. Our drivers could barely guide our transport through the wildly enthusiastic masses to the hotel. Of all the trips I made with Presidents all over the world, I never witnessed a city so consumed by temporary fanaticism.

I can certainly say that it was not easy for any of us to manage a decent night's rest anywhere we stayed in Germany. In Weisbaden, my room was on the front side of the Von Stuben Hotel, and I was kept awake half the night with the presidential fleet of helicopters landing one after the other, only to lift off minutes later from the front lawn. That shrill noise was accompanied the entire night by thousands of Germans chanting; "Ken-ah-dee, Ken-ah-dee." But, as psyched as I usually was about getting my sleep, I didn't mind this all nighter. I was thrilled to be an eyewitness to such sights and sounds.

The Communists began building the Berlin Wall in August of 1961, in order to shut off the faucet of fleeing East Berliners. Over four million technicians, teachers and other professionals, had taken refuge in the Western sector after World War II, between 1949 and 1960. In 1961 alone, over 30,000 more fled before the wall was erected. Khrushchev feared they might even lose control of neighboring Poland if this were allowed to continue. He misjudged our young and inexperienced president after their Summit Meetings in Paris the previous June. Kennedy now made it clear that he and the American people (polled at 87%) would go to war to defend a free West Berlin.

June 1963, standing in the midst of more than two million Germans in Rudolph Wilde Platz, was one of the most dramatic days of my life. My crew and I were not moving under our own power, but were propelled by the crush of the crowd who were shoving forward, or leaping in the air to seize a fleeting glance of President John F. Kennedy. He was standing on a viewing platform with German dignitaries atop the Berlin Wall, looking into the bleakness on the Eastern side, which contained only Communist guards armed with powerful rifles. What an antithesis must have struck his mind, when he turned back to witness the adulation on millions of faces and hear the cheering that was deafening to all those present.

En masse, the crowd quieted when he began to speak, only to roar again at the sound of his voice uttering the first few words. He had to begin anew and his short poignant message to them was halted again and again with cheering. When he closed by saying: *"All free men, wherever they may live, are citizens of Berlin and, therefore, as a free man, I take pride in the words "Ich bin ein Berliner."* The German people riveted by his proclamation, reached the outer edge of saneness. I would never again witness the spirit those people demonstrated on that day involving any public speech.

This wall would stand for 28 years, and it is argued that over one thousand people were killed in trying to escape over it to freedom. These deaths, propagandized to the world, proved the oppressiveness of the Communist rulers. There was a stark difference in the economic level of life from one side to the other. It cost the Soviet Union a fortune to keep the East's population in barely more than a subsistent state and was a testament to the world that free people, in a free society, will flourish.

America played a careful game of chess for years, with the troops we stationed on the western side. Kennedy let it be known through diplomatic channels that we would *not* use force to destroy the wall as long as no further overt actions were taken against West Germany.

There was certainly background history between President Kennedy and the Russian Premier. In June 1961, I was still working on Capitol Hill when the President and Mrs. Kennedy went to Paris and later Vienna, where our newly inaugurated leader first met with Nikita Khrushchev. I later learned from Hugh Sidey about the challenges and stress for Kennedy during three straight days of meetings. This summit took place only a couple of months after Russia had begun transporting and installing nuclear weapons in Cuba. It appeared that Khrushchev, being a bully anyway and lacking in diplomatic skills, decided to thoroughly test the strength and conceptive talent of JFK. It was the closest America came to a nuclear war in history.

Many Americans including me were unaware just how real the danger was when Kennedy made the decision to place a blockade in the waters just north of Cuba, while demanding that Russia remove the weapons already in place. It was a terrifying thirteen days in the White House, while JFK called Khrushchev on a bluff.

Our Generals wanted war, but President Kennedy with his brother Bobby, stood hard by his decision. In two weeks the Russian Premier turned his ships back and removed the weapons already in Cuba. It was gutsy, but this forty-three year old leader did indeed make the right call. Our future would have been written very differently in the history books with a wrong decision.

Following that threat, was the failed "Bay of Pigs" attack in April 1961 by Cuban exiles, who were backed by the U. S. However, after the meeting in Vienna, Khrushchev refused to support a treaty prohibiting nuclear proliferation and threatened the security of the Western Berlin Sector.

This thrust against Kennedy was not as threatening, and the Non-Nuclear Proliferation Treaty finally passed in 1968.

Hugh and I had several discussions about the various distinct personalities JFK exhibited. We were both fascinated that he showed total disregard that his reputation would be destroyed if his shameful womanizing was exposed to the public. Even knowing about this, we admitted that he was so mesmerizing to be with that neither of us wanted to sit in judgment of him. Certainly Hugh had more of an insight into the other Kennedy, the brilliant, capable and skillful diplomat armed with magnetic charm. And, we agreed that he was totally capable of compartmentalizing his life, so that he was not distracted from any important decisions. I never felt that he was driven by political polls the way President Clinton appeared to be in the future.

> *"We have always found the Irish a bit
> odd. They refuse to be English."*
>
> —WINSTON CHURCHILL

Following the surreal atmosphere in Berlin, most of us were delighted to go to Ireland, but none so much as President Kennedy himself. He was absolutely thrilled with this opportunity to visit distant relatives and see all the landmarks where his ancestors had lived, loved and died. In contrast to the frenetic enthusiasm we left behind, the Irish displayed a sense of pride in welcoming him as *one of their own.* "Bless you" was the comment we heard most often there.

He did indeed enjoy the little picnics and gatherings planned in his honor and gave everyone his individual interest. It was also his style, whether it be with a King or a peasant. With all his faults, I always believed his passion for the every man was authentic. He loved being in Cork, Galway and Dublin, and it showed in his eyes.

There was a quick stop in Waddington, England, at the Royal Air Force Base. JFK and his sister Jean went without an entourage to visit the grave of their elder sister Kathleen in the English Hamlet of Edensor. Kathleen had died in 1948 in a private plane that crashed in France, just four years after their eldest brother, Joe, Jr., was killed in another crash during a war mission.

An agent who accompanied them, told me later the engraving on Kick's gravestone was, "Joy She Gave Joy She Has Found."

"When it's three o'clock in New York, it's
still 1938 in London."

—BETTE MIDLER

We flew on to London for two nights, and the President spent this time with his in-laws, Jackie's sister and her husband, Prince Radziwill. I never once talked with him personally during this entire trip, just a wave or two at an airport, but I totally enjoyed the sheer excitement of just being along for this unique ride.

From England, we flew to Rome. JFK gave a speech on the smallest of the Seven Hills, "Campidoglio." This has been the religious and political center of Rome for over 2,500 years. The next night he spoke at a formal dinner given by Italian President Segni, and the rest of us did quite a bit of dining ourselves. Rome was like home for me, and we enjoyed our favorite restaurants with many in our entourage.

After the President's speech at the NATO Headquarters in Naples the next day, Captain Jim Swindal directed Air Force One toward Washington, and as always, we were exhausted and looked forward to returning home.

Kennedy's Eleven State Western Charter
September 24–October 30, 1963

"I think the American West really attracts me because it's romantic. The desert, the empty space, the drama."

—ANG LEE

On September 24th, 1963 we departed Andrews Air Base on a seven-day charter with President Kennedy, which would cover eleven states. He would make a total of *fifteen* speeches. It is amazing what one man can do when he has a large jet, literally hundreds of staff and extra part time organizers at his disposal.

A few of his speeches were given at the airports so we never left our plane, but many involved motorcades into the local cities. My more memorable moments were in Billings Montana, Salt Lake City and Palm Springs where I had never visited.

In Cheyenne, he spoke at the airport facility, but a huge crowd showed up to listen and also enjoy their own storied history. Local Indian tribes in full dress regalia performed wonderful tribal dances and their horses were painted, as the war ponies were during the early days of settling the west. I was thrilled to witness such a glorious and colorful display of the cultural yesteryear I most relate to in America. The only DVD I've ever bought is "Dancing with Wolves" because this film represents the hardships of our country's native people *from their side.*

We continued on to Laramie, and then had our second overnight in Billings. JFK left after we arrived to speak at the Yellowstone County Fairgrounds. A local organizer of this visit asked if we would enjoy visiting a working ranch nearby. Several of us in the crew were quite enthusiastic about the invite, and he picked us up at our hotel after we had put on warmer clothes.

The ranch was magnificent. I have loved horses since my childhood when I read all of The Black Stallion novels by Walter Farley. I walked over to a chestnut mare with a white star on her forehead and three white sock ankles. With grain in my flattened left hand, I cradled her head with my right arm. As soon as she finished the grain, she took a bite of me, high on my left breast. Thankfully I was wearing a thick sweater over my shirt for warmth, but even so blood began seeping through my sweater within a minute. I pulled the neck of my blouse out to look down and blood was gushing out. The sight of that shocked me but I felt no pain at that point. I quickly put some Kleenex inside my bra next to the open wound and pressed down on it to slow the bleeding.

The rancher immediately got his truck, and Purser Keri Mette Steiner said she would go with me to the clinic as support. As soon as we arrived, the doctor took me quickly into a room and had me lie on the table where I had to strip my sweater and unbutton my blouse. As soon as Keri Mette saw all the blood streaming from my breast, she began to faint. The doctor seeing this, dashed to her side and steadied her before she could fall. Then he actually walked her for a few moments in the hall to make sure *she was all right!* Wow, it must be wonderful to go through life as a beautiful Scandinavian in America. Here I was, still spewing blood and he is worried about her. In a few moments he attended to me with a few stitches and a thick bandage. A local sedative reduced the pain and I was good to go.

The following morning when I boarded our jet, I found that the press had been busy bees decorating the plane with handmade Cleopatra signs and chidingly asking if they could see my scar. The movie "Cleopatra" opened in theaters that summer and was a huge hit. Because she was bitten by an asp, they related it to my being bitten by a "clever" horse. It makes one wonder if they were taking in enough oxygen while traveling so often at 35,000 feet. Well, the boys just liked to have fun.

154

The President made speeches in several more states during the day before we checked into the Hotel Utah in Salt Lake City. After speaking at Great Falls, Montana and Hanford, Washington earlier in the day, JFK felt he needed some music and laughter before his speech in the Mormon Tabernacle later that evening. He called my room and asked if the gals and I would join him for a drink and some buffet snacks before his scheduled appearance.

"Of course, that would be fun." I said.

"I hear you met up with an admirer so excited he took a bite out of you." Jack remarked.

Surprised I said, "Does *anything* happen that isn't reported to you?"

"Well, that was big news around the camp out here!" Jack noted with mirth in his voice.

When we arrived at his suite, he had the music blaring and the drinks mixed by faithful George. There was plenty of food for all and out of the blue, along with a couple of his aides, we began doing the limbo. I never accomplished dancing under the limbo bar set less than 30 inches because of my back problems, but I've seen people do it at little more than a foot. This maneuvering to music had become popular on the islands in the Caribbean, with its' roots going back to the slave ships that came to the Colonies early in our history. Its' popularity rolled around again during our era.

Jack was totally enjoying our efforts and kept clapping his hands and cheering everyone on. Finally a Secret Service Agent knocked on the door and said, "Mr. President, it's time to leave now." On his way out the door we received a presidential command to, "Keep this party going, I'll be back soon!"

Of course everyone sat down and put on the large TV to watch the presidential arrival inside the Temple. I cannot remember the name of our hotel, but it seems his suite was almost across the street from the Tabernacle. I walked into Jack's bedroom and joined George, who was sitting in the wide window alcove. He had raised the window as far as possible and we could hear the sweet voices of the Tabernacle Choir flow into the room.

It was comprised of over 300 Mormons, both men and women and is arguably the most famous and beautiful sounding choir in the world. It was magical and surrealistic to be sitting on the sill, hearing the music and watching on TV as President Kennedy was being escorted up several levels of the Temple, where I thought only the hierarchy of the Mormon faith were allowed. He was wearing a long robe and looked ever so respectful and reverent.

The speech he delivered that night was very powerful and persuasive regarding the necessity of America involving itself with nations around the world. He deftly explained how science and technology had made it impossible any longer for us to feel protected by two oceans, isolating us from Europe or Asia. So many Americans were angered with our involvement in Korea and by now, Vietnam.

His father had been a devout isolationist, but JFK believed a monolithic nation could not possibly preserve itself without supporting even countries whose values we often disapproved. This was the only way to build the alliances we needed whenever a large threat loomed. The biggest threat then, of course, was the Soviet Union. That exact speech would be so relevant today if you substituted the word "terrorists" as our enemy.

Watching John Kennedy the statesman always inspired my pride in being an American, and I think he raised hopes and dreams for many citizens. It was stupefying for me to witness that same man walk back into his suite twenty minutes after delivering that speech, clapping his hands and asking, "Hey, what happened to our party? How about some music and cocktails?" When I hear that a politician is skillful, I relate that to how easily JFK could compartmentalize totally different personalities within minutes.

> *"There's always some amount of gradual,*
> *slow burning destruction over the course*
> *of partying."*
> —GAVIN DEGRAW

Following our hectic swing through the western states, the president had scheduled a weekend to relax in Palm Springs. Immediately upon his return to Washington, he had a scheduled State visit with Emperor Haile Selassie of Ethiopia, so this would be his down time.

When our flight caravan arrived in Palm Springs, he proceeded to Bing Crosby's estate near Palm Desert. He had borrowed this estate from the famous singer on earlier trips. The White House Press, staff and the Pan American and Air Force One crews checked into a lovely hotel in Palm Springs Friday, September 28.

There have been so many accounts of this infamous weekend by various authors, but I had not read them until recently. The only book I read after the assassination until I began writing my book was William

Manchester's, "The Death of a President." For years this was a period that was painful for me, and I chose not to revisit.

I am amazed that known authors with many works to their credit write such inaccuracies when supposedly they researched and conducted many interviews for their work. I now take with a grain of salt the narrations about famous people when writers are quoting third parties. If that is how they receive their information, then they certainly need to *check* and *double check* the information they receive.

I am relating here only what I *personally* experienced. I have no need to embellish. Even in only telling the truth, these events were beyond the limits of propriety. Before I give you my very different account of this admittedly wild weekend, I would like to *review* a few paragraphs I read in two different books.

Seymour Hersh wrote a scathing account of the Kennedy years in "The Dark Side of Camelot" that was published in 1997. He interviewed Secret Service agents Joe Paolella and Larry Newman who, according to Hersh, related the following. Please note the words in the parentheses are this author's corrections to the inaccuracies as Hersh reported them. "*There was one occasion, during a raucous party in December 1962* (wrong month, wrong year) *at Bing Crosby's huge estate in Palm Springs, California, when, Paolella told me, agents literally rescued a young airline stewardess* (me) *from* (Peter) *Lawford's drunken advances, and left him sprawled in the desert.*" (This is totally untrue.)

"*The Crosby party was the high point—or low point—of presidential partying,*" *Paolella continued. Some of the women at the pool, the agents knew, were stewardesses from a European airline;* (Pan American was not a European airline) *their names, as usual; were not known to the Secret Service.* (They knew most of us as we had flown all the charters so we obviously had been cleared) *The party was so noisy that a group of California State policemen on duty at the front of the estate, which bordered on a desert wilderness area, assumed that the shouts and shrieks of the partygoers were the night time calls of coyotes.*" (My Pan Am girls were never at Crosby's pool, but at Jimmy Van Huesen's house in the compound and left "before" sunset both evenings.) *Newman gave further raw description: "Powers was banging a girl on the edge of the pool. The president is sitting across the pool, having a drink and talking to some broads. Everybody was buckass naked.*" (I was not at the Crosby house on "Friday" night, so if anything like this happened, I cannot confirm or deny this account. The problem is that this reads as though all of it happened with the Pan Am girls there and we were not. Nor did a single one of us ever remove any part of our bathing suits on Saturday or Sunday.)

In March of 2005, Michael O'Brien wrote the book, "John F. Kennedy—A Biography." There is a quote accredited to Newman by Seymour Hersh. Without a word of credit Hersh writes: *In December 1962, Newman was on duty during a raucous party at Big Crosby's huge estate in Palm Springs. At one point Secret Service agents rescued a young airline stewardess from Peter Lawford's drunken advances, leaving him sprawled in the desert, near Crosby's home. From Newman's point of view the Crosby weekend was the nadir of presidential partying. Some of the women at the pool were stewardesses from a European airline, their names unknown to the Secret Service. Because of the shouts and shrieks of the partygoers, Newman intruded on the President's privacy by going poolside for a look. What Newman saw was Powers "banging a girl on the edge of the pool. The President is sitting across the pool, having a drink and talking to some broads. Everybody was buckass naked.*

Neither of these writers did their homework well for this account. And O'Brien simply lifted Hersh's misinformation over to his book. The parents of the Pan Am stewardesses did not need to read embellishments like this about their daughters. My recollection of this particular weekend will be as close to the truth as you will find unless you have a good channeler, who can connect you with JFK or Peter Lawford. There were other books and TV documentaries about our trips, as well that left me shaking my head because they were "*So—not accurate.*"

> "*Sex is one of the nine reasons*
> *for reincarnation. The other*
> *eight are unimportant.*"
>
> —GEORGE BURNS

Jack Kennedy had spent time with the Pan American stewardesses on previous charters, however, I will be the first to admit that this was certainly the wildest. Saturday morning October 28, 1963 was a gorgeous California day. Before noon many in the presidential party were poolside at the hotel having brunch and enjoying the sun. Around twelve, I heard my name being paged over the outdoor sound system asking me to pick up the White House phone. Before any presidential visit, the advance team, including the Secret Service who set up the security, installed special phones wherever they felt necessary to reach anyone in the presidential entourage.

I walked over to the pool cabana suspecting it would be a call from the president's compound. It was Jack himself calling to ask me if I could round up the girls, and he would arrange a van to drive us over to Jimmy Van Heusen's house a few cactuses away from Bing Crosby's. Jimmy was a famous songwriter and a good friend of Bing's. JFK said, "It's a perfect day for a swim party!" Then he surprised me by asking that I not bring Kelly Tangen.

He said, "she came on so strong" the last time we were all together that he would be more comfortable without her around. Ah, here I learned that Kennedy would *not* sleep with just any female available as I had begun to believe. '

Our entire Pan American crew was at the pool so as discreetly as possible, I wandered through the lounge chairs and whispered to the girls one at a time, that President Kennedy had invited us for a swim party, and it was her choice whether or not she would like to go.

"Are you going?" each one asked me. I said that I thought it would be fun if we all went. This was the first White House Charter for one of the girls, but they were all excited about the invitation. Within the hour, off we went. Being fair here, I think most women would have probably joined this excursion given the opportunity.

Only the servers were at the Van Heusen house when we arrived, but soon JFK came striding through the huge cactus plants surrounding the pool area with one of his oldest friends, Dave Powers trailing him.

"My God, it's Dr. Strangelove," Sheila Reilly said to me when she saw him.

Sheila is one of the brightest, wittiest English women I know and was always great fun. Kennedy evidently thought so too. She seemed to be his main target that afternoon, although he was totally charming to all of the young women there. Many cocktails later, he was aggressively pursuing her about the house and patio.

At one point, Sheila came to me and seemed quite upset. While thwarting every advance from JFK, she remembered she was in the U. S. working on a green card permit.

"Layte! You don't supposed he will have me deported if I don't do the deed with him do you? After all, he IS the President and he can do anything."

I promised her that he would take the rejection in stride and loved a challenging woman, especially one with her quick witted sense of humor.

I was quite relieved that I wasn't wearing the bull's eye that day, but after our altercation in El Paso, he was totally respectful while still charming. He knew I would probably work at the White House when I returned to Washington and he would *figure me out* in time. Having women was easy for him, so evidently he loved a challenge.

When calm prevailed for a moment, I told Jack I was disappointed that I wouldn't meet Frank Sinatra on this trip because my mother always had a crush on him, and I wanted to relate what he was like in person. He asked me if meeting Peter Lawford would do and I said, that was close enough. He picked up a phone, and in 20 minutes, Peter arrived at the pool.

At that time in his life, Peter was still quite good looking and was a woman magnet. His charm was the English sophistication without the accompaniment of stuffiness, at least to me. He was very well traveled and more intelligent than people who did not know him well realized. In no way did he come on to me, but was polite and beguiling.

Later I was to learn that this was the weekend that he and his wife, Patricia Kennedy Lawford, were separating, and he had moved out of their home in Santa Monica. She would soon move with the children to NYC, and Peter would move back into the house until it was sold years later.

The afternoon spent itself and as the sun headed toward the horizon, the girls were ready to go back to the hotel and prepare for dinner out on the town. JFK walked back to Crosby's house and Peter asked me to stay and talk longer. I could take another car back to town later. I agreed and then as the darkness began closing in, he suggested we walk over to Crosby's house and sit by the pool there.

We took the cactus walk, and when we arrived at the house, there was no one else outside. Peter said that Jack was probably taking a late nap. I knew that Fiddle and Mimi, the two young aides at the White House who often kept the president company, were on the trip and quite possibly he wasn't napping alone. George brought us a snack, but as we had been eating all afternoon, I had no appetite for anything more. We talked about our lives, and I was fascinated listening to his version of the Rat Pack adventures and his youthful travels of the world.

His life was so different than any man I had ever met. At this moment in time, Peter just needed to talk and someone to listen. Unbeknownst to me, the Secret Service assigned to the house were not only stationed at the front gate down a long driveway, but also behind cactus plants surrounding the pool area where we were.

It's probably no surprise if I mention here that I was casually dating one of the Secret Service men who happened to be stationed at the front gate. It was a platonic relationship for me once again because of George Smathers. Many of the agents knew me after traveling together on the charters, or from my visits to the White House. The agent at the gate kept calling the cactus agents to ask them if Peter had touched me or tried to kiss me. They kept assuring him that we were only talking.

The later it became, the cooler the desert was and Peter and I had moved to the terrace steps *in the pool* where we could keep ourselves warm from the heated water. We were still talking at almost four A.M. I told Peter I really needed to get back and get some sleep. He leaned over and very gently kissed my lips. We walked into the house and Peter said it was too late for me to go back to the hotel and suggested that I sleep at Crosby's. Big mistake on my part! I thought he meant "sleep with him." I spat out my disillusionment.

NO! Not in his frame of mind, on the eve of his separation from Pat, was he interested in sleeping with ANYONE. He firmly took my arm and led me down the hall to the nursery where he pointed to a beautiful baby crib and told me that my comprehension was that of a child and I should sleep there. He thought we had made a connection on a friendship level and I did as well, however I was overly distrustful since so many men had made cheap come ons to me for years.

We were both insulted now, and he marched to the phone to request two cars. One was to drop him off a couple of houses away where Pat Kennedy Lawford and one of her sisters were also staying. But, there was only one available for me, so we had to make a few minutes of the trip in the same car. The agent I was dating wanted to drive, but the agent in charge said, "no way."

Peter sat in front, which I was later to learn he always did because of carsickness. I sat alone in the back. I don't remember what I said when he got out, but I did mumble something trite and his response was "fuck you." No one in my entire life had ever uttered such a vulgarity to me and I was dumb struck. I felt absolutely sick to my stomach the rest of the way to the hotel in Palm Springs.

The agents certainly disliked Peter, but I hardly think that Agent Newman's (supposed) description that Peter was "left sprawling drunk in the desert after agents saved me from his advances," meets the truth here! In fact, it's very difficult for me to believe that Larry made any of the statements that were later recorded in books, as he cared about Jack Kennedy and surely he would not so crudely have described all the events ascribed to him this particular weekend.

"You know, of course, that the
Tasmanians, who never committed
adultery, are now extinct."

—SOMERSET MAUGHAM

Well, a new day and a renewed outlook. Sunday's weather was as beautiful as Saturday's had been, and when I was once again paged to answer the White House phone by the pool, I had no doubt who would be on the other end of the line.

Jack said, "Yesterday was great fun. Can you get the gang to come back over?"

I wasn't sure that some of the girls would want a repeat engagement, but I said I would ask them. I was a bit surprised at the enthusiasm they all showed when offered the second invitation to swim and lunch with "The Man." Power has always been an aphrodisiac to women, and I probably haven't known many who would not like to share time with the most powerful man on planet earth.

Kelly was devastated, but I had to be truthful and tell her that Jack personally requested that she not be included. My relationship with her was never the same after that weekend because she felt abandoned. The bond we had shared would shred in the future.

The pool party at Van Heusen's was more tranquil than it had been the day before. There were lots of laughs, great food, drinks and silliness, with more decorum shown by Jack Kennedy. Peter was not there, and I was disappointed. I wanted to apologize to him for assuming he was no better than some guy on the make at a local bar.

Later in the afternoon, he did show up, but kept a little distance between us. I approached him with my apology, and he was totally gracious. I also told him I was shocked by his last two words to me.

"I am not Hollywood indoctrinated," I explained.

Alcohol always puts a different slant on a conversation and both of us were quite sober now. We knew we had connected on an emotional level. He was emotionally needy and I was emotionally captivated.

This party broke up a little earlier, because we were departing for Washington late that night. Jack walked over and asked me to come up to Bing's house and stay for dinner. He said I could go back to the airport in his car, so I called Kelly and told her that I would greatly appreciate it if she would finish packing my bag.

"Would you take my uniform separately to the Pan Am plane for me? I'm going to join the group here for dinner and go directly to the plane in the president's car. But, please don't mention this to Doug (our Captain). Just say I'll get there on my own."

When Peter and I reached Crosby's pool, we found Kennedy swimming nude with Fiddle, Mimi and his buddy Dave Powers. His faithful butler George was dressed immaculately as always and serving drinks.

It was once again the best acting I could muster that I didn't blink an eye at this scene. I pretended that it was any typical day at the pool with a few friends. It was not suggested that I take my suit off and jump in, as Jack knew I would be straight in a situation like this. If our swims at the White House didn't tell him, then El Paso certainly had done so.

I was wearing one of the beautiful Thai silk bathing suits that I had custom made by the half dozen when I was on Bangkok trips. They were so inexpensive I would wear them to sun and swim a few times and then toss them, as they didn't take chlorine well.

I was relieved that Peter showed no inclination to shed his suit either. We did swim, however, and I continued to pretend I was not uncomfortable in the midst of this rather astonishing setting. Later while I was sitting on the end of the diving board, the JFK swam over and tread water, alternately holding on to the board while we talked. He was forever fascinated with gossip, and I felt complacent trading stories because he always had that charming talent of creating camaraderie.

"Jack, I know you appreciate and love Jackie, but with so many women in your past, have you ever loved anyone else enough to consider marrying her?" I had never asked him quite so personal a question before, and I didn't expect him to give me an answer, but to my surprise he did.

"Yes I have, a really wonderful woman named Florence Pritchett, but I don't think you know her," he replied. "She's intelligent, worldly and is married to a good man now."

I didn't know if he was being truthful, or if it was just a sentimental thought on that particular day. Weeks later I asked Peter about her and he told me that she was a fantastic woman, married to Earl E. T. Smith, our Ambassador to Cuba. He thought Jack had given me a pretty honest answer as he knew they were in love years before.

From there however, JFK immediately launched into a sneaky plan that could use my help. He knew from Smathers that Joe Tydings, the handsome young U. S. Attorney for Maryland, had a crush on me. So, he actually suggested that I should agree to go off for a weekend with Joe, thus leaving his beautiful wife alone in Washington and available for a White House dinner invitation. This was to be while Jackie was at the Cape.

Hello again? I don't have enough creative imagination to make this kind of stuff up! It's too silly for fiction, especially in a conversation involving the "President of The Free World."

Startled I said, "You can't be serious! That's crazy and I have absolutely no intention of taking off for a weekend with Joe for your convenience. You continue to amaze me, sir."

After looking at me with amusement in his eyes, he snickered and said he'd have to think of another way. I agreed that sounded like a much better plan. The Tydings marriage did break up shortly after that, but it most certainly had nothing to do with me.

Joe and I dated as friends after his divorce, and in fact, after his next marriage as well. We dined in London, or New York, or wherever our schedules crossed. And now as a U. S. Senator, he traveled often. And because his father had married the incredibly wealthy Marjorie Merriweather Post, he was quite worldly.

Meanwhile in Palm Desert, I sat quietly by the pool while everyone else left to dress. We were leaving for the airport immediately after dinner. I, of course, was going to show up in my bathing suit, sandals and a matching Thai silk cover up sundress.

The gathering at the dinner table was a little surprising to me, because Patricia Lawford joined us. What a cozy little group it was. JFK, Dave the court jester, the two young sexy presidential aides, the president's sister Jean, sister Pat, her husband the brother-in-law, and me.

It must have felt like the last supper to Peter, as Pat was returning to their California beach estate in Santa Monica and he was flying east with the president. JFK had told him he should stay for a while at the Carlyle Penthouse duplex in NYC. It was always reserved for presidential use and Jack told him, "stay until you pull yourself together."

After dinner, before we got into the president's limousine, Peter pulled me aside and asked if he could see me while he was in New York. I told him I really needed to think about it, but asked him to call me after he arrived. My casual dating was not a threat to George, but I knew that Peter would be a very different story. The Senator was well aware of the many conquests this English actor had made since his arrival in Hollywood.

Off to the Palm Springs airport rolled the presidential limousine with Jack Kennedy, Peter Lawford and me in the rear compartment. I loved this 1961 Lincoln Continental convertible in navy blue and custom built beyond imagination. The luxurious shades of leather in the interior belied the fact that machine guns were stored under the front seat and in the trunk. There were custom rear stands where Secret Service men stood when the president was on review. Flagstaffs rose in the front, but this was a late night private drive most certainly without ceremonial flags flying in the desert winds.

Actually this would turn out to be the *only* time I ever saw Peter ride in a back seat. It was a pretty long drive, but the time passed quickly while I overheard a good deal of family talk. Even facing the first possible divorce within the Kennedy family and another campaign, Jack managed to find humor along the way, and as always, he made me laugh out loud.

It's more than a little unbelievable now the way the press operates and the tabloids go berserk over any and everything a famous person does. In those days, they *got away* with much more. The presidential limousine pulled up to the rear door of the Pan Am press plane and out I popped. I dashed up the back stairs and straightaway into a rear lavatory where I changed into my uniform.

Many of the press guys were already on board, and Kelly was a good sport to cover for me. If any of them were looking out the windows when JFK's car arrived, they never mentioned it to me, or the newspapers and networks they were serving. I was baked from the sun all weekend and the trip home was exhausting. Fortunately, everyone on board seemed as exhausted as I was, and no one complained about the service. Having flown together on so many trips, we were like a large family now.

*"No friendship can cross the path of our destiny
without leaving some mark on it forever."*
—FRANCOIS MOCURIAC

There was something else happening before and during this Palm Springs visit that would forever alter Peter's friendship with Frank Sinatra and the Rat Pack. Frank had worked hard to help get Jack Kennedy elected and brought in the Hollywood elite to produce the most glamorous galas ever held during a Presidential Inaugural celebration. When Sinatra learned the president was going to make time for a couple of days in Palm Springs following a political swing out west, he was thrilled. Assuming the president would stay at his home, as he had in his pre-presidential days, Frank set about remodeling part of his home and even built a helipad on his compound.

There had been quite a bit of press regarding Kennedy's chummy association with the Rat Pack. It became very problematic to Bobby. It was fairly wide knowledge that Frank had ties to the mafia and had legal problems with the Cal Neva Club on Lake Tahoe's northern shore as well. Bobby felt the last place his brother should stay would be at Sinatra's house. The publicity would be extremely bad for the president's image, and Bobby was adamant he should stay at Bing Crosby's, who was known as more of a family man than that of a swinger.

Frank refused to believe that Jack would listen to Bobby on this and blamed Peter for not stepping in and persuading JFK to stand by him. Peter did, of course, try to get Jack to do just that, but he knew that in this case Bobby had a strong argument. Frank blamed Peter until the day he died, because he couldn't admit to himself that he was not reputable enough to host the President.

Peter Lawford
Pre-November, 1963

"Safe upon the solid rock the ugly
houses stand: Come and see my
shining castle built upon the sand."

—EDNA ST. VINCENT MILLAY

Peter did indeed call me the day after flying east with the JFK from Palm Springs and settling into the duplex penthouse at the Carlyle Hotel on Madison Avenue. I agreed to see him for dinner the following evening, and afterward, we went back to the suite and talked for at least two more hours. He asked me to stay overnight, totally disregarding my disclosure of my serious relationship with George. I also said I hadn't been with anyone else since George and I had first become intimate. But that would not be a problem yet.

I did stay with him. We talked ourselves to sleep, and he did nothing but hold me the rest of the night. He clearly didn't want to be alone, and I was more like a Linus' blanket for him. If I learned one thing about his psyche in our years together, it was that being alone *ever* was fearful for him. I love alone time because I'm not afraid to go inside, knowing and accepting who I am. I did not analyze him at this point. If I had, it would have been a big warning flag whipping in the wind.

He did not want the divorce and felt his life, as he had known it, slipping away. Looking back, I realized that near the beginning and much more so in the end of our three-year relationship, I mothered him. He made enemies in Hollywood during Kennedy's presidency and now turned even more to self-destruction than self-preservation. His relationship with Sinatra ended with the Palm Springs problem, which was absolutely not his fault. Sammy Davis was the only one of the Rat Pack who kept a close bond with him.

He talked about his experiences growing up and moving all over the world with his titled, but penniless parents. He told me about the German governess who fondled and had sex with him when he was about ten years old. On top of that his mother never forgave him for being born a boy, and she dressed him as a girl for years! No wonder his reasoning regarding relationships with women was so complicated. He was terribly damaged.

It was inevitable that we would consummate our "friendship," and it took him only two solid days and nights to break down my emotional barrier. Our chemistry was intense, and my heart had no intention of listening to my brain. Once we mated, we treated that duplex like a bomb shelter from the rest of the world. I didn't stop to reason that for Peter it was out of need and for me it was out of desire.

He kissed my eyelids with such passion, I became dizzy. It was a time when our appetite for one another couldn't be satisfied. During that point in time when new lovers become mesmerized by the exploration of one another's bodies, the rest of the world ceased to exist for us.

The Carlyle was a chic hotel, and if I had to fall in love with a man so completely wrong for me, this hotel provided the ambiance. It was the Presidential Penthouse duplex and available to JFK whenever he was in NYC. Every comfort was available to us. When we met, Peter had a lithe well toned body with perfectly portioned hips and shoulders always sheathed in a good tan. I, like so many women before me, was susceptible and eager to love him. We might have lived on mating and room service for a month, but I had a job, and Peter couldn't stay at the Carlyle indefinitely.

Dinner with the President

It was November 1, 1963 when the President called Peter in New York and asked him to have dinner at the White House the following night. Peter told him he would love to, but wanted to bring "a friend." Jack said that he had invited a lady himself and had wanted Peter to be the "extra" man. He acquiesced and said he would call another male friend to be the extra. Jackie was at the Cape, but in those days a married man had to have a cover or a "beard" as it was labeled (even in the White House). Jack had no idea that Peter and I had been dating since the Palm Springs trip in June, and that the sparks we felt out there had turned into a bonfire in NYC. I hadn't wanted JFK to know because of his friendship with George Smathers and his own advances toward me.

We took the Eastern Shuttle down the next evening, and a White House car picked us up at National Airport. After arriving at the south entrance and taking the lift up to the family quarters, Jack came over to greet us as the elevator doors opened.

> *"It is a mistake to try to look too far*
> *ahead. The chain of destiny can only be*
> *grasped one moment at a time."*
>
> —Sir Winston Churchill

"Oh my God Layte, I am so sorry. I had no idea Peter meant he was bringing *you*."

Before I could understand the problem, Bill Thompson arrived in the hallway and said, "Well, Layte, what a surprise to see *you* tonight!"

Bill just happened to be one of George Smather's best friends and one of the last people I wanted to see me with Peter before I had the opportunity to confess everything to my "boss/lover." George had introduced Bill to Jack Kennedy while he was still in Congress as Bill was as big a ladies man as JFK.

Those three were hugely popular with women and liked to think of themselves as "The Three Musketeers." Jack got a big kick out of Bill's sense of humor and practical jokes, but their friendship was not general knowledge. He was never part of the inner circle, as Jack's long time friends didn't think he was a good influence, but more of a vice enabler. That would be hard for me to believe, as Jack was the biggest philanderer I would know in my life, having all ready inherited strong sexual vices from his own father during his youth.

However, Jack would not have chosen Bill to join us because he wouldn't have intentionally put me in such an awkward and uncomfortable position. The damage was done, and now I was "outed" with Peter. We went into the family living room, and Jack introduced me to Piety Gimbel (of *the* Gimbel family) who was his companion for dinner.

We had a drink and then went into the family dining room for dinner. Everyone joined into a lively engaging conversation. JFK always made an occasion amusing with his quick wit and intelligence. Later, he leaned over his plate and pointed his finger at Bill (for whom JFK had arranged the job of President of the Florida East Coast Railway and often referred to *Bill* as Mr. President when just friends were around).

"Mr. President," JFK addressed Bill. "I unintentionally put Layte in an awkward situation, and I'm "commanding" you not to say one word about this evening to George. It wouldn't be fair to her. Do we agree on this?"

"Absolutely," Bill declared.

And I thought to myself, *you'll call George as soon as you are awake in the morning.* He and George had been too close, too long for him not to scurry to a phone and relate every gossipy detail of this night.

Even if Jack was secretly delighted that I was finally cheating on George, I appreciated that he at least pretended to be gallant on my behalf. It was only part of his little game with me, part of the chase. And the chase was most likely the main thing he enjoyed about me. There were so many more glamorous women available to him than me, but he did enjoy a challenge.

As soon as dinner was over, I told Jack that I needed to call Smathers because he knew I was back in New York from my last flight. I had been keeping up a big pretense since meeting Peter about my schedule and my inability to get to Washington to see George. This call couldn't be on a White House line. The operators always announced, "Just one moment, this is The White House calling."

JFK took me into his bedroom and gave me the private phone beside his bed so I could pretend I was in New York making the call. Before leaving the room, he tried to reassure me that he honestly had not set me up and I believed him. However, Peter and I together was most likely a happy surprise for him. As Jack left the room, he turned and gave me a smile that was as intimate as a kiss.

I returned to the group in the living room to talk and finish my wine. Soon the phone rang next to Jack's chair. After answering, he listened for several minutes before asking questions. I knew by his words that it was something very serious regarding Vietnam. When he returned the phone to its cradle, he said in a very strained voice, "President Diem was just assassinated." We sat in stunned silence until Peter asked him if he had known this would happen as part of the coup in Vietnam.

JFK said, "Nothing that has happened in Vietnam has turned out as I hoped it would."

I read in another book that JFK learned of the assassinations during the Monday morning National Security Council meeting, but I know absolutely that phone call came after we had dinner on Sunday night November 1. Saigon time is twelve hours ahead, and it would have been November 2 about 10 am their local time which is actually when it happened.

A military coup had overthrown Ngo Dinh Diem's government the previous day. Diem and his brother Nhu were offered safe exile out of the country by the U. S., but they would not accept this escape plan and instead tried to sneak out of the Palace that night on their own. They were caught and killed by officers involved in the coup. JFK had his emissaries in Saigon trying to negotiate with the Generals not to go through with the coup without success. Kennedy was quite upset by the murders, and said it was a very bad omen for America's future involvement there.

Vietnam had been in a civil war with very little commitment by our military until now. Diem, also a devout Catholic, was a diehard anti-Communist. Who now would be as effective in fighting Ho Chi Minh in the north? Our generals, however, had secretly promised the military officers in Vietnam that the U. S. would *not* interfere with the coup itself. Judging by Kennedy's reaction, I don't think he expected *Diem to be assassinated.*

Jack Kennedy was *certainly not a hawk,* and the last thing he wanted was another war like Korea. He knew the risk of getting involved in a major war in Asia. After his death, however, some of his aides felt that he might have been *sucked* into it little by little just as Johnson had been. After all, MacNamara and several others were his men and LBJ kept them. They would most probably have advised JFK as well that this war was a necessary one. Just how deeply America would become involved was not a decision he was allowed to make. Jack Kennedy would also be dead within twenty days.

My comprehension of just how much this would envelop all our lives in the near future was zilch. My immediate thought which I expressed to him, was that he expel Madame Nhu from San Francisco where she was visiting and ban her from America, period! With that said, I tilted back my goblet and drained it. I disliked Madame Nhu immensely, but that was hardly a priority issue at this point.

Nhu served as Diem's First Lady. He was wifeless and she was married to his brother who was slain with him. She was an absolute witch and extremely unpopular after making a joke about the Buddhist Monks, who burned themselves alive in protest to the ethnic cleansing by the governments' Catholics. She was quoted as saying, "If they want to have another barbeque, I'll supply the gasoline." She was not my idea of a First Lady for any nation, nor even a decent human being.

This new development was obviously very troubling to JFK. Peter and I told him we needed to make the last shuttle back to New York. We knew he had a lot of thinking to do before the morning and the onslaught of the Press Corps as well as strategic meetings with his top aides.

New York City

We arrived back in New York City late, and I slept very poorly knowing that I now had to face George Smathers sooner rather than later. I was quite emotionally in turmoil. I hated confrontation on any level, and I took more of a Scarlett O'Hara attitude, "I'll think about that tomorrow." I simply was not slick enough to maintain such a surreptitious relationship with Peter, much less carry the guilt any longer.

> *"Will those of you in the cheap seats*
> *clap and those in the front rows, if*
> *you'll just rattle your jewelry."*

—JOHN LENNON

Peter and I had dinner the next night at the "21 Club." Our visit proved to be a continuing lesson on where you were seated in the more important restaurants depended on who you were, that is if you *were* anyone. Peter was extremely welcome at "21" and of course was seated in the first room straight back, so that you could observe and be observed by whomever came and went. There were always famous people who preferred a dark corner, but most chose the status seating. It was just the two of us. George was coming up to NY for our summit meeting regarding my seeing Peter.

When my entrée arrived, the waiter set the plate in front of me. When he lifted the pewter dome, I simply stared. There was an exquisite sapphire bracelet decorating the edge of the plate. It was the second piece of jewelry he had given me. This, as well as future jewelry gifts, would be from Van Cleef and Arpels. I had absolutely no idea that he could not afford gifts this expensive.

Peter bounced around from the White House family quarters to friends' homes and to hotels in NYC. We saw one another whenever possible that month. I had been leading a triple life now. The time was overdue to confess to George that I was not just seeing Peter, but *sleeping with him*. This was not going to be easy for me, as I cared deeply for George, and we had been together so long. I don't know how I managed to carry on this charade for the month I did so.

Confrontation in an Elevator

It was quite soon after our dinner at the White House with Jack Kennedy and Bill Thompson that George flew up to New York so that we could talk things over. He checked into the Sherry Netherlands Hotel on Fifth Avenue which was just dandy because Peter was also staying there, and I had been with him the night before following our dinner at the 21 Club. He was aware that I would be seeing George on this day, but was also surprised he would be in the same hotel. The whole affair, or I should say affairs, had become emotionally debilitating for me.

It was a very awkward afternoon for me, and George could not believe I would consider leaving him for Peter *of all people*. I didn't believe for a minute that George did not cheat on his mistress once or twice at this point, but heaven forbid I should finally do the same! He felt that it was a terrible infraction on *my* part even though *he was married*! Peter had an enormous reputation as a ladies man. Many glamorous women in Hollywood and high society had fallen in love with him. I believe the shock came down to big ego damage for George.

> *"I have a healthy sense of humor, but it fails me when the ridiculous occurs."*
> —LAYTE BOWDEN

He told me now for the second time that he and Rosemary would be divorcing, and if I were patient, we would be married. My mind went back in time when we were in his car driving along the Potomac going I can't remember where, when he first mentioned this. I should have been thrilled, but I don't think I ever saw our future as together forever, and only now could I understand why. He had been omnipotent in my life on many levels, but I wasn't passionately in love with him. Oh how passion can detonate one's world and mine would eventually cause me so much pain.

I was all ready more romantically invested in Peter than I had been with George. It wasn't the safe harbor I had lived in for certain, but when your heart refuses to communicate with your brain, you're not thinking safety. George *demanded* that I get this out of my system and told me he would not accept my deserting him!

So, what does a woman do at this point especially when she can't handle confrontation? *She lies*, of course! I promised George I wouldn't see Peter anymore and would meet him in Miami at the end of November for a holiday on Key Biscayne which we had planned months earlier.

With this settled in *George's* mind, we got into the elevator to go out to dinner. My heart was the heaviest organ in my body. I felt a darkness of being closed in and no longer seeing a bright light ahead of me. There was absolutely no flutter left in my wings.

I have mentioned how terrible my timing in life is, haven't I? Well, a minute or so later, on a lower floor in The Sherry, the doors opened and who is waiting to step into the elevator? Oh my God, this could only happen to me!

George shook hands with Peter and said as though nothing in our little world was askew, "Well Peter, I haven't seen you in quite some time. I understand you've met Layte." "Yes, it has been awhile and yes, we have met, Senator. You're looking well," Peter added with a straight face. He was an actor after all and this was a cool scene . . . *icy*, in fact.

I was not inhabiting my own body at this point, but was witnessing this play out from another dimension. The doors opened again and we three said adieu, as George and I walked out of the hotel.

Of course as soon as George left the city the following day, I was on the phone with Peter. I would have four or five days off before heading out on JFK's Presidential Charter to Dallas, so we planned to go quietly to Lake Tahoe.

Dangerous Flight

I flew to LA on Friday, the 15th of November, and the next afternoon Peter and I took a private Charter flight to Lake Tahoe. His dear old friend Jimmy Durante had booked him to do a routine they had done together many times before. This would be fun for me as I had never been to Tahoe. They were scheduled to play at Harrah's Club there. We were dressed in heavy sweaters, pants and après ski type boots, because there was quite a bit of snow in the mountains and at the lake.

We flew northeast and the further east we went, the worse the weather became. A real front was moving in and the snow was heavy. It was already dark because of the time of year, when our pilot came back to tell us that a private craft about half an hour ahead of us had radioed that the weather was deteriorating to the point that he was going to turn back. It couldn't have been more than fifteen minutes later that our pilot yelled back to say that we were turning back to San Francisco *immediately*. It was a faster route from the storm than LA.

> *"Gratitude is not only the greatest of*
> *virtues, but the parent of all others."*
>
> —CICERO

He had just heard from the tower controlling us that the small aircraft ahead of us had gone down. Whoa, I looked out at our wings and saw a big build up of ice on them as well. Thank God, we hadn't taken off earlier, or we could have been caught in the same tragic circumstance. The front had moved in much faster than predicted. We heard more about that crash the next day.

When Peter and I arrived in San Francisco, we checked into the Fairmont Hotel and still had time for a good dinner. He took me to Ernie's which I had heard about, but had never visited. Saturday night at Ernie's in those days was a big deal and a very dressy affair. Women even wore long dresses to dine with no affair to follow! Fortunately the owners had known Peter for many years and really liked him, or we would never have been allowed past the front door in our "mountain apparel." We were shown to the upstairs because it was the only area where the maître d' could steal a table for us.

I felt like the main act of a floorshow. Every pair of eyes, nestled in every socialite's face, was focused on us. Not only because it was Peter Lawford, but because the impropriety of our dress was so shocking. That's called flaunting it! NOT having crashed in our plane a few hours earlier, made me realize I could not have cared less about something as trivial as this. That attitude was not new for Peter, but it surely was for me.

Sunday afternoon we flew over to Lake Tahoe's southern airstrip through a clear sky and bright sunshine. Following the big snowstorm the day before, all of Tahoe and the Lake sparkled like millions of scattered diamonds. This Florida girl was thrilled with the view. I never have tired of a day like that when I'm so privileged to enjoy one.

We were met at the small airport by a swanky Rolls Royce that I barely had to lean over while entering the back seat. Over my lap the driver put a white mink throw which matched the soft white leather seats. We drove along the lakeside surrounded with virgin snow glistening on every tree and bush, before arriving at a stunning lakeside home with *no* snow on the driveway. I learned that Bill Harrah, owner of Harrah's Club, had installed a *heated* paved drive, which melted snow away. It was a pretty new engineering feat those days.

Mr. Harrah offered this home to the stars he hired as entertainment for his club. Since Jimmy Durante preferred to stay at the club's hotel, he had Peter use it in his stead. Well, that was a sweet treat for us. The large living room had huge windows overlooking Lake Tahoe. Peter laughed when I said, "Lights, camera, action!" For me, the entire day was like starring in a glamorous movie.

The next day we went snow sledding with Sonny King and several others. Sonny was blessed with great looks and a most amusing personality. He was in Jimmy's act until it came to a close years later. I loved the sledding and the snowball fights, but they were here to work after all. So poor me, I had to roam the casino playing an occasional bout of Black Jack while they rehearsed later that afternoon. It was an act Jimmy and Peter had done so many times over the years in different clubs, that they only had to refresh it together.

Peter had made as many enemies as he had friends due to his relationship to the Kennedys and the Rat Pack. Jimmy was very fond of Peter and this was the only reason he was booked for this engagement. That would be the case for several movie and television contracts in his future. I wasn't aware of all the negative background noise while we were together because, for me, Hollywood truths were difficult to unbraid.

I would have loved to stay two weeks straight in Tahoe, but had to leave on Tuesday morning in order to repack and go to Washington for a White House Press charter accompanying President Kennedy to Texas. I was to return to Tahoe when I got back from Dallas and I was very much looking forward to it.

Kennedy Dallas Charter
November 21–22, 1963

"The courage of life is often a less dramatic spectacle
than the courage of the final moment; but it is no less
a magnificent mixture of triumph and tragedy."

—JOHN F. KENNEDY

Very early in the morning November 21, we departed Andrews Air Force Base for what none of us could possibly know would be our final Charter with President John Kennedy. This was the first charter that I had flown where Mrs. Kennedy had agreed to join him. That was a huge plus politically.

We stopped in San Antonio for his first speech of the day. My crew and I remained at the airport because we would be airborne again shortly enroute to Houston for another speech. We arrived that night in Fort Worth, Texas, and entered The Hotel Texas a little after eleven o'clock, totally spent from the Texas stopovers. JFK and Mrs. Kennedy attended a dedication dinner for Texas Congressman Albert Thomas before arriving at the hotel for the night.

About midnight, my room phone rang, and I was so hoping it was the bellman telling me our luggage had finally arrived from the airport. But, it was the President calling. He was really on a high from the huge receptions Texans were giving them, I was experiencing a down slide from getting only five hours sleep the night before we left. If only I could have brushed my teeth by now, I would have sounded cheerier.

Enthusiastically JFK said, "Hi, I just got here, why don't you come up for a drink."

"*You can not be serious.* Is this invitation from Jackie, too?"

"Jackie was so exhausted, she went straight to her room, and I'm sitting here with Mac talking about how well the day went. The crowds were great to us!"

Ordinarily, Pierre Salinger would have been with JFK, but he was on a jet with some of the Cabinet members headed to Japan. So, Malcolm Kilduff, the assistant Press Secretary was going over a few things with the President.

"Wow, you never cease to amaze me! I'm sitting here, still in my uniform with my roommate Kay Johnson, waiting for our luggage," I complained.

"That's fine, bring Kay with you.

"You've got to be kidding, Jack. There is no way I could be that disrespectful to your wife."

"Oh she's sound asleep, and I'm only suggesting one drink, not a noisy party."

"Good grief, I thought there was nothing left you could say to surprise me, but this is amazing. You really live on the edge don't you? I'm looking forward to the barbecue at the ranch tomorrow night, and maybe we'll have a chance for a few words then."

Sarcastically, he returned, "Yeah, that'll be a *real treat*—Lyndon's ranch. Okay, I'll let you get your beauty sleep. See you tomorrow."

I wonder how many times I have played that conversation over in my mind since the assassination. As wrong as it would have been, I often wish I had just taken the elevator up to the eighth floor and had a last drink with him. I am happy to know that he truly enjoyed his last whole day and was so enthusiastic about his Texas welcome, especially as it was a trip he had not wanted to make.

Surely many people who have lived a long life have at one time or another had the thought, "If only I could live yesterday over." Amidst all the turmoil and news that exploded like a bomb around the world on November 22, that thought invaded all the other emotional thinking racing in my brain.

If I had made his last invitation public within a few years of his death, *no one* outside his Secret Service detail, or some of his intimate friends, would have believed me.

With his wife in the next room, how could he possibly have been so reckless to suggest such a thing? But decades later and a mountain of published books about President Kennedy's fearless philandering, I think my disclosing this completely truthful fact will surprise fewer people.

Dallas, Texas, Fort Worth was rainy and cloudy when we went out to the airport the next morning and prepared the cabin. The Press was covering the President's speech at a Chamber of Commerce breakfast meeting.

The rain slowed to a trickle by the time the motorcade arrived. I went up to the cockpit just before JFK's car passed by. He actually looked up and gave us a big wave and smile. Doug had the side cockpit window open, so I leaned out and waved back. Captain Moody said, "He's still attentive to you, I see."

> *"If anyone is crazy enough to want to kill*
> *a President of the United States, he can*
> *do it. All he must be prepared to do is*
> *give his life for the President's."*
>
> —JOHN F. KENNEDY

"C'mon Doug, he's just being nice," I replied leaving the cockpit.

It was a puddle jumper flight across to Dallas, and there was a huge welcome at Love Airport especially from the women terribly excited to see the beautiful First Lady who rarely made political trips with her husband. The crowd was dense with squealers and jumpers echoing, "Jackie, Jackie." She looked absolutely radiant and was such a huge asset to JFK, there is no way that he did not deeply appreciate and love her. I am not a psychiatrist, but he certainly was wired strangely when it came to women.

As usual, it looked like total chaos on the tarmac while the press, the aides, the regular detail, plus all the local Secret Service, local politicians and their aids were all jockeying to hop in the motorcade vehicles. I was standing two or three feet from the Presidential limousine by the time JFK and Jackie got into the car. Jack gave me a huge smile and one of his underhanded half-moon waves. There is a picture of me in the book "The Four Days" with a silly grin, just as his car had pulled forward.

Sometimes we would join the motorcades, but this time I had decided to wait at the airport and have lunch with a few from my crew as well as a few of the Secret Service men who were not on duty until that night. There was a large contingent of us around a big table joking about saving tummy room for the surely to be delicious Texas barbecue we would be having at LBJ's Ranch that night.

Suddenly an announcement came over the airport address system, "All personnel associated with the Presidential Party return to their aircraft immediately." We were all perplexed, but quickly paid our bills and left the restaurant.

When we got to the area that had been cordoned off for the planes and Presidential entourage, I went up the ramp of Air Force One with one of the Agents. As soon as we were on board, he asked, "What's going on?" Another Agent announced that they received word that The President had been shot and probably killed.

The next thing I remembered, two people were leaning over me in the aisle and one was trying to get a little brandy into me. That was the last thing I needed after fainting in the middle of two rows of seats. I'm sure I was only one of many to faint upon hearing news so shocking that my system crashed. After I regained my balance, I went down to the tarmac beside Air Force One and used one of the only empty phone booths. It had been set up there for the Press's use upon return. I needed to call Peter whom I had left in Lake Tahoe only two days earlier.

Peter was hysterical and crying while telling me he was having a hard time getting through to the family and was only getting his news at that point from TV. We called back and forth probably ten times, as I obtained more information from the communications center on Air Force One, and he obtained anything additional from the Kennedy family. We both cried when Jack's death was confirmed.

I was standing near Kennedy's plane when LBJ and Mrs. Johnson, along with a few of his aides, arrived. I watched them board this jet, not Air Force Two. It seemed forever until the hearse arrived bearing the coffin of the slain President. I was standing near the back ramp while Kenny O'Donnell, Godfrey McHugh, General Clifton, Dave Powers, Agent Kellerman and Clint Hill struggled to lift this heavy bronze, 800 pound casket upward.

Captain Jim Swindal, with a couple of flight stewards, rushed to help them. It was only their sheer determination that accomplished the near impossible even breaking off the handles. I saw Godfrey a few minutes later and his uniform was drenched with sweat. It was an out of body experience for me because my senses were all playing games within myself.

Mrs. Kennedy had been standing at the bottom of the ramp with Pam Turnure and Evelyn Lincoln, their eyes glazed over watching and hoping as I was, that the men could keep their burden level. The ramp was so narrow and steep. When Mrs. Kennedy climbed up past us, she looked to be in a catatonic state. I was mesmerized by the amount of blood not only on her suit, but also caked on her legs. Numbness was moving down my own body as they pulled the back ramp away, I don't even remember propelling myself back to the Press Plane with some of my crew.

The reporters were disheveled and operating in a state of confusion like I had never seen. Sidey, Doug Kiker, Peter Lisagore, Chuck Bailey and some of those I felt closest to relayed the news they were getting from the activity aboard Air Force One. Photographer Cecil Stoughton told them that Johnson was going to take the Presidential Oath of Office on board before take off. They were all waiting for a Federal Judge.

It was so hot on our plane, I thought it must be unbearable for those crowded on AF One with the rear door closed and no air conditioning hooked up to the fuselage. Indeed, when I saw Cecil about 20 minutes later, he was soaked through and racing down their front ramp. The flight attendants and I were just wandering about at this point, with no organized job. We had set up a full bar in the front and rear galleys and large pitchers of ice water as a do it yourself system for the return flight. The reporters would be so harried mentally they might not want to be bothered with even the simple question, "Would you like something to drink?"

We heard that the atmosphere on AF One was volatile between the Kennedy faithful and the trespassing Johnson with his aides. There were several compartments on this jet and at first Kennedy's Irish mafia (as everyone referred to Dave, Kenny O'Donnell and Larry O'Brien) including others were shocked to see that the new President's group chose to return to Washington on Kennedy's plane. But, it was Johnson's right to do so, and they would simply have to grit their teeth.

Later we learned that Johnson would not begin the swearing in until the former First Lady stood beside him and Lady Bird for the picture that would be wired around the world. He was correct in believing it showed solidarity for the succession of our new Commander in Chief. Captain Swindal had all ready started the engines before the Judge and two others were hustled off AF One and down the front ramp.

I watched Jim taxi the craft to the main runway and climb at a steep incline toward the sky, demonstrating just how eager he and his passengers were to leave the City of Dallas. He was Captain of the most important airplane in the world, and now he flew it with a very heavy heart into the earlier time zone. At over 500 miles an hour, the dark would quickly blot out the light of a terrible day in all our lives. The Secret Service had coded Air Force One as Angel. Never had that symbolic name seemed more appropriate than now as it bore the body of the slain leader of the Free World home on power driven wings.

We departed Love Field as soon as all the reports were filed with the available ground phones. I never before traveled when every single person from the Captain to the last passenger was immersed in so much grief. The cockpit crew had no choice but to operate professionally as our lives depended on that. As for the rest of us in the crew, we were anything but stoic. It didn't matter. Almost no one in the Presidential entourage was in control of all their senses that day. For the first time since we landed in Dallas, the Press Corps could slump in their seats, close their eyes for a few moments and think back over the sheer pandemonium of those hours.

Pandemonium was the perfect summation for that day. This day in November brought to the surface all the emotions humans are able to experience . . . *excepting acceptance* . . . joy, excitement, fear, shock, disbelief, denial, pain, sadness and now grief.

I went back to the row of seats where Hugh Sidey and Peter Lisagor were typing with their heads bent low toward the keys. I sat next to Hugh, and when he looked over at me, the tears were streaming down his cheeks. Of all those in the White House Press, I think Hugh had the most special relationship with Jack Kennedy and was perhaps suffering the greatest loss.

In the years since, I thought it interesting that two such different men, especially in character, should like one another so much. Hugh was something that JFK was not. He was a straight arrow, faithful loving husband. Admittedly, they did share a finely honed sense of humor with that amused glint in their eyes, but in their private closets. Hugh could open his wide for public view with pride. John Kennedy needed padlocks and a sealant around the door of his.

Nonetheless, I felt the same pain Hugh was experiencing because I too was caught in the magical web spun without effort by Jack—the man.

John Kennedy, The President, was a bolt of lightning, striking the American people, as well as diplomatic leaders around the world with a spirit, youthful vitality, intelligence and a uniqueness unknown in the history of the White House. His death brought the powerful and the powerless to tears and prayer.

Kennedy Funeral

"The fear of death follows from the fear of life. A man who lives fully is prepared to die at any time."

—MARK TWAIN

When our jet reached Andrews Air Force Base, almost every trace of Air Force One and it's trappings had been cleared. Jackie had refused to remove her blood stained suit, ignoring the urging to do so by those near her. It was reported that she said with conviction, "No, let them see what they've done."

Bobby met Jackie inside the plane, and together they accompanied the casket to the ground on the elevator lift drawn to the side of the fuselage. Those pictures were also wired around the world.

From Andrews, Bobby, Jackie and those who had stayed near the casket on the flight back, departed for Bethesda Naval Hospital in Maryland where the President's body would be prepared for the funeral. (I only learned this later from a television report.) Mrs. Kennedy was determined to stay with her husband's body until they returned to The White House, which would take until almost dawn.

The entire crew on Pan Am flew back to home base in New York, but I remained in Washington and checked into the International Hotel on

Thomas Circle. (In the land of coincidence, my future husband and his partner would purchase this very hotel years later.)

Peter had called to tell me that although several of the Kennedys were not enthusiastic about him joining the family for the funeral, Pat insisted that he and their oldest daughter Sidney accompany her to Washington. She felt Jack would certainly want him to be included. I admired her for taking that stand. Sidney would be a comfort to Caroline as they were close friends within the cousins group.

Saturday night, or actually Sunday at one A.M., Peter left Milt in a White House car in front of the hotel and came up to my room. We held each other and cried for many minutes, and then stared at the TV coverage while exchanging very few words. We were both in pain and feeling we were in the bizarre Land of Chimera.

Finally he began describing the activities at the White House. The Kennedy relatives as well as close family friends were popping pills and washing them down with wine and liquor. But the shock was absorbing their bodies faster than the tranquilizing drugs. Peter had trouble adjusting when they shared funny stories of years past around the dinner table, with too much laughter following. I told him he had been around the Irish long enough to understand that *this was their way* of mourning.

"It's known as an Irish Wake, Peter, and I imagine it will continue through the weekend. They're hurting even more than you, so it's surely not meant as disrespect. You of all people know that family. When one hurts they all hurt. *Nothing* comes between them excepting death!"

Peter replied, "Bobby and Jackie are much more somber, and they sit in the East Room beside Jack's coffin not even talking, just staring into space. I can identify more with their mourning."

He left after an hour or so, and I went back to my all night vigil with television rehashing all things Kennedy. My sleeping pill was ineffective. By morning I must have slept a little because the telephone awakened me around noon. It was Smathers saying he wanted to come over and talk. I had called him from Dallas to let him know where I would be in Washington because I knew he would be very shaken over Jack's death too.

When he arrived, he didn't break down in tears, but was obviously devastated. George shared so much with Kennedy including all their days in Congress and the Senate. He was also in his wedding. Fortunately he was close to LBJ and also part of the Senate Leadership. It was a good thing he had been kept quite busy.

The new President had requested his presence at Andrews when he landed and also at the White House later Friday night. George told me that Johnson had the leadership meet in his Vice Presidential office in the Executive Office Building across the street from the White House to discuss the transitional process in the government. He was considerate in leaving the mansion for the Kennedys' private use during the funeral. His admiration and affection for Jackie at least, would never dissipate.

George would be caught up in the transfer of power involving the U. S. Senate, and it would help him through this period. But when he described praying beside the coffin in the gloomy, dark shrouded East Room, I saw emotion in him that he had never exhibited in my presence. He said the President's casket lay on the same catafalque as Lincoln's had one hundred years earlier.

Both Peter and George came by the hotel to talk with me several times during that dreary weekend. I thought it appropriate when Saturday's cloudy sky brought forth pouring rain, the perfect accompaniment to the bleak depression that was already saturating Washington's psyches.

After midnight on Sunday, Peter was even more broken. His upstairs stories of the family's anguish and continued drinking and pill taking made sense to me. Who could blame them? Their lives were changed forever. Peter's slow, painful decent into his own personal hell was on a direct path now.

Together, we watched the thousands of civilians standing in an endless line in order to pass by the catafalque, which had been escorted to the Rotunda in the Capitol earlier in the day. In my life, I had never seen the entire Nation so united in their grief over a single event. Churches and synagogues everywhere were overflowing with mourners and television was relating stories of strangers embracing strangers in sorrow.

I could have had an aide take me inside the Rotunda, but I was so drained I preferred to remain in my room transfixed by TV. The ice machine down the hall was the furthest I walked those four days. Room service suited my few needs.

Between Peter and George's visits, I was hearing the inside stories of both the activities inside the White House and Johnson's eagerness to take the reigns. George described LBJ's manic energy tempered by his desire to do the right thing in respecting Kennedy's wife and family's wishes for the funeral.

Monday was declared a National Day of Mourning by President Johnson. This seemed superfluous, other than putting an official stamp on it.

Monday, the Funeral Cortege departed the Capitol at 11 A.M. The sky was a perfect shade of blue, which I'm sure was greatly appreciated by the more than one million people lining the route that day. I had room service breakfast in bed once again and continued my fixation with the TV screen. For all those who didn't travel to the Nation's Capitol to view history in person on the funeral route, it was what most Americans did that day.

As the screen flickered from one scene to another, I saw Peter several times and George on screen as well. When the First Lady chose to walk from the White House to St. Mathews behind the casket in the cortege, the family, friends and world dignitaries gathered in the street behind her. With Bobby on one side and Ted on the other, images were created that none of us have ever forgotten.

Compared to the enthusiastic cheering that had greeted the Kennedy's every time they came into public view, the million plus men, women, and children lining their route stood in consummate silence with respect and awe at this surreal procession.

I can't explain why I had NO desire to go outside a single time during those ninety-six hours, since only blocks away, I could have stood and watched in person. I think this was only the second time in America's history that a major event became a collective experience for the entire nation. Television changed our lives. It took us places where only dignitaries or the rich, famous and involved were able to go before.

So armed with yet another box of Kleenex, I sniffled my way through that agonizing day mesmerized by the black and white images passing before me on the flickering screen.

For those who were too young in 1963 to grasp the gravity of the assassination on the entire country, I can only say that it was awesome to witness. The First Lady, who rarely enjoyed the public part of her job and kept privacy for herself and their children as tight as she possibly could, suddenly became as resolute as steel. She was now the person who wielded the power to make or break the legend of John Fitzgerald Kennedy. She had suffered so many indignities by choices he made. There were so many insiders who felt their marriage would not last long after the next election, whether or not he remained President.

But somewhere in those hours between the assassin's bullets and the time he was brought back home to the White House, I think her persona was reborn. She no longer had to share Jack Kennedy with anyone, not for his official duties, or his aides and certainly not other women. Her youthful beauty in sadness and her perfect demeanor throughout those emotional days captivated not only America, but the entire world. She became his living monument.

In Theodore White's book, "The Making of the President 1960," he writes that Mrs. Kennedy makes the analogy to their 1,000 days in the White House to Camelot. The press loved this as did the American public, who for years accepted this as appropriate in reference to Kennedy as the fallen hero and Jacqueline as the surviving Queen. I admired her more than any other woman, both for her dignity and for devoting the best of herself to raising two wonderful children until the end of her own life.

Break Up in Key Biscayne

"A dilemma is an argument which presents an antagonist with two or more alternatives, but is equally conclusive against one, whichever alternative one chooses."

—DEFINITION OF DILEMMA

Somehow, in different ways, we all found a way to stumble through the end of November, then the months and years that followed the assassination, but some fared better than others.

This tragedy brought Peter and me even closer emotionally. He once told me, during a very sentimental moment, that he felt Jack must have put me in his life to comfort him in the future. I quite seriously doubted that, but I did know that I had to finally settle everything with George.

It was a week since JFK's funeral, and it felt as though I was facing another as I prepared to meet George in Key Biscayne. I had lied outright to him in New York, thinking in the back of my mind that it would buy me time to make sure I was making the right decision. I knew George was definitely depressed following the assassination, and I had to see him this last time after the wonderful years we had spent together.

It was always easy for George to put in a phone call and get me a leave of absence from Pan Am, so it wasn't difficult for me to get down to Florida for a few days. He had his entourage as well, and I liked everyone who worked for him or accompanied him in Washington or on trips.

Bill Thompson, Scotty Peek, Billy Vessels (the football great who won the Heisman while at Oklahoma University), Jake Jernigan, Bud Luckey, Bebe Rebozo and several others were around at any given time, not always at the same time.

A driver picked me up at the airport when I arrived in Miami and took me out to the Key Biscayne Villas, where everyone often stayed while there. George welcomed me with a warm hug. We had all been friends for years and I wasn't uncomfortable at all. In fact, I had this unexpected feeling of being back home. George's world had felt like my only real terrestrial body as an adult, and I knew this is why it was so difficult for me to end our relationship. He was the caretaker in our time together, and now, I would be switching my role in being Peter's.

It was only a week since the assassination, and even had Peter not been in the picture, I don't think intimacy would have been on either of our minds. George was down and I was down. We all went out for a late luncheon, and afterward just he and I walked barefoot in the twilight, hand in hand along the beachfront. He needed to talk more about Jack and told me over and over again how uncanny it seemed now that JFK had talked so often about death during the previous year. George admitted that for the first time, he felt more mortal than he ever had and it frightened him. He couldn't stop thinking about the violent way Jack died.

In all the time I had known George, I had never ever seen him so close to breaking down, not even at the hotel during the funeral weekend. But suddenly he just sat down in the sand and sobbed. My God, I was actually the stoic one for once. I had never seen him so vulnerable.

I sat down beside him. He put his arm around me and told me that he couldn't understand how I could leave him now. I don't think dilemma is a word strong enough to convey the depth of my emotional embroilment.

I slept very poorly that night even with a sleeping pill. The next day, we spent some time at Bebe's home, and when we went back to the Villas to get ready for dinner, I didn't see how in the world I was going to get alone long enough to call Peter as I had promised. I certainly couldn't do it from our suite, so I needed to get to the lobby and call collect from a phone there. George knew me well, and knew I was acting strangely. I finally mumbled something about needing to go to the lobby's convenience shop for a cosmetic item.

In the hotel foyer, I dialed Peter. When we had talked less than 3 minutes, Jake walked over to me and said, "Honey, you really better come back to the Villa, *now*." Dear sweet Jake had been sent on the mission.

When I returned and went into George's room, he didn't say a word about the phone, only that I needed to hurry to dress for dinner and that he would be leaving early the next morning for Washington. I had embarrassed him in front of his friends and totally bruised his ego at a very vulnerable time in his life. Other than that, I knew Senator George Smathers would be just fine thank you. He had a very big life and a great deal of money and power.

In time, he would forgive me because he genuinely cared for me as friend, a lover, a daughter and as a woman with whom he had shared his deepest secrets and fears. I wasn't sure which was the most important. But, his lover had made a choice, albeit she felt another gut wrenching loss at that moment herself.

My world was very small before I met George, and he turned it into a large, fascinating universe. Subconsciously, he became the father I never had, and so importantly, the powerful man who could be my protector even when I wasn't with him. Our comfort level was perfect, and we remained friends until his death. Long after I was married, he would still call when he was troubled over a personal matter, and he would ask my opinion.

Those of us who spent a good deal of time with him would kid about what a total hypochondriac he was. So in later years, I knew he was quite afraid of death. He talked to me several times about what I thought about the afterlife. He expressed his fear of nothingness.

Peter Lawford After Dallas

*"My candle burns at both ends, it will not last the
night; But ah, my foes, and oh, my friends—
it casts a lovely light."*

—EDNA ST VINCENT MILLAY

Peter and I low keyed it socially, and I loved his life with his friends. We would go over to Hope and Otto Preminger's townhouse to see films. (Ironically, after marriage, I would find myself living in the Edward Durell Stone townhouse directly across the street on East sixty-fourth.) We'd go to Hamburger Heaven with Odile and Porfirio Rubirosa, which was funny to me as they lived in Paris and ate fabulous food there. But in NYC, Ruby absolutely loved Hamburger Heaven. We often went into the back room at P. J. Clarke's for their deliciously famous chili. It was pretty much a late night stop with more drinking and talking until two or three in the morning.

One evening we had dinner at El Morocco with Odile and Ruby, and as was my habit, I once again stirred my champagne bubbles to the point of overflowing with the large sugar cube stick that accompanied it. Peter grabbed my wrist and took my stir stick away saying, "This is the LAST sugar stick you get. You ruin good champagne, and I'm left with my suit elbow soaked from a wet tablecloth." I only remember that because Ruby laughed as though it was hysterically funny. I drank my champagne properly from that night on and no longer sucked on the sugar cubes.

A little later when I was dancing with Ruby, my lack of sophistication surged once more. I said to him, "When I was a very young girl, I would read about you in all the movie magazines and thought you must be the most glamorous man in the entire world. And here I am dancing with that man in El Morocco—still glamorous and still turning women's heads!"

It was the *very young girl* part of my statement that caused him to ask me, "How *young* were you Layte?" Suddenly I feel VERY old and NOT very glamorous! In truth at 54 years old, Ruby was a delicious man.

I mentioned Rubirosa earlier, but if you are younger than fifty you probably don't have a clue who he was, or that he lived a life outrageous. True books about him would read like total fiction. He ranks up there as one of the most famous playboys in history—men such as he, were called Lotharios in earlier centuries. And, a seducer of women he was—of the richest and most beautiful women of the twentieth century.

Born in the Dominican Republic, he gained the favor of their Dictator, Trujillo, and was given his daughter's hand in marriage—along with a Diplomatic post in Berlin. It was not long however before he began seeing other woman and a divorce followed. He then married the beautiful French Actress Danielle Darrieux, on whom he also cheated.

He followed these two ladies with marriages to two of the wealthiest women in the world, Doris Duke and Barbara Hutton. Ms. Duke gifted him with a Paris mansion, Polo ponies, (he loved playing the game), several sports cars and a B-25 Bomber as a gift during their divorce.

After only *thirty* days of wedded bliss with Ms. Hutton, she showed her great appreciation by giving him *another* B-25 (what was this with B-25s?) and several million dollars along with a coffee plantation in the Dominican Republic! His final and fifth marriage was to another beautiful young (nineteen) French actress, Odile Rodin. He was forty-seven at the time.

Along the way, he managed to romance Rita Hayworth, Marilyn Monroe, Ava Gardner, Kim Novak and the feisty Zsa Zsa Gabor. Their public fights grew into hotel lore. He also returned to romance several of his earlier wives. It seemed they all found him the most suave man in their lives. It was no secret that he was well endowed and for years in Paris, the French often referred to the large pepper mill grinders as Rubirosas.

I may have missed the experience of knowing Picasso and Hemmingway, but I am delighted to look back at my youth, picturing the time spent with a third incredibly fascinating man from my young fantasy dreams.

Surely one day Hollywood will make a wildly romantic film on Ruby's life. He lived in the fast lane, and he died while speeding his Ferrari in the Bois de Bologne. It would not have been his style to die of old age.

> "Anytime four New Yorkers get into a cab
> together without arguing, a bank robbery
> has just taken place."
>
> —JOHNNY CARSON

Peter subbed for Johnny Carson a few times on the Tonight Show, and it was good fun for me sitting in the audience and going backstage to visit with that night's celebrity guests. After the shows, it was a custom that some of the band and associates with NBC would hang out at Hurley's Pub on West 48th Street. Perhaps this is why I'm such a night owl today. I never seemed to get to bed much before 3 or 4 A.M. while with Peter.

We went about our life without public scrutiny. The reason we went unnoticed is that Milt Ebbins, Peter's long time business manager was always with us. We went everywhere by limousine. It was a discreet color of grey, and Peter always sat in the front seat and I would sit in the back alone, or with Milt.

Judy Garland was one of his best friends, and we spent so many evenings with her. At that time, she was going with Mark Herron whom she would marry in 1965 for only two years. We spent night after night at Jilly's on West 58th Street sitting at the piano bar with Judy, who now and then sang along after several drinks. I took it all so for granted, forgetting my adoration of her in the movie, "The Wizard of Oz." Now she was just one of my favorite people, and my sense of humor mixed comically with hers. We both talked almost totally tongue in cheek.

She was frightened silly every time she had to get on an airplane and was fascinated that I flew for my salary. She was even more incredulous that I could do it *sober*.

Her comment was, "At least, if I am ever killed in a crash with 200 people, I know I'll get the headlines!"

Another place we often ate was Patsy's, also on the West Side. I learned that if you wanted *great* Italian food in New York, you might very well have local Mafia sitting at nearby tables. One night we were upstairs with a few friends when Sinatra came up with his crew. To my surprise he left his group, came over to our table and talked graciously with us for a little while. It is the only time I know of that he ever saw Peter in person after the Palm Springs trip with JFK.

In December of 1963, I was with Peter at the Sherry Netherland Hotel in NYC. I answered the telephone one evening surprised to hear Sinatra on the other end of the line.

He said, "Layte? This is Frank and I really need to speak with Peter please." After they talked, Peter hung up the phone and told me that Frank Jr. had been kidnapped and the kidnappers were asking for $250,000 in ransom.

Frank wanted Peter to get hold of Bobby Kennedy as soon as possible and ask him to do everything plausible to help him get his son back. For some strange reason, the kidnappers didn't go through the act of picking up the money that Frank was willing to pay, but returned Frank Jr. unharmed two days later. The criminals were caught however and Bobby, as Attorney General, saw to it that they served long sentences. Frank did call to thank Peter, but to my knowledge that was the final contact between them. Frank was known to hold a grudge.

I heard hundreds of stories about the Rat Pack from Peter over the years. I cannot say that I was left impressed by the aura of Sinatra. The man could surely sing a song, and he left us with so many musical gifts, but that magical charm of his could turn to snake venom when he chose. He and Peter had shared great times. I don't know whether it was because Peter had women (Ava Gardner in particular) as lovers whom Frank loved, or that *he* wasn't President Kennedy's brother in law. He turned on him several times. Peter always idolized Frank.

Publicly, Peter never said a single negative word about Frank. In his heart, he hoped one day they would be friends again. People blessed with the sort of talent Frank had, be it an entertainer, artist or scientist, live in an unnatural world compared to the rest of us. I think down deep emotionally, they suffer as much pain as they might dole out to those close to them.

"There cannot be a crisis next week.
My schedule is all ready full."

—HENRY KISSINGER

The Family, and especially those close to President Kennedy, had made it their mission to keep Pat and Peter's separation and pending divorce a secret from the press. Even though Peter and I had been in public many times, it was usually with friends, and if Peter was asked about me, he lied. He and I were more intent to protect JFK than he was himself. Jack personally told us that if he wasn't reelected, it surely wouldn't be because his sister got a divorce. He asked why we were worried when he wasn't. In today's world, the Press would have eaten us alive. Well, for once, my timing was good.

We were still blind itemed in gossip columns. There was only one in which I read a snipe from Pat Kennedy Lawford. They had dined at the Colony Club the night they *formally* signed a legal separation, and Pat made a comment to reporters waiting outside regarding *that stewardess.* It was a little ironic that we had all dined together in Palm Springs the weekend I met Peter. She must have assumed that I was another toy of Jack's that evening and paid little attention to me.

My life had been on fast forward for years, but now it went to warp speed. My job with Pan American was hard work, and time zones were constantly changing my sleep schedule. Peter wanted me in California with him if he couldn't be in NYC or elsewhere with me. I couldn't keep all that we did and everywhere we went in chronological order, but there was rarely a quiet hour.

There is no time so sweet as when you are falling in love. Color seems more vivid, the air seems fresher, and even a rainy day is glorious. Peter and I had pet names for one another that now seem absurdly silly to me, but when you are in that *zone,* it is endearing. When we were with other people he called me Charlie as often as Layte. Everyone in his Hollywood circle seemed to call everyone else Charlie, women and men alike.

When Peter was in New York, my schedule was doubly busy combined with my job and the international time changes. He talked me into playing the TV game show "Password" when he and Angie Dickenson were on one week. Angie was one of my favorite people in show business. She was ecstatic at this point in her life having just fallen in love with the songwriter Burt Bachrach. I must say when she introduced me to him, I would have had to put him on my top ten *most physically gorgeous men alive* list. They did marry and have a daughter, but sadly it didn't end as *happily ever after.*

Burt was such a talented songwriter and played the piano beautifully. One of the most dynamic shows I ever saw on Broadway was the night I took my mother to see Marlene Dietrich. The stage was dramatically dark, then we heard her voice begin a song accompanied only by the piano when the light pin spot circle aimed far left stage, Dietrich glided toward the center with a small mike in one hand and the other dragging an eight-foot white fox stole which she let it slide from her body. She wore a skin tone stretch gown that looked sprayed on, embroidered with soft crystal sparkling designs that covered only what was necessary to keep her from being led off to jail.

She was the sexiest diva I have seen on stage to this day, and her age was about sixty-three! Her body was perfect. Burt was at the piano, now lighted as well, and they needed no accoutrements. She enthralled the entire audience. She certainly lived up to the legend she had become. There was a huge standing ovation and roses were thrown, covering the stage. I couldn't count the curtain calls.

Our New York City life was good in that I didn't have to hop on another plane to LA following a flight home from Europe, or the Far East. The William Ashers (Elizabeth Montgomery) were good friends of Peter's and Bill had been his partner in projects with Chrislaw Productions. Peter had set this up thanks to Joseph Kennedy's connection with Arthur Krim, head of United Artists.

The first night I met them for dinner, I was charmed by Elizabeth who had starred in "Bewitched" on television for years. She and Bill had helped get Peter through some rough nights in Santa Monica during the marital breakup with Pat, but they were wonderful to me. In fact, when I complimented Elizabeth on her beautiful broach and earrings, she immediately took them off and insisted I take them. She told me in the ladies room that she was so happy to see Peter laugh again and thought I was very good for him.

Chrislaw produced "The Patti Duke" series on television when Patti was very young. I think she had a little crush on Peter because she wasn't terribly pleased when he gave me a bit part as Miss Channing in the movie "Billie." (If you blinked you missed me.) Patti starred in this, and I would hang around the set when I was in town. I had a strong feeling that she was not happy to see me at any time.

Peter also produced a film called "Johnny Cool" which opened in October 1963. He convinced the money people to star a fairly unknown actor named Henry Silva. Henry did a great job, and it looked as though the film would be a big hit here as it was in Europe, but then the assassination happened in Dallas, and people suddenly didn't want to see a movie with someone being shot. So, it fell short.

The night they were showing a blind preview of it on Long Island, I met Helen Feibelman, who was to become one of my very best friends in New York. Peter called me from the limo (at the time I had an apartment on 55th Street and 6th Ave.) I came hurrying down. Milt, of course, and Helen were all ready in the car. Peter introduced me to Helen and it was deep friendship at first sight.

Helen was a tall rather statuesque blonde who had lived with Eddie Safranski for years. He played bass in the "Tonight Show Band" for Johnny Carson. They were great fun together. A couple of years later, I moved into an apartment on the eastside just below theirs, and I'm not sure which of us made the other's life crazier.

Helen really hadn't known Peter very long, but certainly by reputation. When I bounced into the backseat, she seemed quite surprised.

"My God," she said, "you're adorable and so—well, so all American— and dawling, what a great sheath you're wearing." She was further amazed when I told her that I had just *made it*.

"You mean you *sewed* this linen creation?"

"Sure," I said, "I make lots of my clothes." It was a timeless snug fitting aqua sleeveless sheath that hugged my body in a most flattering manner.

We all made the long drive out to Long Island in the limo and watched Peter's movie from the balcony seating. The star, Henry Silva and his wife, an absolutely darling Broadway dancer, met us there. The film was well received and when the lights came up, the crowd gave a big standing ovation for Peter and Henry. Peter was really *up*, and we all had a great dinner to celebrate the night.

Another evening we dined at The Colony Club with the Producer Joseph E. Levine and his wife Rosalie. Peter worked on the film "Harlow" which Joe had produced and they got along very well.

In the summer of '65, he suggested we use his yacht, which he had docked in the East River. We invited a few friends including Sammy Davis and spent an amusing afternoon eating fine food and soaking up the sun's reflection from the East River. I told Sam he wasn't improving his tan at all!

Even after his separation, Peter was invited to join one or another of the Kennedy clan, even though the Press said they never spoke to him. We had dinner at an old established blue blood restaurant La Caravelle, with Joe Kennedy in his wheel chair, his niece Ann and Jean and Steve Smith. Jean was one of Pat's sisters, and they were all terribly nice to me. The Kennedy's were so naturally outgoing.

We even stayed over several nights in Joseph Kennedy's apartment on Central Park South with Milt as well, with that stinky cigar he constantly smoked. Milt had as many movie people stories as Peter, and told them in such a witty manner. I liked him. I saw what he went through, always on the front line of every Peter predicament. Their relationship lasted longer than any other in Peter's life. I'll never know how he managed to stay sane. I couldn't have.

I certainly had nothing to do with Peter and Pat's breakup. Pat could have had Peter back if she had desired. Peter and I had very honest talks about this, and I knew that what he really didn't want was a divorce from the Kennedy family. Peter and Pat had had it with each other years before I knew him. He was incapable of fidelity to her, so I totally understood where she was coming from as well.

He was not the devoted father he should have been to his son and beautiful daughters. He certainly loved them, but had terrible role models in Lord and Lady Lawford. Peter simply didn't have parenting skills for dealing with young children. The years I knew him, I felt he was pretty much all about Peter, but in fairness, he honestly didn't realize it. He was insecure, but charmed his way around that reality in public.

Some of the best times I had during our relationship were during the many months that Sammy Davis starred in the Clifford Odets play, "Golden Boy" on Broadway. We went down to Philadelphia to see the *out of town* opening and sat fifth row center. This was our major public outing as a couple alone. I couldn't believe how many women approached me in the ladies room during intermission to ask me who I was. "Oh, you are soooo lucky. Peter Lawford is *gorgeous.*" It was amazing the effect he had on so many females when they saw him in person. At this point, he was still a physical eyeful enhanced by his English charm and chic style of dressing.

One night we were watching a new young singer at the Copacabana while having dinner, when a big haired blonde came over to our table and practically laid her breasts down on Peter's plate as she introduced herself.

He said in an icy voice, "Madame, would you kindly remove your *things* from our table. Perhaps you didn't notice, but we are trying to eat our dinner."

Whoa, she certainly huffed away in a twit. He could be as effective as pepper spray when it suited him.

Of course we, along with so many of Sammy's *crowd*, attended the Broadway opening of Golden Boy. Thank heaven it was a good play with good musical routines because I would see it quite a few times before it closed. Sam was absolutely great and was nominated for a Tony. Often when Peter was in New York, we would go back stage after it ended and a gang of us would head over to Frankie and Johnny's for a midnight dinner.

It was a hangout for the show biz crowd located in the Broadway district. Not that long ago, I went again for the first time in all the years since the 60's with my best friend Jenny. We had the lamb chops. . . . two inches thick, and they are still the tastiest in the city, no, succulent should be the adjective.

Most nights after the Broadway shows, we would end up at Sam and May's townhouse on 93rd Street right off Fifth Avenue. It was a *happening* social salon. One never knew who might drop by. Actors, singers, politicians, or famous athletes might be there on any given night. It was here that I first met Pierre Salinger's new lady, a young French journalist Nicole Tillman, who would become the second of his four wives. Pierre was a character who spoke perfect French and played the piano pretty well too. After Kennedy's assassination, he spent much of his time living and writing in Paris.

At the Davis' house, we played board games, charades, or poker. Perhaps we would belt out a song or two. Sam would run around taking pictures of everyone with his newest camera. He had quite a collection. He would have gone crazy with all the photo technology we have today. I'll never know how May could constantly be around so many triple A personalities in one house.

Sammy married May (My) Britt, the lovely young Swedish actress in 1960, and they had two children, Mark and Tracy by the time I knew her. She and I got along so well that even when Peter wasn't in New York, Sam would send a limousine for me to accompany them for dinner, or parties. May was quite shy, but for whatever reason felt very comfortable with me. I would also visit her on afternoons to play with the children. The Saturday nights in Harlem clubs were really something new for this little southern gal. Sammy could DANCE and I learned what rhythm really is from him.

Mother was astounded hearing some of my tales from The Cotton Club and even more so, the times that Peter wasn't with me. May and I looked *pretty white* with that crowd. This was the sixties, and in Hollywood your career could be over (May's cooled down) if a white woman married into another race. It was a difficult challenge for their relationship. In Europe, and especially Sweden, the races had mixed comfortably for years.

Mother and I had one of our few arguments because I was socializing with people of color, as she put it. But, her prejudiced attitude never affected me. If I liked some one, I wouldn't have cared if they were purple, and I adored Sam. Whatever else people thought of him, no one was ever allowed to even say a swear word around May or me. It happened one time, and he gave the fellow a real tongue lashing. He certainly treated me with respect, and I didn't think of him as unattractive because the person inside was so captivating.

I can't remember how it happened, but when Sam learned I was a good bowler, he sneaked me on the Golden Boy Team in the Broadway League. That was a blast, and the young singer from Golden Boy, Lola Falana and I became fast friends. She had enormous talent and was beautiful to boot. Like many of my Pan Am friends, she'd pop into my apartment on fifty-fifth street, during the afternoon before the show.

Lola always knew she would make it big after Golden Boy, and she did become a big singing star in her own right. Bob Hope also took her with him on trips to entertain the troops in Vietnam. I read she wowed them all.

Peter loved that I was talented enough to make my own stylish clothes, and one day he proudly presented me with the finest sewing machine Singer produced that year. He admitted that he took a lesson from the sales girl and insisted on showing *me* how to thread the machine. When he returned to LA after that visit, I told him as a thank you, I was sewing a very personalized gift for him.

Our phone conversations became almost intense over this homemade creation for him. He loved surprises. I don't know if he thought I was sewing a stylish tuxedo or what, but when I finally presented him with a pair of boxer shorts with dozens of rows of lacy ruffles, he was REALLY disappointed. I thought it was a super joke, but for a guy who had pulled pranks on everyone he knew, he found this not amusing at all. His mother had dressed him as a girl much too long when he was a child, and I truly hadn't realized the impact that part of his childhood had made. I should have sewn him a tie!

> *"Fall is my favorite season in Los*
> *Angeles, watching the birds change*
> *color and fall from the trees."*
>
> —DAVID LETTERMAN

I was only around Peter's children a few times. As I mentioned before, he didn't really do the *father* thing often enough. But once, when we entertained his three daughters at the Sherry Netherlands Hotel, I took some cute photos of the three girls with stuffed animals as big as they were. He had bought them from FAO Swartz that afternoon.

In LA, I organized a tenth birthday party for Christopher. The dinner was at a restaurant on the beach with some children of friends, including Joey and Lorna Luft, Judy Garland's younger children. They were all so adorable, polite and innocent then. However, it was not easy growing up in those famous fish bowls. There is a lot to be said for anonymity while you are growing into the being you hope to become one day.

After Pat moved permanently with the children to a condo in New York City, I spent more time at the house in Santa Monica. Irma Lee Riley had stayed on as the housekeeper and was absolutely fantastic to me. I was not terribly comfortable being there in the beginning, but she, as well as old friends of Peter's like Molly Dunne made me feel very welcome. I just loved the dog of the house, Blackie. He was a sweet friendly black terrier, and I bought a couture leather collar on the Rue St Honoré in Paris to show my affection for him. Blackie was a gift to Sidney Lawford from Caroline Kennedy, and his ancestry was more interesting than most people I know. He was a "Pupnik." News articles related, his grandmother, Strelka, orbited the earth 18 times in a Russian spacecraft.

Life at the former L. B. Mayer home was certainly not the same as it had been when the Lawfords began their life there together, but it was still usually filled with people and activities. We played poker in the intimate card room next to the bar on certain weeknights. The hard core group didn't rotate much any given evening.

Robert Wagner who was married to Marian then in between his marriages to Natalie Wood, and David Janssen (star of The Fugitive TV Series), and his beautiful wife Ellie, Ben Gazarra and his wife, singer Martha Raye, and Judy Garland were most often at the green felt table. I was still living my other life with PAA out of New York, so I missed quite a few games.

Judy Garland spent a lot of time with us at the beach house, and she could be terribly funny. But, she had a very sharp tongue and could get nasty with people when she drank. One night after a poker game at Peter's, she became quite ill tempered from booze and had something nasty to say to everyone as she was leaving. I was standing by the door quaking a bit, having no idea what her exit line would be to me. I was such an innocent observer on the Hollywood scene, she just put her palms on my cheeks, looked at me long enough to make me even more uncomfortable, before she said, "And, good night to *you*—my little angel."

I certainly can't remember boring nights. One began quietly however until Judy called Peter about 4 am and told him she had slit her wrists and was ready to die. Peter was still traumatized by the terrible debacle surrounding Marilyn Monroe's death, and he was out of bed in a shot, yelling at me to hurry.

" Layte, get dressed. We have to go NOW."

We raced over to Judy's house and ran upstairs to see what her condition was. Lying in bed her wrists were covered in blood, but she was very much alive as the cuts were superficial. This was more like another call for emotional help. I hurried down stairs to the kitchen and got baking soda. After cleaning her wrists, I made a paste of it and smeared it thickly over her cuts to soothe them and help stop the bleeding. Ah, finally those medical tricks I learned through Pan Am training came in handy. Peter sat with his arm around her the whole time reminding her, "Judy, you CANNOT kill yourself ever! You are a fucking National Treasure!"

I was terribly saddened in 1969 when she was found dead in the bathroom of her London Hotel. We spent many crazy fun days and nights together, and I honestly adored her. She really never had the chance for happiness as most of us know it, because Hollywood power brokers recognized her enormous talent when she was only a small child. When MGM signed her contract in 1935 they bought her life as well, and they were willing to use threats or drugs to keep their little money machine singing and acting.

Peter loved the beach and the ocean, having spent much of his life living on islands in the Pacific. He enjoyed our early evening walks along the ocean. We would either walk south toward the Pier, or north past the long chain of mansions lining the beach. Several evenings we heard, "Peterrrrrr," and the voluptuous Mae West would be waving from her upstairs balcony about seven houses from his. I got a kick out of her raunchy way of talking and the interaction with her pet monkey whom she invariably had outside for company.

Any time spent with Eileen and Jonathon Winters was a hoot. Jon was such a mental genius that I can see why Robin Williams looked up to him as his mentor. I don't know if this is actually true, but supposedly Jon was working at a Comedy Club in Hollywood one night, and in the middle of his act, he simply walked out the front door of the club and into the middle of the street where he began directing traffic! It sounds like the Jon I knew. He was talented in so many areas. He was a wonderful painter (with great humor in that as well). I still have his art book gift, which is full of satirical renderings. He played a pretty good piano too, so he was obviously touched on the shoulder by the Goddess of Talent.

Some parties in LA were fascinating to me, like the time we went to Neile and Steve McQueen's house. He actually had a moat, and the house was built around a huge stone paved circle, lined by garage after garage. He loved motorcycles, and I imagined a fleet stored inside next to the cars. Steve was one of those intensely intriguing men who oozed sex appeal. In the sixties and seventies, he was the highest paid actor in the world and like James Dean and Brando, could carry any film to box office heights.

That night the biggest stars were present. Of course the little girl in me who had devoured movie magazines while she was young was quite excited to sit beside Moses, in the form of Charlton Heston.

During the filming of Harlow, we hung out with the actors involved, and I would visit the set now and then. One night Raf Valone, the popular Italian starring opposite Carole Baker, had a dinner party for the cast, and I went with Peter (who had a challenging role as the ill fated husband of the actual Jean Harlow). I was quite surprised when I realized that the wife of one of the most famous actors of all time was Raf's dinner date and would be spending the night with him.

By this time however, I was beginning to think that in Hollywood, everyone was related by only three degrees of separation at most. At the very least, everyone seemed to be sharing their DNA with everyone else in *that* world. Fortunately it was before AIDS hit our continent.

MGM had quite a stable of thoroughbred actors earlier in the movie making years, before the studios were taken over by big corporations. Their rules were law. It was amazing how they absolutely invented the public persona they wanted their stars to represent. They nixed marriages and all in all played God over these people including Peter.

But by the sixties, much had changed excepting the nonconformist lives many of those in the industry chose. Level headed actors came into the business and bought homes anywhere but Hollywood and lived pretty normal lives away from their work. I drove golf cart one day for Peter, Mike Connors and Robert Redford during their game. I was forever impressed with Redford's sense of self and community. He was serious and very intelligent. He and his wife Lola were active in saving the environment decades before it became the *in* thing to do in Hollywood.

When we were on the coast, I always drove Peter's Dual Ghia, which was one of only seven in the country. I was told that the eighth one, on its' way to America, sunk with the Andrea Doria. The Ghia was elegantly sporty and gleamed with 27 coats of a deep grey metallic paint. People would often call over at red lights, "What are you driving? It's a gorgeous convertible." One evening, Peter gave me the keys and said, "Charlie, the Ghia is yours, I never drive it anyway."

Living in New York had me addicted to taxis and limos and allergic to monthly garage parking fees, so I thanked him and told him that since I always had it to drive in LA, I really didn't need it in my name. Foolish girl! I read it sold for over a hundred thousand some years later at an auction. I told Peter that he needed to put that car on blocks and save it for Christopher. It was probably sold to help settle debts when he lost the Santa Monica house.

Peter loved giving me jewelry surprises. One of the first pieces of jewelry was a darling gold cat brooch that had a black onyx belly, emerald eyes and a ruby nose. I took it to Central Park one day, leaned it against the base of a tree and proceeded to paint it with the oils and canvas I had just purchased. Peter was very impressed with my art present as a thank you. Thus, my future career in art was born.

One evening when I was at his home in Santa Monica, we were just relaxing in the den when I decided to create an oil pastel painting with the pastels he had bought for me as encouragement. It was a mermaid swimming in swirling water. Peter was thrilled with it and the next day took it out for expensive framing. He loved the ocean so this was appropriate and with the gorgeous frame, I had to admit it looked pretty artistic. He hung it in the foyer entrance with pride.

He certainly enjoyed making me go on treasure hunts whenever he would gift me with jewelry. I would have to go all over his house on the coast, or wherever we were at the time and follow the directions of note after note until I found it. He was very generous, and I still had no idea that he could not afford to be. I have eight lovely pieces left, all in 18 kt yellow gold, from Van Cleef & Arpels, but I rarely wear them now.

My most sentimental piece is not the most valuable, but the memory that stirs whenever I run across it in my jewelry chest still makes me smile. We had been dating for over a year, and one evening as I was sitting in the back seat of the limo as usual, he said something comically funny. I laughed and then said, "I just love you!"

He leaned over the back of his seat quickly and asked, "What did you just say?"

"Ah, I don't know, I was just laughing."

He said, "No, after that. What did you say?"

"I said, I love you."

"That's what I thought you said!" he declared with a big smile.

Peter had told me many times that he loved me, but I never verbalized my feelings even though he was separated from Pat. Evidently he was very pleased to hear these words from me. Soon after, he presented me with a beautiful heavy gold St. Christopher's medal on a chain, to keep me safe on all my travels. Engraved on the back in quotation marks were the words, "That's what I thought you said!"

Peter and Henry Ford had been friends for ages. Every year, Henry would lease a brand new Lincoln to him for the friendship price of one dollar. It was the car Peter preferred driving, having enjoyed the Ghia in earlier years. Henry was a very interesting fellow, and when I first met him, he was deeply enthralled with Christina Vittore a vivacious blonde Italian. They did marry later and it lasted for fifteen years.

I had mentioned to Peter that when we were with him, he was such a wild and crazy kind of guy it surprised me. I had always thought of him as a sophisticated industrialist, but wow he could shift into the out of control gear after a few drinks. When Peter explained to me how much responsibility was thrust on him at such an early age, I thought, "go for it Henry—you deserve to enjoy life."

His father died very unexpectedly in 1943 and President Roosevelt personally deactivated Henry from the Navy in order to run the Ford factory, which was helping in the War effort. He had married right out of college before the Navy, and consequently, this man of privilege had had few opportunities to live out any *young man* fantasies.

One day while Henry and Christina were west, they called Peter on the spur of the moment and said they and their houseguest from Italy, Gianni Agnelli (the Fiat scion) had decided to go to Las Vegas. "Why don't you two come with us?" So only hours later, Henry's jet arrived at Santa Monica airport to pick us up. This was the first time I had met Gianni, but I had certainly read about him. I was in the midst of *tall cotton* on this little flight!

It was such a short hop between California and Las Vegas that Henry didn't have a flight attendant on board. HE served the drinks. Well, that was quite a switch for me and I offered to take care of the galley, but he seemed to take delight in serving a stewardess. I don't even remember which of the luxury hotels we checked into, but it was one of the newest ones.

We had dinner and then began making the rounds of the casinos. I would be dishonest to deny that I was a fairly attractive and voluptuous young woman, but Gianni Agnelli turned into a bloodhound near me. I knew nothing about him personally, only that he was an automobile scion in Italy, just as Henry was in America. In Vegas however, he was a predator, and I was the prey. He played a simple European, naive to gambling. I, with my tiny knowledge of the roulette wheel and black jack, proceeded to advise him in getting the gist of the games.

By now, I should have been much more aware of howling male wolves, but I had a long way to go before I would understand the social sophistication of a Gianni Agnelli. In fact, I never aspired to it. That level of European society for me was something you needed to be born into in order to feel comfortable socially. This Tyrone, Pennsylvania girl would *never* cut it.

Later, Henry told me that Gianni's love of gambling had grown to the point that *he had himself* blacklisted at the casinos in Europe. How gullible was I in explaining the rules of any casino game to *him*. I felt like a fool totally flaunting my "unworldliness."

Later, I was intimidated again, when he called me at The Kensington Palace Hotel during a layover in London to tell me he was *also in town* and wanted to take me to dinner. NO thank you. It happened again on a Paris trip, and I made it *even clearer* to him that I was exclusive with Peter, period. Obviously he had no problem getting my schedule from Pan American. He was much too powerful and sophisticated in a world that held no interest for me.

On another occasion, Peter and I went to Vegas for an overnight to see Sammy on stage. We shared a *stage front table* with Eydie Gorme and Steve Lawrence for dinner. The waiters weren't allowed to serve any food during Sam's act, so he and Peter really set me up. Sammy took the stage and was singing away, when halfway through a song he suddenly came to a frigid stop.

He stared with a disgusted look at a waiter coming through the nightclub carrying a tray with a huge banana split. The server came right to our table and put it down in front of me. I turned three shades of purple when Sam walked over to me, looked straight down from the stage and said, "Folks, I know this young woman and she really LOVES to eat!"

"I knew you couldn't make it all the way through my show without your desert Layte, so feel free—have at it."

As I shook my head no, Sam pushed, "No, I mean it. Take a few bites at least."

Okay, so I played along and filled a large spoon full of the whipped cream on top, raised it in a toast to Sammy then put it in my mouth. Aaaach, it wasn't whipped cream. It was a truly rancid tasting *shaving cream*. I couldn't help it. I just spit it out all over my plate. Everyone in the room was laughing when Sam told them what it was.

Then added, "Layte, I thought you would eat ANYTHING a waiter would set in front of you. My mistake!"

'Not so funny in the retelling but one of those times you had to be there. It was the kind of silly prank the Rat Pack used to pull on each other according to Peter.

I never attended an Academy Awards event, but in 1964 we went over to the dress rehearsal for a couple of hours and sat with Sidney Poitier to watch the musical productions. The following evening at Barbara and Jackie Cooper's house, we joined a mountain of actors *none of whom were nominated* for anything that year.

I can tell you, that was an experience. Whoa, I had never before or since heard more sarcasm in one night. The TVs were on in every room and whether it was an actor or actress on stage during the program, this *group* slashed and burned each and every one. Either they laughed at how terrible the plastic surgery was, or verbally shredded every gorgeous gown . . . and certainly each body underneath.

I didn't hear a single compliment about one actor on stage that night. As Jackie Cooper had been in the business since childhood, the house was filled with the "old guard," like the Milton Berles—well you get the picture. Ruth Berle and Barbara Cooper were close friends and formidable in my eyes. They were *not* women to be trusted. And appropriately, as "Uncle Miltie" was a founder of the original Friar's Club, I listened as every actor winning an award that night was "fried" to a crisp.

In the summer of 1965, Warren Beatty rented the Santa Monica house from Peter. He and the lovely French actress Leslie Caron, with whom he was having an intense affair, wanted to stay at the beach while she was in LA filming. We were going to fly out to New York the day before they arrived, but her schedule was moved forward a day which meant we would have to schlep off to a hotel for a single night.

Warren told us that he wouldn't hear of it, and since Leslie would have to be in bed early with a 5 a. m. studio call in the morning, we should just come in late that night. The next day she would be off so early that she'd never know we were there and we could get off to the airport later, no problem.

All went according to plan, and we stayed that night in Peter's bedroom. At the house there was a door that closed off the master wing from the rest of the house. Pat's beautiful salmon colored bedroom was on the beachfront. Across a small foyer was Peter's room done in a masculine, but very attractive plaid design.

I was shocked the first time I went to the house and saw for myself separate bedrooms and bathrooms for the husband and wife. It made *perfect* sense to me years later!

Peter said it was really a very civilized way to live as you could still sleep together, but if one partner had a problem sleeping and wanted to watch TV or keep the light on to read, he or she could just go to the other room. The rich do live differently. At the very least, they have a comfortable den off the master bedroom where one can achieve the same comforts.

The next morning when we got up, Warren called us to join him in the front bedroom for coffee and Danish. It was an on going thing with people in the entertainment world (at least all those whom Peter knew) to carry out practical jokes and sneak pranks on someone, even people they especially cared about. For no good reason, the three of us thought it was such fun that Leslie had not suspected that she was not alone with Warren in the house their first night.

Peter and Warren had been friends for years, and I had met and talked with him at parties, so I was comfortable while still attired in my jams and robe. Ah those days when at 29, you have lovely skin and a youthful glow with no need for any makeup in the morning.

How it started I don't remember, but suddenly the three of us became embroiled in one hell of a pillow fight. It was a huge room and there were couches along the front rounded windows also loaded with pillows. We had a great deal of feathered ammunition to fling at one another. It got pretty vicious, but I think I held my own until the three of us collapsed in laughter.

To relate that incident to today's world. I would be flinging pillows with Brad Pitt and Hugh Jackman. I think thousands of women would have loved to trade places with me that morning. Between them, I can't think of a single beautiful woman in films, high society (or low) who found one or the other resistible.

> *"Hawaii is not a state of mind,*
> *but a state of grace."*
>
> —PAUL THEROUX

New York and LA were the cities where we spent most of our time together, but Peter always loved Hawaii. He lived there for a short period with his parents before moving to California for good. He was a beach boy at heart and fell in love in the islands before he romanced most of the glamorous women I saw in films as a young girl. I had only been there once when we accompanied JFK on the Press Charter, and Peter wanted to show me *his* Hawaii.

This holiday would have been a happier invitation, if I had been able to plan ahead and not have it *sprung* on me by Milt Ebbins. I arrived at the airport in New York after working a full flight from London and raced over to the TWA terminal to hop on a flight for Los Angeles. In fact, I had done this many times in the past, even changing out of my PAA uniform and into my civvies in a ladies room after a tight connection. I arrived at the LA terminal bone tired, expecting Peter to meet me. He often did so with the helicopter he leased, and we would reach the house in minutes landing on the beach. But this time it was Milt giving me a welcome hug at the gate.

"Where is Peter?" I asked in a worried tone.

"He's in Hawaii and wants me to put you on the next flight out there. It leaves in an hour, so you don't have much time."

"WHAT?" "Please tell me you're not serious!"

"He knew you would balk and that's why Peter left me the job of convincing you to go."

"Milt, this would be my *third long flight* in one day! He's so selfish to expect me to do this. I'm not just angry, I am exhausted. Get that coward on the phone for me."

Milt got Peter on the phone, and I told him that I just had to sleep, but would go out the next day. As usual, Peter got his way, and I was back up in the wild blue yonder within the hour. After sleeping all the way, I arrived in a better mood, and Peter's enthusiasm told me I had made a good decision. It was for me however, *one of the longest days* of my life crossing all those time zones.

Friends of Peter loaned him their stunning house overlooking the ocean, and the main thing I remember is the swimming pool. It was ocean fed by a mechanism that emptied, or filled it, with *fresh* salt water when you wanted it changed. I had never seen anything like it. With the windows open and the ocean waves breaking below us, I slept like a baby.

The second night as we were entering a hotel cocktail bar, we ran into Marlon Brando. After talking for a few minutes in the lobby we ended up having drinks together. Brando had such a mischievous sort of humor that he sprinkled over our conversation repeatedly. Peter had never even mentioned knowing him, so our first evening out was a nice surprise for me.

> *"Consumption of alcohol is the leading*
> *cause of inexplicable disagreements*
> *taken to the pinnacle of dumb."*
>
> —Barbara Burkhardt

In the later part of 1965, I felt more and more stress being with Peter. We had some terrible arguments. I wish I had realized at the time that drinking gin really does something chemically to many peoples' mental state. It just makes them plain mean. I felt it in myself and certainly saw it in Peter who also had me on Tanqueray. One night while we were having dinner at the place we ate most often in LA, Mateos, we were both mad as hell about something. Who remembers how those stupid arguments get started?

Matty Jorden was a super nice man and had befriended Peter through thick and thin by this time. Peter and Pat ate at his restaurant, on Westwood Boulevard for years. It was Peter who made it, *the place to eat great Italian food* for many of the Hollywood stars, and Matty never forgot that favor. You could walk in on any night and think you were on a set at Universal, or any other studio, there were so many big name actors there.

I almost never went into the ladies room without running into some gorgeous woman with whom Peter had slept. That night I remember putting on my lipstick, when in walked Lana Turner. She was still beautiful and my first impression was that I never realized how petite she was in person. Every star had looked bigger than life on the big screen

She said, "I see you're with Peter. I've known him forever and he's a really nice guy."

I was angry enough to retort, "Well, maybe so, when *you* knew him."

When I returned to our table, our argument escalated. It became so loud and bitter with both of us that we literally ended up in the kitchen throwing a pan or three at one another. I *definitely* had had too much to drink. Any other restaurant owner would have thrown both of us out the back door. But I heard later that Matty was also patient with Pat and Peter during many of their rowdier quarrels, so he let ours play out as well.

That was not the first night I was incensed enough to need a sleeping pill. Peter had a running prescription for Placydil, and I took one that night. I've never had a sleeping pill so effective. It never left me groggy in the morning, and it worked within fifteen minutes. You *knew* a couple of minutes before you were going under, because this euphoric feeling would fill your mind. I'm sure they were not good for me, but I missed them after we broke up.

> *"The difference between life and the
> movies is that a script has to make sense
> and life doesn't."*
>
> —JOSEPH L. MANKIEWICZ

Fortunately, we went to Palm Springs after that fray at Mattie's and the week greatly improved our attitudes. We stayed at Bullets Durgom's house. Bullets was a short, rotund, baldheaded fellow with a fast quip who had managed or been an agent for many big celebrities in Hollywood.

That particular weekend Mickey Rooney was also one of his guests. Being around Mickey for one hour made you feel as though it was four. He was exhausting, one of those people who had to be the center of attention all the time. At the pool, he was a little boy screaming, "Look at me, look at me," every time he went off the diving board. I surmised that being an actor since childhood, he could not help needing to be the central focus.

I only got back to Florida twice with Peter and these visits were not shared with my friends, but as always with his. We flew down to visit with Earl E. T. Smith in Palm Beach, but this was after his beautiful wife Flo died. This woman was the same Florence Pritchett whom JFK told me he once loved. The home was exquisite and reflected in every way the lady about whom I had heard so much from those who had known her. Former Ambassador Smith (to Cuba) was a lovely man, and we enjoyed the best of Palm Beach, from The Everglades Club to the Monkey Bar.

Peter knew Palm Beach in his teens while living there, not in style but with his parents and parking cars for the wealthy, including Joseph P. Kennedy, his future father in law. He also explored the major clubs and parties as a suave young movie star dating the most eligible socialites. Eventually he spent time at the Kennedy mansion as one of the family, so he had many memories to share with me.

On another Florida visit, we stayed on Bob Neal's boat and we cruised out of Miami. He was Peter's long time friend from his beach days. I didn't even mention these trips to my parents because Peter's world was so different.

He would have taken them out to dinner with us, but I would have been very uncomfortable. He wrote them a couple of nice letters telling them he was taking good care of me and they did speak on the phone several times. It was just too awkward for me, but certainly in a different way than Peter not wanting me to meet his rather "crazy" mother.

We mainly stayed on his turf with the usual trips to Palm Springs, easily reached on friends' planes or even driving. The only time I can remember being out of the U. S. with him was when he filmed a commercial in Montreal. Milt was with us, or I was with them as their relationship outlasted any other in Peter's life. We stayed at the Ritz-Carlton Hotel in the Suite named after Elizabeth Taylor and Richard Burton. It was pretty swank, albeit not stocked with cases of champagne as it was for one of Miss Taylor's weddings to Mr. Burton.

I loved Montreal and was fascinated with their city under the city, or as it is properly named, La Ville Souterraine. There were shopping malls galore and pedestrian walkway tunnels connecting you to all areas. I think the more than any city I knew then, they were more prepared for a nuclear fall out!

After leaving Montreal, we returned to NYC where I remained because I was scheduled for stand by with Pan Am over the Christmas holidays in 1965. Peter flew back to the coast. My birthday is on December 24 and at one minute after midnight Peter called from LA and said, "Hi, I wanted to be the first one to wish you Merry Christmas."

"That's very sweet Peter, thank you." I said. "And if you had called two minutes ago, you could have been the LAST one to wish me a Happy Birthday."

There was stone silence. Finally he uttered, "I can't believe I did it AGAIN this year."

Yes, he had forgotten *yet again*. Several of our friends who were at the house that night for dinner told me later that he never returned to the dining room table, but just sat in the kitchen and drank from nine P.M. until they all left. My dear friend Helen was there from New York and said later that he was, "Sittin' and cryin'. . . and it didn't help when I told him, 'shame on you.'"

New Year's Eve 1965 was probably the most glamorous New Year's of my life. It *almost didn't happen*. I was called by scheduling the afternoon of the 31st to fly to Rome. Peter rode out to the Pan Am Terminal with me. We were both disappointed not to be spending New Year's together. Alas, for once timing was on my side. My flight was cancelled, and when I called Peter, by now back in NYC, he was delighted. He sent the car back out for me, and I joined him for dinner at the Radziwill's condo on Fifth Avenue.

Lee Radziwill, Jackie Kennedy's sister, was a professional interior designer, and her rooms were beautifully done. There was also a painting by Francis Bacon in the living room and it was to die for.

The settings on the large round dining table were stunning. It is the first time I remember seeing four mismatched exquisite crystal glasses beside each plate with two wine decanters placed between each man and woman. He could then assume the pleasure of pouring for the lady and himself, either the white or red wine. I was for sure a country bumpkin, but in my defense Lee was on the cutting edge of design. I was more impressed with her style than her sister Jackie's in so far as home décor was concerned.

It was a good group. Lee, her husband Prince Stash Radziwill, Charlotte Ford Henry's eldest daughter, Chuck Spaulding, JFK's friend since college, and Alan Jay Lerner the song writer. There were ten of us in all including a few Broadway actors. After dinner we went to El Morocco en clique for more wine and dancing before heading to Alan's East Side townhouse where he played on his own piano and several of the musical versions from his Broadway musicals. It was magical. I loved those famous songs, and to have the pleasure of hearing their creator sing and play them himself was a dream. We ended the special evening on Park Avenue for a 6 A.M. breakfast at the Four Seasons Restaurant. New Year's Day 1966 began beautifully, but the year was to end badly for me and Peter.

We broke up that year, but oddly, he sent me flowers on my birthday for years to come, even after I married. Our mutual friend Helen Feibleman called me right after he died on December 24, 1984. She had been at his dinner table that Christmas Eve in 1965 when he had forgotten it. "Well Layte, he let you know he remembered your birthday until the end, he even chose to die on it!"

> *"I feel so miserable without you;*
> *it's almost like having you here."*
>
> —STEPHEN BISHOP

When I read a book about Peter recently, I found it terribly sad that he had slipped into a very dark world of drugs and had sexual proclivities that were abhorrent to me. I couldn't have related to his deterioration in the future.

When we were together, lovemaking was normal excepting after heavy drinking at night. As I wasn't driven so much sexually and certainly preferred going right to sleep after a big dinner and several hours of drinking, I was quite happy we made love during late afternoon naps.

If he had *ever* suggested that another woman join us, he would have become *history* within minutes. He knew me well enough to realize I was far too straight an arrow and would find that repugnant. Evidently chorus girls didn't mind the group thing. Peter could hold his liquor very well in public. I was never aware that he did drugs a single time when we were together, so he was conscious enough not to attempt trying to get me into *anything* kinky.

Our relationship continued until May in 1966, but it had been rocky for months because his drinking was getting worse by the day, and I decided I needed Al-Anon in my life more than Peter. I felt every cell in my body rejecting his behavior. One afternoon on the coast, I told him that he had to give up liquor, or I would be out of his life. He chose Jack Daniels. I flew back to NYC *that* very night on the red eye. I was finished.

He called me constantly for two days and then flew in to NYC and pleaded with me to reconsider, but *he* would not agree to completely give up drinking. I again saw a large Dead End sign ahead, and I just wasn't masochistic enough to go back with a man who was using up my very blood supply.

We both had that pit in our stomach that shrieks emptiness, but that was normal for any two people who had spent several years together. He went back to the coast, but continued calling. I had my mother come up and stay with me so I wouldn't break down and go back to Peter. Dear Milt should have told the truth of this to a couple of writers who wrote books about Peter. But as his manager it had always been his job to make Peter sound irresistible to any woman. Who was I to leave him? Milt knew very well why I did.

I took a vacation week and flew down to Miami to spend time with my friend Barbara Storer. She was incredibly kind and assured me I would live to love and become undone again in the future. She and I had shared experiences in NYC and with George as well, so she was someone who could relate to the life I had been leading. In fact, her life had been as crazy as mine in Hollywood.

"Layte, just cry yourself a river, build a bridge and get over it honey," she said.

I replied, "You know I will. I absolutely don't miss him as he is. I miss the man I wish he could be."

I did begin dating again late that summer, but preferred being with friends. I had no interest in any intimate relationship. By 1969, when Peter was shooting the film "April Fools" with the French beauty Catherine Deneuve, I was totally cured of all things Lawford. When he called and asked me to come out to the TWA terminal at JFK Airport where they were shooting, I accepted. It seemed strange to be once again on a movie set watching Peter act. In the beginning, I had found it interesting, but now six years later, it was a totally incongruous world to me. It was actually boring!

After the shoot finished, I told him I'd wait outside the terminal until he changed, and we could go into the city for dinner. I was wearing a designer mini skirt outfit I bought in Paris, with patterned stockings. I felt I looked fairly chic. I had only been on the walkway a couple of minutes when a rather attractive man walked over to me and tried to pick me up.

Every thing he said or asked me, I answered in very simple French, which was definitely all I knew anyway!

I commented several times, "Je ne comprends pas. (I do not understand.)" Had he himself spoken French, I would have been pretty embarrassed as my *vocabulaire* was pretty damn pathetic.

But, he was undeterred and kept up his attempt to give this French chick a ride into the city. Peter walked out, took my arm possessively and said, "Let's go Charlie, we're running late." I looked back over my shoulder and said, "Later, Gator" to a rather confused man with his jaw dropping.

Our dinner that evening wasn't particularly comfortable for me and probably not for Peter. I told him I was seeing someone else exclusively, and he told me he had a lovely woman in his life. After catching up with news about some mutual friends, there wasn't anything left for us to discuss.

He was the only man who had loved me and was important in my travels through this life, who was unable to remain my friend. I understood. His life was sinking ever so deeply into quicksand, that dark world of drugs.

President Lyndon
Johnson Press Charters

*"Ambition is an uncomfortable companion many times.
He creates a discontent with present surroundings and
achievements; he is never satisfied but always pressing forward
to better things in the future. Restless, energetic, purposeful, it is
ambition that makes of the creature a real man."*

—LYNDON BAINES JOHNSON

Traveling on the White House Press Charters with President Lyndon Johnson was different in many ways from the Kennedy Charters. The White House guard and top advisors always change, but many of the long time WH staff remain and that included the Transportation Office of the President. Jiggs Fauver was still in charge, so the communication with Pan American remained excellent, and we continued as the crew for the Press Charters.

Air Force Colonel Jim Cross replaced Colonel Jim Swindal as Captain of Air Force One. He would become a good friend of mine. The gals on the Pan Am flight crew would change by a few from trip to trip, due to marriage or departure from the company, but these flights remained extremely special and always an adventure for the gals lucky enough to fly them.

Lyndon Baines Johnson was always a larger than life presence to me. I first met him when he was Majority Leader of the Senate and King of Capitol Hill. His fellow Texan was his mentor, Speaker of the House Congressman Sam Rayburn, so Texas ruled! LBJ was a *big man*, from a *big state* in the most powerful country in the world. Not too much quieted down in Washington when he arrived at the White House.

Johnson was formidable, complicated and a man of excesses. His Presidency would be tumultuous for many reasons. With the nation grieving, he had to overcome the legacy of the Kennedy elites and intellectuals. He kept Bobby Kennedy as the Attorney General and he worked hard to carry out what the brothers began in overcoming segregation and moving Civil Rights forward. It was a difficult decision for him to keep Bobby and it was equally difficult for Bobby to work for a man he absolutely didn't like, however, both men had a common cause. They were sincere and dedicated in establishing some semblance of equality for black people. A social revolution as up heaving as this one caused the ingrained hate and passion, white and black, to escalate and boil over.

An enormous cauldron of pain and misery for so many was bubbling all around us. The fires from years and years of prejudices would soon physically burn cities all over America. So much death and destruction arose from pent up hate and this in the nation that was originally founded to flee from and avoid oppression. What irony! Although this was almost more than we could emotionally handle, we were now being drawn deeply into a war in Vietnam. Johnson inherited this war, and it haunted him throughout his Presidency.

This was unlike any war we had fought before, causing riots and marching by black and white alike to object. Our military leaders lied in order to carry out operations that we as a population would never have approved. In 1995, Robert McNamara, Secretary of Defense during the war, wrote the book, "In Retrospect" admitting the mistakes he made in directing the war and acknowledged his guilt and regret.

I lived two blocks from the United Nations Building in New York City, and I would often leave or return to my apartment by climbing over roadblocks. Try doing that in a mini skirt which was très fashionable in the 60's. Entire families were shouting and lifting home made signs in the air. From my vantage point, this definitely was home born, not generated by any particular political power. Our nation would lose almost sixty thousand of our loved ones before this war of eleven years ended in April 1975. Vietnam was on the other side of the world from us, and most people had never even heard of this country before, much less be able to find it on a map. *Why* were we sending our young and strong over there to die and spread so much pain here in America?

To make it worse, we lost a war for the first time in our young republic. Today, early in the Twenty-first Century, many feel we may well be repeating history.

LBJ Charter to Florida

*"Paradise can be anywhere
you want it to be."*

—TESS VIRMANI

The *style* of the Presidency certainly changed from the sophisticated to the folksy. I was not around LBJ the man in private settings for conversation after he became President, but he was usually magnanimous when I was able to observe him.

We took a domestic charter to Florida in October of 1964, and when we stopped in Ft. Lauderdale on the way to Miami, he was generous in walking over to meet my parents and grandmother at the airport. He said all the things a mother wants to hear about her daughter and gave them some White House mementos. LBJ didn't have to make that effort, but I always appreciated his thoughtfulness. My folks really enjoyed that opportunity to meet for the first time in person a sitting President.

Then our Captain, Doug Moody said, "C'mon Mr. and Mrs. Bowden, you can ride down to Miami with us. They had a short, but fascinating ride sitting in the cockpit with our crew. They had never seen a take off and landing from that viewpoint, and it is unique. Over a metropolitan area like Miami it is brilliantly lit and crowned off by the runway lights rushing at you before touch down. I wish more regular passengers could have this experience.

LBJ Manila Conference Charter
October 17–31, 1966

*"We live in a wonderful world that is full of
beauty, charm and adventure. There is no end
to the adventures we can have if only we seek
them with our eyes open."*

—JAWAHARLAL NEHRU

My first big international trip with President Johnson was in October 1966 and it provided my first visit to cities I never flew on my normal flight schedules from the New York base. It was a major journey covering several continents and if you fly from Washington to New Zealand, you won't find it a hop, skip and a jump. This trip was labeled overall as "The Manila Conference."

We left D. C. at 9 A.M. on a Monday morning and flew non-stop to Honolulu. We in the crew took to our rooms for sleep, but Johnson began a round of meetings. At times like these, it's good *not* to be President of the United States. LBJ had helped Hawaii achieve its' Statehood and he reveled in visiting our newest citizens.

At sunrise on Tuesday, we flew to Pago Pago (pronounced Pango) in the American Samoa Islands in the Pacific. Physically this is the only

American territory south of the equator and is composed of seven small volcanic islands halfway between Hawaii and Australia. Samoa is on the very edge of the International Date Line and is one of the first places on the planet where the new day *begins*. Consequently, we lost an entire day between Honolulu and our overnight destination in Wanganui, New Zealand.

Besides refueling, the President made this a special visit for the Samoan Islanders and met with their King Malietoa Tanumafili, who was in full dress regalia. Greatly admired, this King was the world's third longest reigning Monarch before dying in 2007, at the age of ninety-one, thus proving to me that a fruit and veggi diet is definitely good for you!

Our entire contingent was invited to a ceremonial area where native people displayed their very festive attire, danced and sang to entertain us. They wore traditional old island styled coverings made from parrot feathers, nautilus shells, and kilts of ti leaves over grass skirts with floral sashes and tree bark as anklets. Some of the women were bare breasted. The men were nude to the waist except for the elaborate necklaces and headpieces. Their instruments were drums and other handmade objects that projected their music. It was primitive, but very effective in stirring emotions.

LBJ made a complimentary speech, and then the King spoke and chanted in a language none of us could begin to understand. When he finished, I leaned over to photographer Cecil Stoughton in the midst of our crowd and asked him if he had any earthly idea of what the King had just said.

Cecil declared, "Honey, he just married us!"

Cecil had been Kennedy's official photographer and remained in the White House to work for the Johnsons. He was definitely a character with a great sense of humor.

New Zealand

From Pago Pago, we flew to New Zealand. The Pacific is *one big ocean* and that's more than a mental note when you fly in one day's time from Honolulu to New Zealand!

I would think that the only city in New Zealand many Americans could name would be Auckland. I thought earlier on that it was the capitol as well, but I was wrong, as it is Wellington at the very base of the North Island. From the air, the hills and valleys appeared a rich emerald green. We landed in Wanganui, on the west coast of the North Island with an entire population of about 3,000. Prime Minister Holyoake chose this warmly gracious town to meet with our President before their upcoming Conference in Manila. The people there were thrilled and so hospitable to our entire contingent.

> *"New Zealand is a country of thirty*
> *thousand million sheep, three million of*
> *whom think they are human."*
>
> —BARRY HUMPHRIES

This country is overall the most lushly fertile of any I have visited other than Ireland and Scotland. After marriage, as a guest at the King Ranch in Texas, I learned the ranch raises cattle down there. Due to the rich vegetation, many American cattlemen joined the King Ranch in raising part of their herds there as well.

During the three nights we spent there at a dinner in one of the lovely restaurants, I couldn't bear to order steak or lamb! I did, however, coax one chef to share his recipe for the salad dressing. It is totally delicious. I made it for friends under the name, Layte's Wanganui Dressing.

Australia

Off we flew to the Australian Capitol city of Canberra, which is inland about ninety-five miles between Melbourne and Sidney on the lower eastern coast. In fact, it is the only major city not located on the coastline. It reminded me of our own capitol, and then I learned that it had also been a planned city, built to become the new seat of power for Australia in the late 1920's. The architect was an American, Walter Burley Griffin, whereas President Washington commissioned the Frenchman Pierre L'Enfant, to design our own capitol in the late 1700's.

This was not only *my* first visit to Australia, it was also the first for an American President!

> *"Once a jolly swagman camped by a*
> *billabong, under the shade of a coolibar*
> *tree. And he sang as he sat and waited*
> *for his billy-boil, You'll come a-waltzing,*
> *Matilda with me."*
>
> —ANDREW BARTON "BANJO" PATERSON

While Johnson was meeting with Prime Minister Holt, we toured and spent time with the local people. I loved their accents and everywhere we went adults and children were incredibly polite and friendly. My impression was that this country was very much like America was fifty or sixty years ago, more innocent. They do follow English customs in their governing and also in their sports. Rugby, Soccer football, and cricket were the big draws.

The Prime Minister held an enormous barbeque in Johnson's honor and the entire Presidential entourage was invited. It was set high in the hills near the city and adorable little lambs and baby kangaroos were at play near our outdoor tables. One good perk on these charters was to be included in many Presidential events. The settings were always something a little more special than tourists see.

After Canberra, we flew north along the coast to Brisbane, the third largest city. During the Second World War, it served as the Southwest Pacific Headquarters for General Douglas MacArthur.

This is also a lovely city and was crisp and cleaner to me compared to our cities in the northeast. Unfortunately, it is very vulnerable to flooding, because the majority of it was built on wetlands. The biggest impression I took with me from down under, was the hospitality of its' people. I felt so welcome and comfortable with every single person I met.

Manila

President Ferdinand Marcos was hosting The Manila Conference. President Park of Korea, General Thieu and Prime Minister Ky of South Vietnam (two men who would struggle for years between themselves and their camps to gain the most political power over South Vietnam), Prime Minister Kittikachorn of Thailand, and President Holyoake of New Zealand came together with President Johnson to discuss solutions for the ever burgeoning war in Vietnam.

"Stop worrying about the potholes in the road and enjoy the journey."
—FITZHUGH MULLEN

This was a very serious meeting for Johnson, but for me it was a wonderful opportunity to explore a fascinating city. In the sixties they said it had the highest population density of any major city in the world, and I must say that it was wild in the streets. For short distances within the city you could use the pedicabs, which are nothing more than bicycles with a side car attached as your seat. Jeepnees and buses were also overcrowding the roads.

I didn't love the restaurants, but was wowed by the Basilicas I saw. The interior of the Basilica Minore de San Sebastian is as beautiful as any in the world. I was fascinated to learn that it was designed by the Frenchman, Alexandre Gustave Eiffel who designed *the Tower* in Paris. I had totally forgotten that it was Eiffel who also designed the Statue of Liberty that was gifted to us by France. If I learn that he designed the Great Wall of China in an earlier life, I might almost be impressed by his accomplishments!

> *"If you can't describe what you*
> *are doing as a process, you don't*
> *even know what you are doing."*
>
> —W. EDWARDS DEMING

On October 25, while we were in Manila, most of my crew and a few of President Johnson's military aides planned a three-car caravan for an excursion seventy miles north of the city. We left quite early in the morning. It was two or three hours driving time due to the poor quality of the roads. Perhaps we should have checked out the area. We heard from our drivers after we were underway that it was a bit communist infested in the country side there, but we wanted to go and were young, brave and adventurous enough not to let that deter us. Gratefully we had one another to talk with as this was hardly a scenic drive.

Our destination was the Pagsanjan Falls which created river rapids. It was quite a special treat for tourists to canoe down the fast waters. I read this area named Laguna was where Francis Ford Coppola filmed part of his film "Apocalypse Now."

When we arrived at a rather primitive but charming outdoor restaurant on the river bank, the man in charge had 12 canoes and two oar paddlers prepared for each of us. This turned into one of the most beautiful and exciting days as a tourist, I had never experienced thus far on my Charter travels. The terrain was dramatic because as the river over the millenniums had carved itself into the rock, creating tall canyon walls on either side, covered with lush rich vegetation.

Our boatmen had to paddle UP river for a very long way and stayed along the edges in order to avoid the main down stream currents. Waterfalls cascaded from the cliff tops flanking both sides of the river. It was unique as we passed underneath each of the falls. We were sprayed, but were not soaked because the falls arched out further into the middle.

When we all reached the river's source at the top, a large lagoon for swimming awaited us, with a mammoth waterfall feeding into it. This was more like a movie set than real life to me. In films, a native tribe would hide treasure under the great falls, but alas, only foaming water bounced off the ledges here. Everyone who can should add this to their bucket lists!

The excitement began on the trip DOWN river. It rushed dramatically over the rocks along each of the tiers along the way. Our guides had to be very quick to avoid the jutting boulders in the shallower areas, while fighting the swirling currents. It was exhilarating, although from films I've seen of people shooting the rapids in Colorado, it's a non contest. For me, it was exciting enough.

The manager of the restaurant at our arrival point had set up a fine feast with their local vegetables, meat and fruit dishes. They also filled and refilled our glasses with their local wine, rice wine that is. Trust me on this one. Don't ever drink rice wine in the Philippine countryside! We were all totally inebriated within thirty minutes. I think the sake we have with our sushi in America must be four times less lethal. We took a raucous swim in their pool under the restaurant's roof, and it's rather amazing that none of us drowned considering our drunken water games.

The lengthy drive home to the hotel turned into an exercise of sorts that I was kidded about for years by those who were following behind our lead car. It seems that the five of us were playing musical seats. We were diving back and forth between the front and the back like juveniles in a gymboree game. Not exactly what you would expect from an airline captain or a top aid to a President. My only excuse is that in our car we were most affected by the *surely* 600 proof local wine.

Henceforth, our group was known as members of the worm pile. That seems to be the best description of what appeared through our rear window to the others. They never figured out how our driver kept the car on the road.

Before each White House Charter, Kelly and I always stressed to the stewardesses that we were representing American women while in foreign countries and that we expected them to be courteous and *dignified* at all times. Well, I have no memory whatsoever of this, even today, but when our cars pulled up in front of the hotel, several of the Press were coming through the front door and witnessed quite a scene involving me.

It seems that two fellows were required to carry a very "stiff," similar to a hypnotized body raised up in a stage magic act, Pan Am Purser up to her room. About five A. M. I awoke to find Colonel Haywood Smith in bed with me.

Horrified, I jumped out holding my pillow in front of me and asked, "What in the *hell* are you doing here?"

He sputtered, "You've got to be kidding!"

He described in more detail than I needed that we had made *passionate sex*. I could hardly call it love since we hadn't known each other very long, even though I found him totally appealing and extremely amusing. As he quickly dressed, he told me that he really needed to hurry back to his room before anyone in the Presidential party started stirring in the hallways.

Standing at my open bedroom door, I grabbed him by the front of his shirt and said, "Listen, I haven't had a physical relationship in *ages* and if you think you're going to leave now, you're crazy. We're going to do whatever it was we did, again, as I haven't a darn thing to loose at this point. I'd like to remember it this time!" He acceded to my request before leaving.

If I live to be one hundred, I'll never understand how my timing in life could be so terrible, so often. After six A.M., I fell quickly into a coma like sleep for what I assumed would be hours, since nothing was scheduled for us that day. The phone rang BEFORE seven A. M. The voice on the other end of the wire advised me to dress in my uniform and be in the lobby within thirty minutes, ready to leave for the airport. NO! I couldn't believe it.

Top Secret Vietnam Trip 1966

No one in the crew or in the Press were sure where we were going, but after we were airborne, many of us with terrible hangovers, we realized we were definitely off to somewhere special. About fifteen minutes into the flight, it was announced that we were bound for Cam Ranh Bay in South Vietnam.

This was obviously a top secret trip for President Johnson because we would be landing only a few miles from North Korean enemy lines. We were told the President was going to make a speech to hundreds of troops being brought in from the jungle without knowing the purpose for their sudden maneuvers. Several of the Press guys kidded about trailing a banner behind our jet saying, "The President is on the plane *behind* this one!" We were well within range of North Vietnamese fighter jets by now, and I trusted this was still a very big secret. The long contrails from our jet were too visible for my liking.

"Mankind must put an end to war,
or war will put an end to mankind."
—JOHN F. KENNEDY

We were to land first, as always, so that the Press could set up all the cameras and position the microphones. Our wheels touched down and we glided past a sea of battle weary military who were surrounding the runway held back by a *single rope* on each side. After all the Press Corps deplaned, a jeep with a mounted machine gun waited for my crew of seven at the bottom of the ramp. They were to drive us nearer the staging area for the speech and awarding of medals, which Johnson would personally pin on the soldiers.

"Big mistake!"

As our jeep pulled in between the roped off troops, they went wild at seeing seven very attractive stewardesses from home. Instantaneously they broke ranks everywhere and surrounded our vehicle. They were throwing us kisses and asking hundreds of questions all at once. It was suddenly, "the hell with the President" as they hadn't seen homegrown gals in many months. Pandemonium reigned.

Air Force One was now having to circle, since the air strip had to be cleared and that would not be quick work. LBJ was now up in the cockpit giving Captain Jim Cross an earful as he watched the disruption out the window.

Finally order was restored and Jim landed the Presidential craft. Johnson received a roaring ovation from the men and he gave a heartfelt speech. Afterwards he pinned medals on several of the special heroes. This President brought his sincere gratitude to these troops as well as empathy for the great sacrifices they were making. He was in physical and mental pain from this war, and I felt they could sense it.

In later years, I always read and watched with interest the Presidential visits to the troops on the battlefield. But on this day, I witnessed *in person* the lifting of their morale by their Commander in Chief. Johnson visibly aged in office because of this war. He lost sleep and fought depression over its' daily toll on our troops and their families back home. In the end, it caused him so much heartache that he chose not to seek another Presidential term.

This day however, LBJ stayed on the ground for three hours, and we all mingled with the troops. So many of them wrote little notes with phone numbers and messages for their families or girlfriends and begged us to please call them and say they were sending their love through us. My purse was stuffed with ragged little pieces of paper. We took dozens of pictures with them, and the Press took even more of all of us together. Many articles about our kindnesses on the ground and hospitality aboard our Pan Am Clipper made the local papers at home.

It was a very special day in my life, and I still treasure it each time I look back over the pictures I have saved. The Press was so busy typing up their stories in order to file the minute they hit the ground back in Manila that I had time to cry during much of the flight back. It was extremely emotional for me and others aboard.

Until that day, Vietnam was a war that was happening far away from my world. Suddenly, I realized I had held the hands and kissed the cheeks of many young men who would die in the jungles so near us. I was even more devastated by this war from that day forward. War is ugly, but sometimes necessary. As we later learned, this one was uglier and not really necessary *fought the way we fought it.*

My mother kept every letter I wrote until she died, and I was a very prolific writer especially in the days I couldn't afford to phone home. The following is a copy of the letter I wrote that night I returned from Vietnam. It is very fragile almost fifty years later on the Manila Bay View Hotel tissue paper. In real time it describes my emotions that day.

"Time and circumstances have the power to transform any great city. And certainly when involved in a war."

—DOCTOR PATTI MANNING

Before returning to Manila that day, we spent an afternoon in Saigon. It was certainly my first visit to that Capitol City that was once called the Paris of the Far East. Remnants of the French occupation were most obvious to me by the great mansions, or what remained of them in their deteriorated condition on a once proud wide avenue. Now many families inhabited a single home, and the laundry flapped from the lines draped from porches. The entrance to the city was swarming like a beehive with individual commerce taking place every few yards.

I remember so well a large group of us sitting in a bar/café having a late lunch and watching a small black and white static television set, while

October 26, 1966

Dear Mother and Dad,

Today was so exciting you can't imagine. No one in the rest of the world knew the President was in Vietnam until we returned to Manila. I learned at 20,000 feet up. We thought we might go into Nam on this trip, but no one suspected today. The surprise, however, insured more safety for the President even though we had fighter jet escorts.

Our plane landed twenty minutes ahead of the President and troops—hundreds and hundreds—brought out of the jungles today (unbeknownst to them why, until they reached Cam Rhan Bay) were lining the runway. Such cheering went up when they saw the seven of us—I couldn't believe it. They honestly took hundreds of pictures and I personally talked and shook hand with so many of them.

The Echo Corps gave me their colors to hold while I had pictures taken with many of these very young men. Most of them hadn't seen or talk (sic) to a western woman in eight or ten months. So many were just sweet kids and it was so touching. I barely got through it without crying, knowing they are right now back in the jungles and many of them will never go home again. War is such a tragic thing—no one ever wins—such a human waste.

I talked at length with Sgt. Buck Coffman* whom the President decorated with the Navy Cross. He'd been in the hills five weeks and lost 31 of his 36 men while he has been personally wounded six times. When he came over to me and said, "May I just hold your hand?" It broke my heart—he told me he has no hope of getting out alive.

President Johnson gave an inspiring speech and the whole visit was awesome. I would fly around the world anytime for just three more hours there. This war is so much more real to me now.

We're off to Bangkok tomorrow.

Love,
Layte

---

* I looked for Buck's name on the Vietnam Wall in Washington years later and there are five Coffmans listed, but I didn't see any with his rank. I prayed that his wasn't one of the five. My first visit to the Wall with my friend Barbara Weintraub left me sobbing like a child. It is the most devastating Memorial I had ever visited. My hope is that Buck is a grandfather back home now and that his grandchildren have some understanding of just how very special he is to our country.

eating food of questionable origin. We also bought souvenirs and I picked up (not literally) a pair of the decorated ceramic elephants that one still sees in Oriental shops. The main difference is that I paid only *ten dollars for my pair.*

On a later trip, Haywood brought me another pair of dark green ones and today, thanks to movers, I have only one of the four left. I used mine in my homes all these years always remembering the Saigon that existed during that terrible time.

Bangkok

Leaving Manila the following day, we flew over the South China Sea to Bangkok, Thailand. This was a regular layover city from our New York base, so I felt very much at home. Johnson met with his Majesty, King Bhumibol Adulyade and his beautiful Queen who are still the reining monarchy.

> *"Too often travel, instead of broadening the mind, merely lengthens the conversation."*
>
> —ELIZABETH DREW

The countries I have visited that are monarchies seem to have one thing in common. There is a picture, or painting of their monarchs in every single building and home in the nation. I felt I knew the Thai royal couple personally because I saw their images so often during my many trips to Bangkok.

Thai temples as well as their monks are everywhere dressed in their traditional bright orange robes with nothing protecting their feet. They usually carry a bowl and people will put money or food into the bowl. They bless the person for the gift, but they never look them in the eye. They, as well as so many Thai people with whom I have shared time, have a special spiritual tranquility about them. Ninety-five percent of the population is Buddhist, so that certainly explains the calmness they convey.

Kuala Lumpur

The President spent only a couple of days in Bangkok before he had us enroute south to Malaysia where he met with Prime Minister Rahman.

We spent only one night in Kuala Lumpur, but it was certainly distinct from our usual layovers.

"Travel teaches tolerance."

—BENJAMIN DISRAELI

As Pan Am hostesses, we were very fortunate to stay in wonderful hotels around the world. It helped that the company owned the Inter-Continental Hotel chain, but, these hotels are *not* everywhere! Arlene Nesbitt was my roommate on this trip, and when they showed us to our hotel room, we couldn't believe our eyes. Thank heaven two native boys carried our bags up the stairs of this two story establishment. The narrow, raw cement steps had absolutely no railings. Loose chickens running up beside us were competing for space. As soon as our helpers shooed out the chickens which had gotten into our room first, we entered the very primitive space. We had nothing more than a colorful drop cloth as our front door.

I mentioned to Arlene there were probably more chickens in Kuala Lumpur than people, and there was a good chance we would have more feathered roommates before morning. We laughed at this because it was more amusing than worrisome. The whole crew went native casual for dinner later and took a walk around the exotic island.

Nearly a hundred racial groups populate Malaysia, and they speak dialects unintelligible to one another. The Chinese have been settling there for centuries and are the second largest group. They mainly practice Tao-Buddhism. During the sixties, I gave little thought to my safety or feared people simply because they practiced a religion I didn't understand. I looked at every place through the eyes of an adventuress.

Korea

Our final formal visit on the Manila Conference Tour was South Korea. After the welcoming ceremonies at the airport, we joined the motorcade into Seoul. Over two million people lined the streets waving little American Flags to greet LBJ. That image is a happy memory.

"Even a fish wouldn't get into trouble if it kept its mouth shut."

—KOREAN PROVERB

I enjoyed sight seeing with Haywood Smith and Jim Cross while they were off duty. I can easily say I laughed more than I took in the sights. We talked about the crazy parts of this traveling marathon we had been on for twelve days. Seoul was still showing the scars of the Korean war and many buildings had not been rebuilt. We didn't depress ourselves by going back over our history from those days.

I've never forgotten the beautiful faces on the younger Korean school children. They walked everywhere in groups in their required uniforms, which were black, or a very dark blue. South Korea's strong tradition of equalitarianism stressed the importance of public schooling and even the children of the rich attended those schools.

There was a painting for sale of a strikingly flawless child. I stood on the sidewalk admiring it for fifteen minutes. I developed a propensity for buying art that later became an expensive habit, but I decided that I would not take this exquisite almost museum quality oil painting home. It was only sixty-five dollars, and I've regretted it ever since that day. It would still be meaningful to me because of the angelic faces I saw on those children.

Another perk in traveling with the President is that we were expected to be sensible with our purchases. Upon our return, we didn't have to pass through any customs with their restrictions on foreign spending. Perhaps, we did get a little carried away now and then with jewelry and such. More importantly, we began the long journey back to America with more knowledge and understanding of human beings who live not only far from our shores, but so far apart from us culturally.

Colonel Haywood Smith

"Some people say satire is dead. It's not dead;
it's alive and living in the White House."

—ROBIN WILLIAMS

Haywood Smith was one of the main men in my life, and most certainly the most unusual, having a personality from another galaxy.

We were caught up in the same world, a world where a President's rope line was not meant to restrain us, just the general public. We were in the company of some of the most powerful people in the world during some of their relaxing off camera hours, and it gave us common ground.

A couple of times, Haywood arranged for Kelly and me to attend White House receptions for whatever occasion. It was amusing for me to watch with awareness those who had never been a guest inside The House before. I found their excitement mixed with nervousness quite charming, and I certainly never lost my own *this is special* feeling when I was there.

One day while visiting Haywood in his office, I asked about the "Bomb Shelter" that I had heard about, but never seen. He took me down, and we wandered through out the rooms that were built to lodge the top White House Staff in case of nuclear attack. There were rooms with bunk beds for staff and communications (assuming that communication was still possible) and roomier quarters for the First Family.

I walked into the bathroom of the First Family's space and opened the medicine cabinet on a whim. There I saw several boxes of amyl nitrates. I couldn't contain my curiosity when I took box after box out and looked inside, only to find "spent" capsules.

Peter had introduced me to this "heart" medicine when we were together, and I admit they gave you quite a high while making love. I certainly don't know *who* used these capsules because there had been Presidents and White House aides who were known as ladies men long before LBJ. More and more the White House reminded me of the castles of yore, where the King had secret rendezvous places within its' walls.

As often as I was privileged to be in the Peoples' House, I was never unaware of the history it held. Though I never attended a State Dinner during the Kennedy era, on occasion, I had the freedom to wander through the rooms and especially loved the library. I lingered before the beautiful portraits of my favorite Presidents and First Ladies. They remind you, lest you do forget for a few moments, those who had walked these very rooms and hallways.

*"I never want to do the same
things twice. I like surprises."*

—AUDREY TAUTOU

On one occasion, my roommate Kelly and I invited about twenty people for a luncheon buffet during the middle of the week, including Haywood and Jim Cross, Air Force One Captain. They flew up to NYC in AF ONE! It was quite a rambunctious few hours and with enough wine everybody was in a celebration mode. To everyone's surprise, including mine, Jim announced that if any of our guests wanted to fly in the President's airplane, he would be happy to give them a ride. They would of course have to take an Eastern Shuttle back to NYC. Well, there are few words to describe how quickly our apartment emptied with all our guests heading to the airport. Kelly and I laughed, but stayed behind because we had a ton of dirty dishes facing us. We had flown on One before, or we would most probably have joined them.

I need to clarify here that neither Jim nor Haywood would ever drink when they were due to fly. If Air Force One, or any of the White House fleet had not been flown for awhile, it was necessary to take them up for a safety check ride. They did not simply waste taxpayer's fuel. This was a short run that would be about the same as circling the Washington area with a landing or two.

About ten P. M. that night, our doorman rang up to tell us there was a very rowdy group of people demanding to come up and continue lunch! This was our life and seemed perfectly normal to us. We ordered in several large pizzas. They were so excited about their unexpected opportunity that they just hated to see the day end.

On one of Haywood's visits to see me in NYC, my mother was visiting, and I remember we drove him back out to a nearby base in Queens to pick up his plane to fly back to D. C. He insisted that Jean get up into the fighter jet's cockpit to get the feeling. That was a comical "uplift," and I wish I had had my camera. It was pretty incongruous seeing her up there under the canopy compared to her desk position in the accounting department at Sears and Roebuck.

Many times Haywood came up to NYC to have lunch with me. This was not your conventional lunch date. This Marine would leave the White House, check out a helicopter, suit up and chopper up to the roof of the Pan Am Building on Park Avenue. Leaving his helmet in the cockpit, he elevatored down to street level and took a taxi over to my apartment on East 46th, where he could be more comfortable in his flight jumpsuit than in an eastside restaurant. Of course he never needed to be strangely dressed at any occasion in order to be the center of attention. Perhaps I was drawn to this wild and crazy guy with leftover feelings from my former crush on Steve Martin.

> "I have no idea what I'm doing, but
> incompetence has never prevented me
> from plunging in with enthusiasm."
> —WOODY ALLEN

You've already read about some of our not so mature behavior on the LBJ Press Charters. Our relationship turned into much more back on our home ground. We would be spending more time together, and I decided to return to Washington in 1964 and commute to my PAA flights from there. Many airline people commute from other cities to their base. I could handle this one hour eastern shuttle trip.

After doing the footwork, I found a cozy furnished first floor apartment in a townhouse one block off Wisconsin and close to M St. This put me right in the middle of all the happening places to dine, shop and entertain friends at home. It also had a small garden and one car park in the back alley, so it felt perfect.

When I went to the landlady's house to sign the lease, she gushed over what a lovely sweet young woman I appeared to be, and how nice it would be to have me living in her townhouse. She went on to explain that her last tenant appeared to be a nice young woman as well, but she was shocked when she learned that the Vice President's limousine stopped there for her every morning while delivering Johnson to work. In fact she lamented, it was often there at other times as well.

I knew the young lady to whom she was referring, and it was common knowledge around Washington that they were having an affair. She later married a man I liked very much. I found it interesting that when she married this friend of Johnson's, the President walked her down the aisle and gave her away. Life is strange. Washington is stranger.

My townhouse, just one block west off Wisconsin, was comfy, but perhaps a little too traditional and antique for my taste. The White House phone in the bedroom reminded me why I was living here. It was now the LBJ era in Washington, and the guests for cocktails this particular evening worked mainly for the administration. A few of the Secret Service Agents on the White House detail were present, including Clint Hill.

After awhile and several drinks later, I found myself sitting on the couch with Clint.

This is the first time I remember talking privately with him since President Kennedy's assassination. Films show Clint jumping aboard the Presidential limousine to grab the First Lady and put her safely back in her seat. The bullets that had just struck Jack Kennedy forced her into shock, and she was climbing onto the back of the convertible. He then shielded them both with his own body.

Clint seemed to be sinking into the depths of depression more, not less, according to mutual friends of ours. All the agents felt guilt over the assassination, but his heart was more damaged than the others.

"How are you doing, Clint?" He understood what I was really asking.

"I have good days and the bad days just like everyone else, I suppose."

"Clint you did all you possibly could, in fact, more than anyone else in the minutes that counted. You of all people shouldn't feel any guilt. Everyone who knows you feels you would have preferred taking that fatal bullet *for* him."

At this point, Clint had had enough to drink, that tears began rolling down his cheeks. He appeared despondent.

"Layte, don't you ever feel guilt about his death? There must be times. . . ."

"Why would you ask me that Clint?"

"You know, because of what happened that night in El Paso."

"That little episode with Jack must have really made the rounds with *everyone* in the Secret Service!" I said, a little surprised.

"It wasn't a little episode and you know that. You physically hurt him and he carried so much extra pain through those last months. We all know the first bullet went through the President's neck, but it wasn't fatal. That bullet would have knocked him over, but because of that higher support back brace, he was held upright and the second hit killed him. You mean you've never felt badly about ultimate harm that high back brace caused?"

"Clint, he and I never talked about what happened that night again and he certainly never held any grudge toward me. We were on trips after that and he was always in a good humor with me. I honestly never put everything together with what happened in El Paso."

He looked me in the eye for only a minute, then shrugged and walked away.

In fact, I had heard from aides that Kennedy's pain the next day and thereafter was so severe, that when he returned to the White House, his doctor decided he would need to be fitted with a custom shoulder to groin brace to hold him more rigid. I didn't know for years he wore this in the motorcade in Dallas.

This had to be the ultimate irony in the relationship I had with Jack Kennedy. With women, he always lived on the edge. If not me, it was bound to be another who would cause the ledge under him to crumble.

There's an old saying with which I think Jack Kennedy would have totally agreed. "If you live by the sword, you die by the sword." Jack lived by NO rules when it came to women and he would not be surprised that eventually this could be one reason for his downfall.

> *"There is a foolish corner even*
> *in the brain of the sage."*
>
> —ARISTOTLE

The scenario my own life was following was beginning to make less and less sense."

As he was Johnson's Marine Aide in the White House Military offices, Haywood was at President Johnson's beck and call twenty-four seven. He had a technician wire my place for a White House telephone because he was there so often. This was a delight for me. I could now go through the White House switchboard to call my friends anywhere in the world. I think my friend Eugenia was sick of hearing from me while she lived and modeled in Paris.

Haywood definitely fit the picture of the clean cut, hard bodied Marine. Ordinarily I don't have trouble describing a person's personality, but in his case the adjectives are too numerous to fit one person. Witty, crazy, spontaneous, cool under pressure, great fun, fearless, competitive, off the cutting edge, and totally wonderful . . . are all appropriate!

I was fascinated by how unique he was, compared to every other man I had known. This is like exam time when you wish you had taken better notes during the course. If only I had written down all the insanity that ruled during our time together.

One night in Georgetown when a few of my Pan Am girlfriends were over for dinner with a couple of Haywood's military friends, we drank a little too much wine which gave birth to one very immature idea. For the hell of it, we decided to head down the street and just check out the neighborhood, as in who is careful to lock their doors. We went up the stairs of one entrance that welcomed us with a simple turn of the front door knob. One light was burning in the front parlor. The seven of us went in and witnessed a scene that told us there had been a wonderful dinner party, where ten people obviously had rushed off, leaving dirty dishes on the table. We decided they probably went to the theatre.

"My God, why would these people forget to lock the door of a beautiful townhouse like this?" I wondered.

Jim remarked, "They have beautiful antiques in here. Look at that ivory elephant and all the leather bound books. Very classy."

"They must be world travelers because there's a Tibetan Alter with embedded semi-precious stones," Helene Harper added. "And check out that Nikon camera on the coffee table."

Looking back at the dining table, I spied a very tall pepper mill. "Let's take the peppermill, and it will drive them crazy trying to figure out where it went! They'll never believe some thief in the night swiped a pepper mill with all these other valuables sitting all over the room."

Impatiently Haywood said, "Okay Bowden, grab it and lets get out of here before they get home and make us do all these dirty dishes for trespassing!" We couldn't have had more fun if we had lifted the "Hope Diamond" from the Smithsonian. We were higher on that caper than on the wine we consumed earlier.

The next day it was more like, "What in the world were we thinking?" Three military aides to the President of the United States illegally entering and robbing a house in Georgetown! The Press would have had such a party, even though these men were so popular with everyone who knew them. 'Fairly petty now—but pretty serious then.

> *"If love is the answer,*
> *what is the question?"*
>
> —LILLY TOMLIN

One evening, having left one party and now arriving at the Shoreham Hotel for a dressy event, Haywood spied a worker's wheelbarrow near our parking place. He swooped me up, set me in the ding-dong thing and wheeled me through the front doors. With the help of our friends, he leaned the barrow up, so that I slid out on my purple tulle covered fanny, in the elegant marble lobby.

I had to have had a pretty good sense of humor, or at least a false sense of confidence, not to go berserk. But, everyone around us was laughing so hard, I just brushed the sand off my evening dress and walked down the stairs like any normal invited guest. When I was out with Haywood, I couldn't be sure just what sort of entrance I might be required to make.

The World Series 1964

Haywood just loved baseball and often attended World Series Games. In 1964 the St. Louis Cardinals played the New York Yankees for the title and won. The Major (prior to his becoming a Colonel) came up with a wonderful idea that we should invite two couples to join us and he would borrow Air Force One to fly us to Missouri for one of the games.

He invited a fun couple from Tennessee, and I invited Angela and Herman Anstatt whom we visited in Vermont and with whom we often socialized with in NYC. Angela had taken some of the LBJ Charters with us before she married and they both got a huge kick being with Haywood on any occasion. The couple who joined us from Memphis were per- haps crazier than Major Smith, and that is a big statement. From head to toe, they were products of the deep south. I would expect to eat chit- lins, greens and pigs feet if invited to their house for a dinner. Properly English Angela and Dartmouth Herman the conservative were positively astounded and mesmerized by them.

There was no end to the laughter on the flight and this was my one and only World Series ball game in person. After the game, we flew to Oklahoma for a late night dinner with oilman Doyle Cotton, a longtime friend of the Anstatt's and mine. We toured his sumptuous, art laden home and I was very impressed by what a fine connoisseur he was.

*"Twenty years from now you will be
more disappointed by the things you
didn't do than by the things you did."*
—MARK TWAIN

We had a couple of drinks at Doyle's home before piling into the car which we very foolishly let Haywood drive to the restaurant for dinner. The main thing remaining in my memory is everyone yelling at Haywood that he was going the wrong way down a one-way street. I had had enough wine that I didn't let that little matter bother me. I had been through much worse with him in charge. After a delicious couple of hours, we boarded the jet and arrived back at Andrews AFB at daybreak. *Time of reckoning* appeared in the form of Jack Anderson who was standing just outside the terminal. We had no idea who tipped him about our trip west on LBJ'S plane.

Jack was the right hand man of exposé columnist Drew Pearson at that time, and Haywood knew his job was at stake if this little jaunt became public. Johnson was a screamer, and he would be heard round the country publicly condemning his aide, if this got out. A couple of hours later Haywood put in a call to Mr. Pearson, who like so many, had fallen under, the fascinating spell of Major Smith. Drew killed the story—dead.

We favored public transportation for several weeks following that little escapade.

President Johnson's Guam Charter
March 20–21, 1967

"One is left with the horrible feeling now that war settles nothing; that to win a war is as disastrous as to loose one."

—Agatha Christie

By March 1967, more than 10,000 Americans had been killed in Vietnam. Johnson scheduled a personal meeting with Chairman Thieu in his quest to keep our losses from escalating even more. We flew all the way to the Island of Guam, once again crossing the International Dateline and spent only one night before returning to Washington.

They obviously failed in their two days of tactical planning resulting in the beginning of 1968 in the "Tet Offensive" by the Viet Cong. It was so named because it stood for the Vietnamese lunar New Year, January 30–31st. General Westmoreland was aware of the build up brewing in the north, but was unprepared for the massive attacks, many of which came from the south where there had been massive previous infiltration by the Communists. We lost almost 18,000 men in 1968, and we lost an additional 11,000 plus of our troops when the Tet Offensives continued into 1969.

This was a devastating blow to America, and by October, millions of Americans across most of the nation were marching to end this terrible bloodshed. I still lived on East 46th Street, only two blocks from the United Nations. In 1969, I needed ID to even get to my apartment building. Demonstrations had been going on near the UN for a couple of years, and it became normal for me to have to cross police barricades to get home. From reading history, I think only the Civil War divided our nation more than Vietnam.

"Like a teabag I don't realize how strong
I can be until I find myself in hot water."

—KIM ANSTATT

I hardly had any private life now because everyone in my world seemed to know that Colonel Smith and I were an ongoing item. Normally on the Johnson charters, I was smart enough to stay in my assigned room, but Haywood convinced me to stay in his while we were in Guam. Our quarters were a very casual wood hotel with the sort of a western feeling of a motel. Several branches of rooms spread out from the main building which resembled a cabin and housed the restaurant and lobby.

Big mistake in the making. After dinner, we went discreetly (we thought) to Haywood's room. The next morning, he told me that while I dressed, he would go to the lobby and bring back some coffee and rolls for us.

When he returned, he said, "Man, do we have a problem! Four Agents are sittin' right outside my room on the railing, drinkin' coffee and smokin', just 'a waitin' on us to come out. They know they've got us this time."

"Oh shit," I said, in no delicate manner.

There was no escape from embarrassment because there was a two-story drop from the only window to the ground in the back.

"Drink your coffee and let me think about this. I have an idea," said the Marine. Haywood calmly finished his coffee and began stripping the beds.

"What are you doing? I hope not what I think you're doing," I said.

"Yep, we're gonna spoil their day. We're going out the back window."

"Maybe *you* are, but *I'm* not!"

But by now, Haywood was tying the four sheets together (thankfully we had two beds in the room), and then dropped them out the window. They didn't reach the ground, but he assured me that he would go first and drop. Then he could catch me when I got as far down as possible before I had to let go. No big deal for a trained Marine!

Well, he went down and landed on his derriere with a thud. My heart was thumping with all his assurances he would catch me, but I finally, hand under hand, lowered myself to the end of the sheets. He caught me all right, but I knocked him back on his bottom again. We stood up, brushed the dirt off ourselves and walked around to the front door of the lobby.

Quite delighted with our escape, Haywood walked out on the deck and yelled to the agents still waiting outside his door, "Good mornin'. Layte just met me here for breakfast. Any of you fellas want to join us?"

Aside, he said to me, "That was some *stealth* action on our part, Babe."

Adenauer Funeral Germany
October 19–31, 1966

*"Dying is easy. It is living up to the great
challenges of life that is difficult."*

—JEANNE BASS

After I had been flying the White House Press Charters for six years,
there was another unpleasant experience during what we called the
Paris-Philly shuttle. You flew to Paris, then back to Philadelphia where
you also had a layover, then reverted to Paris before returning to your
home base in New York. In the middle of one of these shuttles, I was
preparing for a Paris flight in Philly in April 1967. I heard on television
that Konrad Adenauer, Germany's first Chancellor had died at the age of
ninety-one. I knew from previous experiences that I would probably be
pulled off line and flown back to New York in order to take a White House
Press Charter out of Washington. President Johnson would surely attend
his friend's funeral, and therefore, so would I.

Out of consideration, I called the Philadelphia Station Manager of Pan
Am at the Airport to tell him that it would be a good idea if he could find
another purser because I would probably be pulled off my flight. When I
explained why, he avowed that no one was going to usurp his authority,
and the flight would depart with the designated crew including ME.

I'm sure New York flight service would have advised him sooner, if they had learned earlier that the President would indeed be traveling to Germany. But, as LBJ had chosen not to attend Sir Winston Churchill's funeral in 1965, they were not assured he would go to Adenauer's. Many of his friends felt that Johnson snubbed Churchill because he had revered President Franklin Roosevelt, and Churchill had not attended his funeral. Johnson honored Sir Winston in kind and sent an emissary.

Later, when I was in the midst of boarding the Paris bound passengers that evening, the station manager stormed on board himself and furiously told me that I had been ordered to fly back to New York as soon as possible. He had arranged for me to be on the next plane.

"Now get your bags and get off this airplane!" he ordered in a nasty tone.

Unfortunately, the flight left with only one purser that evening, and I felt badly for the under staffed crew. I can tell you, I made it a point NOT to bid any flights through Philadelphia after that.

> *"Live as if you were to die tomorrow.*
> *Learn as if you were to live forever."*
>
> —MAHATMA GANDHI

I felt so fortunate making this transoceanic crossing for the funeral of Chancellor Konrad Adenauer in Cologne, Germany, in April of 1967. This man shaped the destiny of Europe more than any leader following The Second World War and the downfall of Germany. He was 73 when he became Chancellor in 1949, serving for 14 years and died at the age of 91. It has been said by many that no other man could have done more to resurrect a nation so despised after the dictatorship of Hitler. Heads of State from more than a dozen Atlantic nations attended to pay their respects. It was such an honor for me to be present for this great man's funeral, and it once again reminded me I was viewing history.

This was an excellent time for LBJ to have informal meetings with those leaders. He especially appreciated the opportunity to meet with West Germany's Chancellor, Kurt Keisinger, regarding the Berlin Wall. The Wall was built at the end of 1961, dividing Germany's most vibrant and important city. It also ignited even more animosity between America and Russia, who was responsible for this iconic structure.

It would stand for 28 years. One hundred and fifty two East German citizens were killed trying to escape over the wall. Around five thousand however, escaped in a variety of clever methods. One even used a hot air balloon to slide along aerial wires. Before security was tightened, one fellow drove his sports car at full speed through the initial fortification. Zigzag approaches and steel barriers were put in place after his escape.

In 1987, President Reagan delivered a powerful speech including the words, "Mr. Khrushchev, tear down this wall!" Finally in November of 1989, over a million East Berliners protested and this was the impetus to end the divide. Passages at many check points were opened for any one wishing to cross over, and though technically the wall stood until it's dismantling in June of 1990, it was no longer serving its' original function.

Thankfully the Chinese military treatise, "Divide and Conquer" devised by Sun Tzu in the 6th Century was not the case here, if, in fact, *that was* the thinking of the Communists by building this icon. Philosophically they felt they could destroy intellectual freedoms through censorship. *They failed.*

Around the World in Fifty-Five Flight Hours
December 19–24, 1967

*"If you look like your passport photo,
you're much too sick to travel."*

—Bill Huegele

Well not exactly, but using a circuitous route, you could say that we were in for the wildest ride around the world in Presidential travel history. It is mind boggling, when I think back to those five days when Johnson dragged those of us capable of with standing the lack of normal niceties like sleep and showers, from Washington to Australia, to Pakistan and Italy before allowing our weary bodies to return to D. C.! In complete honesty, I was able to take three showers, but we had short naps, not real sleep. The Press guys kidded about putting in for additional hardship pay. They clearly deserved it.

On December 19th in 1967, we were off to Australia again, but sadly for the Memorial Service to honor Prime Minister Holt, who had drowned while swimming in strong currents off Cheviot Beach near Portsea. He served Australia for only one year before his life ended so suddenly.

President Johnson had very much liked him when they first met, and he made this grueling trip to show his respect.

Many of the same leaders who had gathered in Manila the year before were gathered there again as well. This included, of course, Prime Minister Wilson from England. They had a shared history as nations during and after Australia's colonization. It gave LBJ another opportunity to meet with far East leaders and to discuss the continuing war in Vietnam.

From here we jaunted over to Pakistan, where finally, I saw a room and bed. The noisy city traffic never made it conducive to sleeping whether it was summer or winter. I think most of us were so overly tired at this point that we could get no more than a nap.

The next morning *very* early, we were up and uniformed for our little hop over to Rome to see the Pope. Has anyone ever chosen to go via Pakistan to the Vatican from Australia? Johnson seemed indefatigable and everyone who worked or traveled with him should have had fitness gurus with them! We needed energy drinks and perhaps *those college stay awake to study for exam pills.*

LBJ had an office, a bedroom, bath, and a server and chef on board AF1, but the guys in the Press Corps were really feeling overwrought with this 55 hour flight around the world! They were expressing out loud their anger at his lack of consideration for all the rest of us, slumming it, as it were.

In fact, two men in the press checked into hospitals along the way they were so fatigued. Our wordsmith, Hugh Sidey began calling LBJ "President Magellen."

The President, however, felt this opportunity to meet with Pope Paul VI was very important in helping him somehow end this terrible war in Vietnam. Our losses were weighing heavily on Johnson now.

We didn't arrive back in Washington until late on Christmas Eve, my birthday. Everyone commiserated with me, but these were people with whom I loved sharing my special day so it wasn't a hardship. Lady Bird was happy to have her husband back for Christmas and they shared in the White House with their brand new grandson, a gift from their daughter Lucy.

Assassination of
Dr. Martin Luther King

"If one morning I walked on top of the water
across the Potomac River, the headlines that
afternoon would read, "President Can't Swim."

—LYNDON JOHNSON

The sixties had been tumultuous enough that had the final two years of this decade passed fairly quietly, outside the Vietnam War, it would have still been thoroughly discussed by historians. However, some of the worst was yet to come.

We were sitting on the tarmac in the Pan Am Press plane at Andrews Air Force Base, waiting for President Johnson to arrive from the White House for take off on a domestic charter. The Press had boarded, but it was a trip we would never make. News came over the transmitter to Captain Doug Moody that Martin Luther King had just been assassinated in Memphis, Tennessee, on this fourth day of April 1968. The Press grabbed their belongings on board and darted out every open door in the cabin.

It was a horrifying event, because Dr. King had been the most dynamic and unifying leader black people had known in their history in America. I admired his goal to achieve equality for his people through peaceful means, and I realized that this goal could die with him. All hell would surely break loose after he was shot by a bitter white man.

Lyndon Johnson was always a strong force for the black cause, but he decided to send Vice President Humphrey to the funeral in Atlanta. I thought this was bad judgment and also a slap in the face to all people who recognized the importance of this great man. I was stunned by this murder. Everyone was stunned—black or white. Many of us were questioning the level of sanity in America. Had we returned to the early days in the Wild West where the gun was the law? Hell, we weren't even fighting the war on drugs yet. But, between 1963 and 1973, while we were rioting and marching against the Vietnam War and losing over 58,000 of our military, our society lost 84,644 citizens murdered by firearms! It really staggers one's imagination.

By 1967, there had been a great deal of animosity between LBJ and the Reverend King over the Vietnam War, which King strongly opposed and vocalized in public speeches. Presidential advisors and the Secret Service also felt Johnson's safety would be in jeopardy at the funeral in Atlanta. So in retrospect, he may have made a wise decision.

Robert Kennedy gave perhaps the best speech of his life as a beautiful eulogy for the Reverend, with no warning that only two months later, Bobby himself would be murdered. President Johnson's attention *was* required almost immediately to the rioting that broke out all over the country following Reverend King's murder. In reaction, 110 cities suffered race riots, most notably Detroit and Newark. Factually however, the Watts California riot in 1965 was the largest disorder in two decades in the U. S.

King was a great leader and I personally hoped his message of bringing about change in a *peaceful* manner might make a difference. For me, his loss would mean every bit as much to the white race as to the black people, because now there was no one of his stature preaching peace. Our nation was ripping apart.

As a child growing up in Lauderdale, I had no concept of integration, or the total lack of it, in the south. I didn't understand why black people weren't ever allowed to walk on our downtown streets after dark. And certainly, I couldn't conceive that when they traveled in the south, they were not allowed to eat in restaurants, or even use a bathroom, or a water fountain.

I lived in a bubble of segregation, and I am ashamed now that I could have been so oblivious to others' suffering. When I first moved to Washington, I met and worked with wonderful people of color, whom

I genuinely liked. We lunched together and shared happy social experiences. I've met many more undesirable whites than blacks in the entirety of my life.

Lyndon Johnson was eligible, but chose not to run again for the Presidency in 1969. So many who knew him well, felt that the Vietnam War had broken his spirit. The casualties were more than his heart could carry. Our nation was heartbroken as well. The sixties were an incredibly challenging period in America's history. We needed more time to heal from three terrible assassinations and to extract ourselves emotionally from the devastating war and violence in the Far East. Here at home, it was difficult to believe we would ever stamp out bigotry and the simple ignorance in some people.

LBJ Texas Charter
1968

"Every man wants a woman to appeal to his better side, his nobler instincts and his higher nature— and another woman to help him forget them."

—HELEN ROWLAND

In December of 1968, I remember one incident that was rather blatant on Johnson's part regarding his philandering. We worked a charter flight to Texas, and one of the guests aboard Air Force One was a college friend of one of his daughters. After the President made his speech, the motorcade passed through a small town where the young lady spotted a dress she liked in a store window and insisted on jumping out of the car in order to go inside the shop. The aides tried in vain to tell her that there was no time, and they would NOT be able to catch up with the motorcade if they dropped out now. Well, she got her way, but with a price I assumed.

What she didn't realize was that half the townsfolk around an outskirt town like this would jump in their cars and trucks and join behind the motorcade back to the airport to watch Air Force One take off, leaving her transport to assume the roll of a caboose.

The rule was that when the President boarded his aircraft, the engines were already roaring, and the door was closed immediately so they could taxi away without delay. This was for the safety of the President as well as his aircraft to prevent it from becoming a sitting target for destruction by an enemy.

On this day, President Johnson arrived on schedule and boarded the craft. All the photographers took their required pictures, and we assumed the plane would taxi off.

The Press was always required to wait just in case there was a problem, or heaven forbid, the Presidential craft would crash on take off. The world would expect pictures of the tragedy! Well, after about ten minutes, I left my Pan Am plane and walked over to one of the Agents I knew and asked him, "What's going on? Why isn't he taking off?"

The Secret Service Agent replied to me, "I probably shouldn't tell you this, but his girlfriend got stuck behind the motorcade, and he instructed Captain Cross to wait for her to get here."

I still don't know how much the Press was told, but I knew that some were aware of Johnson's latest object of fancy. She was not a beauty although she was a tall strongly built young woman. Finally, she showed up and was promptly ushered up the back stairs to the cabin, the door closed immediately and off taxied the Presidential craft. I think she probably received a good tongue lashing from LBJ.

That was the only time I personally saw Johnson being indiscreet. Somehow this slid by the press. But soon the repercussions from the incident at Chappaquiddick involving Ted Kennedy would equal opening a modern "Pandora's Box." Following the death of Mary Jo Kopeckne, and the cause attributed to Senator Ted Kennedy, politicians became fair game for the Press. It was a lid that will never be closed now that the age of gossip has overtaken most serious news.

> *"Sometimes I wonder if men and*
> *women really suit each other. Perhaps*
> *they should just live next door and visit*
> *now and then."*
>
> —KATHERINE HEPBURN

The White House Press Release on June 29, 1968 announced that Haywood would now officially replace Colonel James Cross, as the overall

Armed Forces Aide to the President. Jim had made the decision to go to Vietnam and serve. That would probably raise his rank to a General's star.

LBJ raised Haywood's rank to Bird Colonel because he felt more impressive hardware on his uniform was necessary for him to deal with the Joint Chiefs of Staff from the Military Aides' Office. I can't say this changed his personality, not any one of them, as he was still pretty unpredictable when I was with him.

Life had been become difficult for me after I returned to Georgetown from my hospital confinement on the PAA Lisbon trip. I began having unbearable headaches at the base of my brain to the point they were crippling my ability to work, or even go out for a meal. I can remember one painful evening when Haywood and I went over to Wisconsin Avenue for an early dinner. After half an hour sitting upright, I had to bend my head between my knees and hang my head as low as possible. It seemed the only way to bring any relief. After a week of this, I was convincing myself that I must have a brain tumor. Haywood was at a loss and quite worried as well because he saw the extent of my suffering.

Finally, I picked up the phone and called George Smathers. We had salvaged a solid friendship after our emotional breakup and the passage of time. He was also alarmed because he knew about my spinal tap in Lisbon and was convinced it must be some delayed reaction. George was one of the all time hypochondriacs. I mean this in the kindest way, but he *was* a worrier and kept the Mayo Clinic on his speed dial.

Immediately he said he would call the Clinic and arrange for me to go up there for a thorough physical. First, however, he wanted his personal doctor to see me for an evaluation. The doctor ran quite a few tests and came to the conclusion that I had contracted the Hong Kong Flu, which had spread through much of the world and had killed so many people.

The Lisbon doctors hadn't detected it and misdiagnosed me with spinal meningitis. Now I needed some serious medication. Thank heaven I was put on the proper protocol. I should thank George for saving my life. Because by then, I thought I might very likely die.

At this point as hard as it was to believe, I learned Haywood was *not* separated and not divorcing his wife. He simply lived in Washington and his family lived in Tennessee.

The deepest truth is, I wouldn't even have wanted him to divorce. Neither of us would have been able to carry the guilt of that. I didn't need a psychiatrist to tell me I was now with this unavailable man for a reason. Having lived through mother's terrorization by my step father, the last thing I could emotionally deal with was a *life commitment*. Marriage still scared the hell out of me, plain and simple.

Looking back at my relationship with Haywood, I was the warrior and quite prone to cause an argument, allowing me to fling at least one plate in his general direction now and then. We spent so much time away from one another between my flying and his life with the First Family and his own family that I felt at times it was the only way I could communicate with him. It must have been his military discipline, because if it wasn't Johnson screaming at him at the Ranch, I was pounding on him at the townhouse. He always kept his cool. I didn't know at the time I had such a bitchy side, and I think it really became stronger when he refused to at least do verbal battle with me. He was much more in control of his emotions than was I. That also ticked me off.

As 1969 moved forward, Haywood chose to deploy to Vietnam as Jim Cross had done the year before. At heart he was not a deskman, but a fighter pilot with deployments all over the world to his credit. He was with the First Marine Air Wing at Iwakuni, Japan and served in Korea, the Philippines, Okinawa, and Formosa. He was a Sky Hawk Jet aircraft attack pilot with VMA earlier and then during the Cuban Missile crisis. In the year before his assignment to the White House, after training in helicopters, Haywood qualified and served with his squadron aboard the U. S. S. Guadalcanal.

It wasn't hard for me to understand why he wanted to do his part in Vietnam. I told him I would fly out to Los Angeles to see him for a couple of days before he reported to base. He arrived in Los Angeles with just a couple of days before having to report to Camp Pendleton for active duty. This was my former turf, a teeny tiny bit of it anyway, compared to Haywood's exposure.

I introduced him to some of my friends from the Hollywood days. We ended up at Eileen and Jonathan Winters' house for a party. Jon absolutely loved him, and Haywood became the center of attention by telling his stories of traveling the world with President Johnson. Haywood embellished his tales with his southern accent, and his exchanges charmed the powerful in that Hollywood crowd that evening.

I was almost to the point of believing he actually said, "Well howdy there Mister Emperor," to the diminutive Haile Selassie, who's full title was Power of the Trinity, His Imperial Majesty Haile Selassie I, Conquering Lion of the Tribe of Judah, King of Kings of Ethiopia and Elect of God. It wouldn't have been a variant of Haywood's personality to carry off this kind of behavior. Jonathan was rarely upstaged when it came to humor, but this night he was equaled.

Haywood's deployment into the war zone would be far different from flying into Cam Rahn Bay on Air Force One. Soon after he left, I wasn't very surprised when Colonel Smith sent me some pictures of his new home, which was an ocean front villa, *war zone architecture,* in Danang, Vietnam. He had taken command of the Marine 16th Aircraft Group based there and was back in helicopters. The pictures I received were of him and his fellow officers at rest. There was a sturdy looking group at his bar and several on lounge chairs on the sandy beach in front. It looked like a pretty good place for R&R between flying sorties.

I can't verify if this is actually true, but I was told by different people that when they filmed "Apocalypse Now," the part played by Robert Duvall was based on Haywood's experiences in Vietnam. It made perfect sense to me. He was known to chopper around with the doors off, and he took his dog up whenever he was able. The Duvall character was a wild and crazy guy in the movie, so who else would they have chosen as their model?

Haywood asked me to fly out to Cam Rahn Bay for a visit after some months, saying he would arrange military transport. We both knew we met at the wrong time in our lives, and we both knew that his life must continue in Memphis when he returned from Vietnam. I now needed to take a different journey as well.

President Richard Nixon

1969

*"A public man must never forget that he loses
his usefulness when he as an individual, rather
than his policy, becomes the issue."*

—RICHARD MILHOUS NIXON

Flying White House Charters when Richard Nixon became President was not as exciting for me as it had been with JFK and LBJ. His staff was rather cold and unapproachable, much as Nixon himself seemed to me. There was certainly no feeling of the camaraderie that had existed previously between the press plane occupants and Air Force One.

His main man, Bob Haldeman, was a stern gate keeper. An intelligent man, he had headed the J. Walter Thompson Advertising Agency before becoming Nixon's Campaign manager in the 1962 Governor's race. He was a Christian Scientist and a *very serious* man, whom I don't recall seeing smile a single time! We felt he and John Ehrlichman had the personalities of Gestapo men rather than the congenial counselors to the former Presidents. But, they suited Mr. Nixon and it mattered not a twit what the rest of us thought nor should it have.

I had met Nixon on several occasions when he was Vice President, and he graciously posed with me for publicity shots to benefit Florida industries. I was included in the pictures by request of those companies or by their Congressman.

Because of Smather's friendship with Nixon, a couple of times I found myself sitting in Bebe Rebozo's back yard on Key Biscayne with him and Pat for iced tea and casual conversation. As Bebe was an available bachelor in those days, I introduced him to my beautiful friend Eugenia. He found her quite lovely, so much so he invited her to join him on a trip around the world with the Nixons.

One afternoon while in Miami, my NYC roommate Kelly and I were enjoying Bebe's little beach behind the house, edged by Biscayne Bay. Bebe walked over and said he wanted to take us for a ride in his new amphibian airplane. In those days it wouldn't have occurred to me to worry about his flying skills. It sounded like a fun adventure. It was one of the few times I have flown off the water and landed with pontoons.

The aerial views of Coconut Grove and Miami Beach at the lower altitude were more interesting than from a commercial jet, and our landing was quite smooth. We helped beach the craft and went back to our sunbathing. It was less than two weeks later when I saw on television breaking news, "President Nixon's close friend Bebe Rebozo crashed into Biscayne Bay this afternoon while flying his amphibian plane. He was rescued, and it is reported from the hospital that his back is broken."

My mother's phone call followed within ten minutes. "Layte Marsha, I don't ever want you to fly with Bebe again, even if he is crazy enough to go back up in that plane!"

"Don't worry mother, that plane is at the bottom of the Bay!"

"Layte, you turned every hair on my head white by just flying with Pan Am, please don't make it fall out by continuing to go airborne with any fool who can get something with wings up in the sky. Now you promise me!"

Now and then I wonder why I am still alive considering all the chances I took without considering the consequences.

Nixon Charter to Europe
February 23–March 2, 1969

President Nixon took office in January and his first international travels began in February. On the 23rd, our press plane shadowed more than three hundred men and women who were accompanying Nixon on his first foray into meetings with heads of state in five European Nations. His first speech in Brussels the following morning was to the representatives of NATO. The real elephant in the middle of every room where he would speak was the ongoing war in Vietnam.

This was the nightmare he inherited from Johnson. The death toll now reached over 46,000 Americans. We denied the accusations that we had expanded our bombing into Cambodia, but in fact, on the very day Nixon was speaking to NATO, Henry Kissinger and General Alexander Haig were on Air Force One (which they knew was totally private as far as being secretly taped) finalizing the plans to bomb Cambodia. Our State Department was against it, but Nixon personally approved the B-52 sorties in that country for fourteen months. He had hoped to keep it secret, but even a little Pan Am employee like me would find that desire naive.

In Paris, Nixon used his meetings with President de Galle to discern where the Russians stood regarding America. Charles de Galle rightfully determined Russia was more worried about China than the U. S. at this point. It was the beginning of the *laying on hands internationally* for this new President.

The capitol cities of the world felt pretty much like home ground for most of us on the crew as well as the press. Other than the enjoyment of being with so many friends again, these White House Charters were far less exciting. For sure, the Berliners didn't show the same electric enthusiasm in welcoming Nixon as they had Kennedy. Poor Nixon, he dealt emotionally with the ghost of the Kennedys until the end of his life.

The President ended this trip with a visit to Vatican City to meet Pope Paul VI. I was then ready to return to New York.

Nixon Charter
Around the World
July 23–August 4, 1969

*"In America, anyone can become
president. That's the problem."*

—GEORGE CARLIN

July 20, 1969 was such an important day for all of us in America. We
watched with great pride, as Astronaut Neil Armstrong stepped onto
the surface of the Moon. The Apollo 11 space shuttle delivered our
Astronauts. It had been eight years since the NASA program first launched
Alan Shepard into space, and in spite of all of the strong competition
from the Soviet Union, it was the flag of the United States that Armstrong
and Buzz Aldrin planted that day.

Nixon scheduled our first stop on his fourteen day "Around the World"
Charter at the Johnston Atoll in the Pacific. We stayed at the airport while
a select pool from the press accompanied him aboard the USS Hornet
carrier that rescued the Apollo 11 space capsule out of the Ocean.

Nixon spoke with them by onboard phone through the glass chamber where they were quarantined following their flight. All space pioneers
were examined by doctors before being exposed to the public. Nixon

congratulated them and related how proud all Americans were of this enormous accomplishment.

I would have so loved to see the splash down. I was in Cape Canaveral to see the lift off, during a Public Relations Assignment, which I describe later. But, of course, our crew was not allowed aboard the USS Hornet.

From Johnston Island, we continued on to Manila, where Mr. Nixon met with President Marcos. Several of us went to an evening event and had a turn on the dance floor with Marcos. We were so fortunate to accompany the Presidential party on many of the special events.

Our next short stop was Jakarta before we continued on to Bangkok, where we spent two days. This was really welcome for me and my crew as we were picking up the beautiful Thai silk clothing we had ordered from Thompson's shop on previous trips. After more delicious Thai meals, we flew off to New Delhi where we were grateful to spend another whole night in a Pan Am owned Intercontinental Hotel, that was always home for us while there.

Review of New York City Life in the Sixties

"I moved to NYC for my health, I'm paranoid and it was the only place where my fears were justified."

—ANITA WEISS

How could I not fall in love with New York when I already had a steady job and was able to find a roomy one-bedroom apartment on West 55th Street, one block off Fifth Avenue? It was hot that summer of 1962, but I was working through my training course for Pan American Airlines, taking medical tests and studying French.

Seventy-seven West 55th was a brand new building and not only was the rent around $275.00 a month, I was given the first two months for *free!* Today it must go for at least three thousand at such a prime location. I still needed a roommate if I was to afford my shopping habit along with the roof over my head.

Most Pan Am girls I knew dressed to the teeth and were able to do so by having very inexpensive tailors in Lisbon, Bangkok, or Hong Kong make up their designs with fabrics bought in Rome, or Paris. Of course, I did so also. But, I so loved spending an afternoon perusing Sak's, Bendels, or Bloomingdales, all of which had their Flagship stores in Manhattan.

And at Christmas, the City was absolutely magical. We skated (badly in my case) at Rockefeller Plaza and Central Park. We used the subway system feeling safe in those days to get from one end of the city to the other. It was cheaper and faster than cabs, and I felt quite unthreatened, even if I was alone. I'd choose a train car that had the most passengers. There is no substitute for intelligent street smarts in a big city.

Living in the center of Manhattan, you could never be sure whether or not you might have to crawl under, or straddle over, a roadblock to get inside your own building.

The Beatles are coming! The Beatles are coming! Yes, in NYC we were all aware of the hyped to the sky invasion of the *Fab Four* on February 7, 1964. What I didn't realize was that they would be staying at the Warwick Hotel on the corner of 54th Street, one very short block south of my apartment on Sixth Avenue.

For a week, while they performed on the Ed Sullivan Variety TV Show and managed to be photographed at every landmark in NYC, I learned in real time just what "Beatlemania" meant. Of course there were roadblocks all over our streets, but worse were the thousands of screaming young women and girls stalking these young Brits. The chanting and hysterical screeching did not stop until the musical sensations left for Miami. I enjoyed their performance on TV, but was very happy when they left NYC. Had it not been for a good set of ear plugs, I would not have been able to sleep at all.

For me, New York will always be my heart city. I only go up from Miami once or twice a year now, but I always feel I have *come home*. Perhaps that's because I lived there during different stages of my life, married and unmarried. It is a melting pot like none other! I love the street vendors (warming bagel smells and hot dog aroma especially) along with various languages from the world over, being spoken everywhere I went. Because I was a world traveler and often needed guidance in a strange city, I made a point of being overly courteous to foreigners with poor English skills.

It was never a city where one had to feel lonely. You only needed to put on high heels, a fairly short skirt, definitely a hat and walk down the street, preferably Park Ave where they always seemed to be constructing a building. Every construction worker would call out conversational comments towards you, and you would smile and think—it's a beautiful day to be young and attractive.

My girlfriends and I learned early on that men *love* women in hats! We made a special point to wear them for our ladies luncheons. One afternoon when I was probably 32 years old, I was walking down Park when a construction guy, sitting on one of the low granite walls, called out a compliment to me. I must not have been in a great mood because I haughtily tossed my head to one side in response.

Without loosing his rhythm, he said, "Honey, you ought to be smiling back, 'cause you don't have many years left to get a compliment that good!" Now *that* did elicit a smile from me, and I indeed thanked him. I think without realizing it that was my first tiny lesson in living in the now with gratitude.

My social life was ridiculously busy and fun. Besides having had George in my life, and after that Peter, I began dating several men in the entertainment world, CEO's, and some not so famous, yet awesome young men.

Warren and Jack . . . Tom, Dick and Harry

After Peter and I broke up, Warren Beatty began calling me. We spent as many hours on the phone, as in bed. You've rarely seen him on the talk show circuit because he was uncomfortable talking in a public forum. Alone with a woman in whom he was interested, he came across as a delicious box of Teuscher chocolate truffles. It wouldn't matter which piece I selected first, the next one and the one after that was even tastier.

He had "IT"—great flavor and perfect packaging. After drooling over him in the film "Splendor in the Grass" with Natalie Wood, he had me even before I first met him. Honestly, however, I did feign little interest in him when I was still with Peter.

He enjoyed sparring, as I did. On one call, I mused, "Warren, you have a stable of fillies, and I don't see a vacant stall."

Warren murmured, "I'd love making you my number one mare." I could bet money that was true for perhaps one whole night.

Oh, that it would have been the case, I would have made myself more available more often. But, not being in the film business and certainly not possessing four long legs, a lovely mane and tail, I knew his whispered sweet nothings were just that. I would have taken acting lessons if I thought it would have snared a few years with him.

He lived up to his reputation as a world-class lover and womanizer, but with a difference. Warren *really loves and appreciates* women! When I knew him, he lived and breathed film and was in the midst of his "Bonnie and Clyde" days. He was intelligent, and I quite liked him as a person, unlike some womanizers I've met.

Later, Jack Jones entered my life and although we did not have a heated affair, we did have good times together. It's fun to date a singer. Once at the nightclub in the Plaza Hotel he was performing and I was sitting at a ringside table. He wandered over with mike in hand and sang directly to me.

Another time he had an engagement at the Shoreham in Washington, and after his first songfest, we drove out to Joan and Ted Kennedy's home in Virginia to attend a party with a tantalizing guest list. There was always that mix of political and entertainment people at the Kennedy homes, but I was surprised to meet the infamous John Profumo that evening.

Anyone of a certain age will certainly remember how the English tabloids printed three-inch headlines for many months regarding the scandal he caused in 1963 by seeing the prostitute Christine Keeler. At the time, he was serving England as Secretary of State for War. He was also a Member of Parliament. That would have been scandalous enough for the married MP, but when it was learned that Ms. Keeler was also sleeping with a Russian attached to their Embassy in London, the press went crazy wild.

Ted Kennedy, like his brothers, was known as quite a lady's man and Joan had been through very difficult years with him. At this party, I was waiting to use the Powder Room when she walked by and suggested I go down the hall and use her bathroom instead. When I turned on the light, I saw a hand written note on top of the toilet seat. I obviously had to move it and couldn't help reading these words, "Joan, thank you so much. This evening has been so much like *old times* and I appreciate it more than you know. Love, Ted." After the assassination there had been far less reason for the Kennedys to party, making this one poignant for him.

I was embarrassed, but replaced it and thought to myself, I wonder if they are going to make it. Of course, they didn't. One could unkindly say here, "Too much water under the bridge." I liked Teddy, but couldn't imagine being married to a man so famous that any humiliation small or large would be headlines above the fold in newspapers.

Jack Jones was a big talent. Frank Sinatra and Judy Garland called him the best singer in the world. He was better known by most for his pop vocals and had many hits with a few winning Grammies for him. To me Jack was unaffected by his fame and a genuinely nice guy. Once when he was performing in Canada, I remember going up for one of his shows. He could have taken advantage of me in my room at the hotel, but after some sensual kissing, he went to his room. He impressed me as a gentleman. In New York one night, we had dinner with his father, the popular singer Allan Jones, who was trendy long before my time. Obviously, Jack came by his talent by way of good genes.

By the time Kelly moved in with me, a great many talented people crossed the threshold at the 55th Street apartment. Several times when the phone rang in the afternoon, while girlfriends were over, it would be President Kennedy on the line. My friends would do loops about it, but frankly I wondered how in God's name that man found time to meet his commitments every day much less put a call in to me, along with the multitudes of women he must have kept up with.

His calls were short check-ins. "Hi, what's happening in your life, 'haven't talked to you in awhile," sort of thing. He would make me laugh with a little D. C. gossip and end with a simple, "Talk to you soon."

One would think I might just lose a few heart beats when he called, but I was not reflecting about the *not terribly normal* things happening in my life at that time. They seemed quite normal to me . . . not that I was out of touch with reality at this point. . . . or anything. . . .

> *"Every drink is liberating, even when it*
> *leads to a terrible hangover."*
> —BEVERLY PERKINS JONES

In the summer of 1966, Kelly and I leased an apartment at 300 East 46th Street. It was on the corner of 2nd Avenue and one block from the United Nations. We chose it mainly because it was directly below our friends Helen Feibleman and Ed Sufranski, and they made it feel like home from day one. It was also an easier commute to the bus and the airport, but not nearly as central as my first apartment. We decorated it together and did a pretty sophisticated job I thought. One hitch was that the two sea foam green couches we ordered ended up taking 18 weeks to reach us.In the meantime, we had a few beach lounge chairs set up in the living room which proved to be very uncomfortable when I ended up sleeping on one all night.

That particular evening, I had dinner with Duke Snider. He was the lead pilot for the Blue Angels and the group was out for a good party. When they had enough time between their air shows, they partied harder than any guys I had ever known. They seemed to favor Stingers then. It was the first time I drank their drink of choice and it would be the last. I had a nice little buzz going before even finishing my *first*.

I cannot even smell Cointreau to this day without feeling nauseous. I have no idea how many I had that night, because after the first one, I was incapable of counting. All I knew was that I reached that deathly ill feeling where you wouldn't mind dying young. Duke got me home and on to one of the beach lounges where I remained for ten or eleven hours, fully dressed including my shoes.

When I regained total consciousness the next day, I stopped at the bathroom on the way to my bed. I then slept another seven or eight hours. That was the Hangover from Hell, and I've never forgotten it. I would never have qualified as wild enough to join the college Cancun crowd from todays' videos out of control young women of springtime. Two or three times in my life was more than enough to experience that condition we call passing out.

> *"Blind dates are for people*
> *with a dog or a white cane."*
>
> —BARBARA LIPSTADT

Very rarely, Kelly would talk me into doing something I wasn't too keen about.

I mean, Arthur Godfrey was very nice and was a good cook, but after dinner you just knew you would have to listen to him play his ukulele. It's one of those once is enough opportunities. Heaven knows, he was big in the early days of television, but life then was simpler and so was his entertainment.

I would NEVER go on blind dates, but once Kelly convinced me to join her and a couple of Texans she had met on some flight. I was late arriving home that day after shopping late in the afternoon. When I got out of the taxi, I found a really long, *really white* limo sitting in front of our building. Oh no, I thought, "Don't let that be the 'Texas transport'." It reeked tacky.

They had arrived early, unfortunately for me, and were having a drink when I dashed through to change for the evening. I'd seen Texans like these before, but only in the movies.

Yep, not only were they sporting diamond tie tacks and diamond pinky rings, but each had his *white Stetson* and alligator boots. HELP! I wanted to strangle Kelly on the spot, but I was stuck. We saw the Broadway show "Chicago" that night. I had already seen it twice and couldn't concentrate. I was too preoccupied trying to figure out how I could escape from the Texas diamond duo.

After the show, we went to a large, very busy Westside restaurant that catered to theatergoers. We sat down and as soon as drinks were ordered, I excused myself to go to the ladies room. When I got there, I thought; "Layte, you cannot handle one more minute with these two (I was sure by then) married dudes." Never had I skipped out on anyone for fear of hurt feelings, BUT, screw that . . . I just had to get out of there—alone!

Fortunately it was so busy with people and waiters milling all around, I managed to sneak all the way out the front door on the other side of the room. The battered taxi in front aided my quick escape, and my Pakistani driver was welcome company on the way home. 'Can't say Kelly was too happy with me when she got home later, but it certainly ended her attempts to get me out on blind dates.

On the brighter side, I would be happy when our DC political friends would drop by if only for a drink on their way to some event in New York City. Hubert Humphrey was such a delight, and in my eyes, much too nice to be in politics.

He popped in late one afternoon with his Secret Service loitering in our hallway. After some laughs, off he went for his engagement. I made one of my usual gaffs one day when Dan Rather stopped by. I said I felt most men weren't really interesting until they were over 40. Dan was only 38, or 39 at that time. Did he still want to write a book with us on the Press Charters? He was, of course, with CBS at that time, and we did at least begin the project of writing about traveling with Presidents on the charters.

New York was much like Washington in that people were constantly coming through for business, or pleasure. I was still seeing John Brademas on those occasions he came to the city. And, Joe Tydings crossed my schedule several times in New York, or Europe, and we would dine and dance. That guy just loved to dance, a true Scotsman. Life was full of dinner parties and interesting people mixed in with my flying all over the world with Pan Am. I considered sleep in any amount to be the biggest luxury in my life followed by great cuisine and dancing of course.

There had been quite a variety of men in my life at this point, but nothing like rounding it out by dating "Batman." No, really! Adam West had starred in the television *Batman* series for years and was a very attractive man. We only went out a couple of times after being introduced by a mutual friend. Jill St. John popped up again. Jill saw Peter, married Jack Jones and dated Adam. She was obviously more competition than I could meet!

There was a funny item in one of the NY gossip columns about the way we were trading men around. Not hardly! Jill was one of the most beautiful of the "Bond Girls" and extremely bright to boot, so she rarely needed to compete with any other woman.

"In friendship I early was taught to
believe. . . . I have found that a friend
may profess, yet deceive. . . ."

—LORD BYRON

Sadly, Kelly and I had quite a falling out after rooming together for five or six years because I was the second Purser, I took over the chief position for the White House Charters.

I took Kelly off the flight service crew. The "misinformation" in a 1995 book, "Fasten Your Seat Belts," written by Valerie Lester about the history of Pan American Airlines was interesting to me. She interviewed Kelly for the chapter on the White House Press Charters, but never called me. I had installed Kelly as the Chief Purser on the White House Charters, and she promoted her importance in Pan Am.

I was surprised reading Kelly's personal account about how she was assigned to the charters. She totally assumed my identity and my experiences with Danny O'Keefe. She went on to tell many tales regarding our flight experiences. Ms. Lester could not know she was talking with a very bitter woman at this point.

In the beginning, Kelly had been such fun. She was very happy that I introduced her into a world of famous people and as I value my girlfriends so much, I was very disappointed that jealousy ended our friendship. Her crush on Haywood was the last straw for me.

Most women I know would have walked away from her years before. I overlooked several back stabbing situations. While we were still living in my original West 55th Street apartment, she had invited quite a few people to a party in my name, as well as hers. She was well aware that I would be out of the city for quite awhile on a Public Relations assignment, and several Senators and Congressmen who attended were quite surprised that I was not present.

She apologized for me saying that I was called out on an unexpected flight. She invited more men than women and told the gals who came, "Don't dress up as it's going to be very casual." Several girls later told me that she was dressed to the nines when they arrived. I can't imagine that she wouldn't have realized that many of the guests would mention the party to me later and express disappointment that I had an unexpected flight assignment arise. I let that slide as I really didn't like confrontation.

Another time was a big "no, no." While I was on a flight, Peter was staying at the Sherry Netherlands Hotel in NYC and in bed with a bad case of flu. She called him and said she had some wonderful homemade chicken soup she wanted to take up to him, so he said, "Okay." She took the soup into his bedroom and then climbed right in bed with him when he started to eat it.

Peter told me about it when I returned, and I said, "I can't believe it, what did you say?"

"I told her to get the hell out of my bed, the hell out of my suite and to take her damned chicken soup with her!"

I laughed and told him he should have at least eaten the soup! Peter had been kind about Kelly, but only because I asked him to be. That situation, however, ended my taking her to California with me.

> *"You are often more captivated by*
> *someone you know you cannot have!"*
>
> —NOANNE GWYNNE

I was always happy when Helen Feibelman, (having moved to LA two years earlier) came to NYC on business. She worked for Warren Beatty when she first got to the coast, but now she was secretary to the President of Warner Brothers. In fact, she and I had spent Christmas with Ken and his wife at their London home the previous year.

Sometimes she would fly into the New York office with her boss. I went over to the Warner Building to meet her for lunch one day near Rockefeller Center. When I arrived in her office, we exchanged an affectionate hug as we really missed living closer.

She said, "When I told my boss you were coming over, he said I should buzz him and have you come in and meet his visitor."

She took my hand and opened the door to Ken's office. I could not believe my eyes. There he sat, only life sized after all, but oh those blue eyes. Ken gave me a kiss on both cheeks, turned to the man across from him and said, "Paul, remember the last time we were in that duck blind together and I told you about the girl with whom I would most like to be stranded on a desert island? This is the one."

"Layte, say hello to Paul Newman."

Wow, I had been star struck a few times before in my life, but never like this. He had the most contagious smile, but seeing him up close and personal with *those* sky blue eyes was next to overwhelming. He could blame that big movie screen for turning him into a walking legend and regular people finding it hard not to gape at him. It has to be easier being a legend, *after* you are gone. The irony is that the eyes he was famous for were eyes that couldn't even give him the pleasure of distinguishing any color.

Public Relations Experiences
The Final Voyage of the Queen Mary

*"She owns a noble history and I was
so fortunate to know her."*

—MIMMA TIBALDEO

Fugazy asked me if I would like to join seven other young ladies and fly to London to board the Queen Mary and act as a hostess during her final voyage of forty days. The star of the English fleet had been sold to Long Beach California and would live out her days in retirement there for all to visit. I had never been aboard a floating city such as this, and certainly forty days was a chunk of my life, but once again I read her history and knew it was a fabulous opportunity.

She was launched in the same year I was born, and I had heard of her and her famous passengers all my life. Her history is unique as a passenger liner. Since she was then the fastest and largest liner in the world, England volunteered her services for the Second World War effort. In 1940 she was refitted as a troop carrier and could then transport 5,500 men compared to her customary 2,410 passengers. My own stepfather told me that when he sailed to England, he actually slept in her indoor swimming pool, which had been stacked full of bunk beds up to the deck level.

Gig went in on one of the first waves on D-Day. The Queen Mary as well was involved that day, however she fared better by staying further off the coast. She experienced plenty of excitement during the six years She served. Hitler's subs were constantly chasing her and She had to use black outs and a zigzag course to evade their torpedoes. But She was never hit and successfully carried 800,000 soldiers to their battle site destinations.

After the war, She was once again painted in the Cunard Line colors and refitted for luxury sailing around the world. By 1967, She had earned her retirement. It was quite an emotional time for the Brits who took great pride in her accomplishments. There were days of headlines about her scheduled departure from South Hampton.

There were also pictures in the tabloids of the eight hostesses sitting on our luggage at the station waiting to go aboard and assist our passengers.

As hostesses, one of our first jobs was manning desks that helped the passengers with questions and directions and for some of those questions we even had the answers! I found that many of the people aboard were older folks who had sailed on this ship for their honeymoon, or an anniversary. I remember it was a beautiful sunny day for our departure, October 31, and I was very excited.

When we pulled up anchor and all engines roared to life, there was a huge celebration at the harbor that teemed with people. Tugboats ahead of us tooted their loud horns, the small fire fighting sea vessels were shooting thousands of gallons of water as high as possible into the sky. Queen Elizabeth ordered a huge jet flyover to salute her final departure, and on deck, I was crying, feeling more British than American that day.

The English Channel can be very rough and our first night at sea we found that the waves were breaking over her forward deck. There was a formal dinner with dancing, and of course, I was drinking champagne. With the lurching and bobbing of the ship, mixed with my sparkling wine, I abruptly excused myself, rushed to my cabin and threw up. Thankfully my beautiful aqua silk gown was not soiled. After lying down for 15 minutes, I went right back to the party. I was not about to miss this night. Fugazy was on board for the first leg, and we were included at his large ringside table with the notables who disembarked with him several days later.

Johnny Mathis was the first singer entertaining aboard. I had always loved his voice, but he turned out to be a super nice guy as well. Entertainers would embark and disembark at our various stops, so the passengers had a nice variety of entertainment.

The sailing was much smoother once we left the Channel and crossed the Atlantic. One of our first stops after the crossing was in Rio de Janeiro, and I was to have quite a frightening experience there.

Our vessel had a deep draft that meant we would have to anchor outside most of our Ports of Call. We would take tenders back and forth to the ship. In Rio, I went ashore with one of the hostesses, a very flashy German named Helga. She had met Hans Stern, a fellow German through family years earlier. He told her that if she ever got to Rio, she must come to his jewelry store, H. Stern.

He said he wanted to have her pick out a nice piece of jewelry as a gift. When we first arrived, she called and sure enough, he was in Rio and wanted to take her to lunch from his flagship store.

It sounded fun when she first invited me to go with her, and I thought great—a good lunch at a fine restaurant with a famous *jeweler*. The taxi we took from the dock drove us to the Ipanema section, and when Helga saw the elegant shops lining the avenue, she told the cab driver, "Stop!"

"Layte we have to get out here and window shop for the last two blocks as everything is *sooo* beautiful."

We had hardly walked a block when I noticed that a group of young Latin men had gathered and were walking behind us. Helga was a leggy platinum blonde with big blue eyes and was causing quite a stir. We hurried to Stern's, and once inside, I was relieved to be immediately escorted to Mr. Stern's office upstairs.

Hans was delighted to see Helga again and began showing us gems so large that I felt as though we were getting the Elizabeth Taylor and Richard Burton treatment. Hans gave Helga a lovely ring and she was thrilled.

We began discussing where we should have lunch when Mr. Stern's assistant came in and advised us that there was a terrible commotion outside the store. He thought it might be safer if we departed by the back door. It seems that word had spread through out Ipanema that a gorgeous movie star was in the famous jewelry store, and the people (mainly men) wanted to get a glimpse of her.

The crowd had now grown quite large and the jeering and whooping so loud, that it was decided we would be better off skipping lunch and quickly returning to the ship. A taxi was brought to the back door to deliver us. Before we could even get down to the door, the huge crowd discerned where our departure would be, and they went to the rear.

It took four men from the store to get us inside the taxi, which was about the size of a small Volkswagen. We quickly locked the doors! The car couldn't move, of course, because it was surrounded on all sides by the people. Then to my horror they began rocking our vehicle back and forth. I was honestly frightened at this point. I was sure we would be rolled over on our side. I was holding onto the door strap with all my might.

My brain had gone into the saving my life mode before I went into total shock. Thank heaven the police arrived to break up the hysterical crowd. They gave us an escort towards the docks. It was headlined in the local paper the following day, noting that no one learned which movie star it was who had caused the riot.

If I ever needed proof that Latin men are excitable when it came to gorgeous blondes, this gave it to me in spades. Stern loved the publicity and did not dispel the rumors that it had indeed been a famous actress visiting his store.

Back at sea, we continued south with a route that would take us around Cape Horn and back up along the west coast of South America, making stops at the major cities. I enjoyed seeing all these places, which I never flew on my regular routes from PAA's New York base. But the most fun was when we were on board. There were parties every night and the latest movies were shown in the theatre along with all the other pleasures these ships provide.

A rock and roll group joined us at one point and this being the sixties, I hardly need tell you what their smoke of choice was. I had never had a joint in my life and didn't even recognize the smell of marijuana. I'd never light a legal cigarette unless I had had too much to drink.

One night several of the hostesses and the band were outside on deck after their performance, and they started lighting up. Then they started passing the joints around to all of us. So, I took my first puffs at sea. After enough coughing, I began getting directions on how to draw the smoke in and hold it for the effect of the drug. I wasn't very successful as I never felt the high. If I had, I think I could have enjoyed the end of the sixties more!

At this point in the cruise, I was beginning to feel as though I had been born on the Queen Mary and was so looking forward to reaching Long Beach. On our last stop before California, Fugazy arranged for some of his Hollywood friends to join the Ship and enjoy the arrival ceremonies on December 9th, 1967.

Unlike them and the paying guests, our cabins were on "D" deck and close enough to the engines driving the huge propellers, that it took me many nights until I could enjoy a good sleep even with my earplugs. We were located so low in the hull, that when the seas were choppy, my cabin's only porthole would be UNDER water.

Fortunately, when I awoke to a bright blue sky with the California shoreline in sight, it was calm and I was astonished when I looked out that porthole. As far as I could see, there were small crafts mixed with large yachts that had sailed or cruised miles out to sea to greet "The Queen" and welcome her to America.

We dressed very quickly and rushed topside with our cameras. From there, we had a 180-degree view of the thousands of vessels surrounding us. It was later reported that over 7,000 boats greeted our ship, and I'm not embarrassed to say that it sent thrill chills up my spine.

What a great morning to be in the exact spot I was in our world that day. Absolutely everyone was excited and dressed in our red, white and blue hostess outfits. We took pictures with Captain Treasure Jones, Vic Damone, Robert Stack, Betsy and Al Bloomingdale, and many other recognizable entertainers, now on board. Shelby Smith, a Public Relations man, well known around Hollywood became a friend to me that day and he would introduce me in the future to show business people whom I had not met in my years with Peter.

The pictures in my photo album and my Certificate for rounding Cape Horn and crossing The Equator declaring from that day forth, I should never again be referred to as a "Land Lubber," are my only mementoes. But, it remains in my mind, an extraordinary experience.

Apollo 11 Moon Mission

*"There is only one thing I can promise you
about the outer-space program is that your tax
dollar will certainly Go Further!"*

—WERNER VON BRAUN

In July of 1969, Bill Fugazy called me once again to ask if I would like to hostess foreign guests of the American government for the Apollo program's first Moon Launch. "Absolutely," I told him before he even explained what my duties would entail along with the schedule of events. By this time, I was a big NASA fan like much of America. We were on the verge of making history for all mankind.

The State Department invited one hundred of the top industrialists from all over Europe as our nation's guests to view the launch of Apollo XI. They flew to Boston on Air France, which had been made available to them for the four-day trip, with U. S. Ambassador Sergeant Shriver (married to JFK's sister Eunice) accompanying them. As I recall, there was only one woman, and she had been involved in Scientific Space Research programs in France.

Bill hired three other hostesses, only one whom I knew from Pan Am, and we were flown up to Boston where we awaited their arrival at the hotel downtown. Our hospitality desk in the lobby was to be available for any problems in reservations, or changes in their agendas. Early the following morning we all boarded the Air France jet which would fly us to Cape Canaveral.

Air France stewardesses served the breakfasts while we circulated in the cabin answering all questions and handing out prepared information for their entire visit. We had been well briefed and as most of these executives spoke perfect English, there were no problem with communication.

After arriving at the Cape, we were delivered by several buses to a nearby hall to attend a special brunch where Werner Von Braun would speak. This famous German Scientist, who developed the V-2 Rocket for Germany, was on the top of America's Black List in 1945. To simplify an extremely complicated and interesting story of his life during the war: He was aware that the Germans would execute him before they would let him fall into our hands, but he managed to get himself and his brother to a small village and secretly surrendered to the first American soldier they saw, an Army Private! The US High Command was immediately notified of this big catch and rushed him to an American sector.

After becoming a Naturalized American Citizen and agreeing to work for our government, the fears of Germany and Russia were fully realized. It might well have been a Russian flag first planted on the moon had they succeeded in capturing him in 1944. Von Braun became known as the Father of the American Space Program, and many films, books and Science Honors have been dedicated to him. He gave a hugely inspiring speech that morning. We were all certainly revved up for the historic launch to the Moon.

The buses delivered us to the launch site where bleacher type seating was the closest civilians were allowed to the launch pad. It was a perfect day, and we needed our dark sunglasses. When the countdown went to ONE, I was holding my breath. The rockets shot pure fire into the earth beneath the capsule and the ground under us felt as though an earthquake was occurring. Being that close, it is a sight and a might to behold. We all lifted our faces to the sky with most of our mouths gaping. We were held mesmerized. The cheering by the witnesses here reached quite a decibel.

Following the launch, we boarded the Air France jet for our next stop in Houston, Texas. The chosen hundred were to be the guests of the City of Houston and NASA's Control Center. After everyone was directed to their rooms and given more reading material about the NASA Center, we used our passenger manifests to guide them to their next transports. They were the guests of honor at a huge Texas barbecue that evening. Between the politicians, NASA hierarchy, the western music, Keys to the City and the great food, it was a *hellova* celebration night.

The next day we accompanied everyone for a fascinating tour of the Control Center. The training equipment there is mind-boggling and many of our guests were able to experience the weightless chamber. I so wished I could have. We also listened in to the conversations with the Apollo crew and the controllers.

Thomas Edison would have been so proud to have witnessed *these* long distance calls. Later in the day, we flew back to Boston where the group was to overnight before departing for Europe the next morning. The girls and I flew back to NYC, very tired and quite satiated from our bird's eye view of history in the making.

I worked on a few more assignments for Bill, including two more ship launchings, but certainly nothing else compared to the Queen Mary or the Apollo XI launch.

There was one short assignment aboard the S. S. Constitution, which was only a three day sail, and it reminds me how rushed my life always seemed. Fugazy was sending a limo to pick me and another gal up, then we were stopping at the Waldorf to get Vic Damone, before proceeding to the docks. I had just returned from Europe the night before and was too tired to unpack and repack so I left it for morning.

Everyone who has ever known me knows that I rarely come truly alive before noon on *any* given day. The doorman buzzed up to say the car was downstairs. I hadn't even started to organize my make up and overnight items for my carry bag. I thought the heck with it, grabbed a big clear plastic bag and tossed all that stuff in the bag.

When Vic joined us in the car, he looked quizzically at this crammed full plastic bag sitting on my lap and asked why I hadn't packed it in a carry on case. I mumbled the fact that I had so much unpacked stuff in my small bag that I just didn't have time to redo everything. Obviously I was beyond worrying that I wouldn't look very chic arriving at the ship.

Suddenly Vic told our driver to stop and he ran into a very upscale luggage store on Fifth Avenue. When he returned, he set a beautiful makeup case on my lap and said, "Now pack it, Layte." It was a very thoughtful gesture and was the way all of the fellows treated us. Once in Fugazi's exclusive club, you were pretty much watched over.

Fugazy's NYC Dinner Club

We would meet for dinner whenever several, or all of us, were in the City at the same time. I always referred to these occasions as "Fugazi's Dinner Club."

I might not have spoken with him in four or five weeks when the phone would ring, and Bill would call to see if I was free that evening because "so 'n so" was in the city and he was rounding up the group. "I'll send a limo around to pick you up at seven and see you at The Four Seasons." . . . or whatever nice restaurant he had selected. He would have limos pick up three or four people, according to how near we were to one another.

"I love New York City; I've got a gun."

—CHARLES BARKLEY

Our usual flock consisted of four attractive women and five or six well known men. I knew Susan Barnett from Miami for years, and we met Carol French and Barbara Mara earlier, on the Queen Mary trip. Bill's close friends were Lee Iacocca, Arnold Palmer, Vic Damone, Hugh Knowlton (President of Smith Barney), and Alfred Bloomingdale. Once in awhile someone else would join us, or one of the others would be absent. But, it was usually no less than seven and no more than ten of us on any given night together.

Male wise, this was hardly a low profile gathering, and we were never a very quiet group, but there was *never* a word in any gossip column about us. There would be constant whispering by other patrons at a restaurant. We were such an odd collection that I suppose no one had a notion of why we materialized now and then at the best restaurants together. The plain truth is our mix just had a blast socially. Bawdy jokes were told now and then, but hanky panky was not on our menu. Considering how beautiful the women were, it was fun just to be one of the guys now and then.

It's a different kind of fun for men and women in a gathering when their married half is not present. When you're married at a social gathering, you tend to be more careful with your manners and conversation. Not that our group was throwing peas across the room, or teething lobster claws. It's just different. No one took offense at what anyone else said and laughter reigned.

The only thing I found unattractive about these dinners were Al Bloomingdale's lack of manners. He didn't join us often thank heaven, as he was very sloppy at the table. His terrible manners were a surprise to me. I met him and his wife Betsy originally on the last leg of the Queen Mary Cruise, and she was the epitome of graciousness and etiquette. She was also one of Nancy Reagan's closest friends.

At one point, Hugh Knowlton asked me to have dinner alone with him some evening. I thanked him, but told him I would not date a man who couldn't produce his divorce papers if asked. I knew he was separated, but I'd been that route before, and even if this man was tall, great looking and cultured, I was not going there again. A few weeks later, I received a call from Mexico, and it was Hugh telling me that his divorce was finalized and he was flying back in time for dinner.

"Will you join me if I produce my papers?" I thought this was a no-brainer and was totally delighted that this now eligible attractive bachelor, who happened to be CEO of Smith Barney, wanted to spend time with me.

I was thirty-three at this point, and friends of my parents were too embarrassed to ask them if I might marry *some day.* But in truth, that was one of the best years of my life. I was dating three very eligible bachelors in New York City, each of whom seemed a bit serious about me.

Hugh and I dated quite often and after a trip to Jamaica with him, I received a phone call from NYC in my London Hotel during a layover. He wanted me to move into his 18 room Park Avenue apartment with him. I was smart enough to know that he was in that unbalanced state of "rebound." Had he been the only man in my life then, my future might have turned out differently. But at that point, I found myself caring more and more for the man I eventually married.

I was more casually dating a very successful young man behind door number 3 who was more interested in having me as a mate than I was him. He entertained me extravagantly and took me to a Park Avenue condo building where he introduced me to his interior decorator. He told her that she should run her ideas past me as he was planning to make me the next Mrs. Robert Wetenhall. That objective hadn't occurred to me even though he did own half the Boston Patriots and several other companies.

Some years later, he had the last laugh. I found myself living unhappily in a lovely townhouse off Park Avenue. Thinking that I just had to get a job and become more independent to raise my self-esteem, I called Bob. I told him I wanted to talk to him about something important to me, so he invited me to lunch. We hadn't seen or talked with one another in years. He had married, had two sons and was divorced by then.

I explained my situation and asked him if he would consider giving me a job, as he was involved in so many endeavors. After one sip of his drink, he said, "Absolutely not!"

I went a little white and felt even more worthless for a few minutes until he said, "I would consider marrying you however." I told him that was flattering, but another husband at this point was not what I was seeking.

What I wanted was a darn job. I had live in help, and my son was attending the private Browning School, so I could easily have worked. The year dissolved around me, and I never did take a job outside my home. I just spent most of the winter skiing in Vermont to shake off the cobwebs.

My first few single days in New York City absolutely were a great place to be in the sixties, and if it wasn't happening *there*, world events reverberated through the canyons, up, down, and across the city, as though they were. When I decided to move to New Jersey with the man I would soon marry, my *single* days ended in my heart city.

Courtship by Future Husband

"There are some people who live in a
dream world and there are some who
face reality. And then, there are those
who turn one into the other."

—DOUGLAS H. EVERETT

My girlfriend Nancy Larson was dating Marshall Coyne in 1969, and Marshall, who owned the renowned Hotel Madison in Washington, was quite the man about town. As I visited Nancy often from New York, he also invited me to a lovely dinner party at his hotel in early October of 1969. There was a good mix of personalities including the younger sister of the King of Morocco, Princess Lalla Nezha, who was married to their Ambassador in Washington, Ahmed Osman Benjelloun. The Princess was seated at our table, as was the handsome Marine, Chuck Robb, who was to my right. He and Lynda Bird Johnson had married at the White House in 1967.

It was a loose, fun party and we had one of the more animated tables. Towards the end of the evening, after many guests had departed, our entire group was still intact and laughing enthusiastically at each of our humorous tales. Without warning, I felt a hand on the back of my chair and Lynda Bird leaned down between me and Chuck. (As was the custom, most married couples were seated at different tables.)

Looking at Chuck she said sarcastically, "Hello, Chuck! 'Remember me? I'm the one who does the dishes and takes care of the baby at home! I'm tired now and more than ready to leave."

Chuck looking very sheepish replied, "Oh Lynda I'm sorry, I didn't realize everyone was leaving. Of course I'm ready to go."

Looking directly at *me*, she replied again quite sarcastically, "I would think you would be."

From a distance, I always thought Lucy Bird was the fun daughter of LBJ, and this rather solidified my judgment.

The following Monday when I answered the phone in my New York apartment, the secretary to Princess Lalla Nezha told me that Her Highness would be pleased if I would attend a costume party at the Moroccan Embassy the following weekend. I told her that I would be delighted and asked if I might bring a date. She said that I could, but Lalla Nezha was hoping I would come with my friend Nancy, as there would be several attractive bachelors in attendance and we might have more fun without dates. I asked the secretary to thank Her Highness for the invitation and said that I would indeed come with Nancy.

> *"At a Washington party, it is not enough*
> *that the guests feel drunk they must feel*
> *drunk **and** important."*
>
> —THOMAS WOLFE

I flew down to Washington a day before the costume party at the Moroccan Embassy. Nancy was working, and she left it up to me to put together some Wild West get ups for us, as the theme was western. Arriving home late Friday afternoon, Nancy was exhausted and said she didn't have enough energy to go out and wanted to cancel.

"Well," I said, "I honestly don't feel like going either, but I've spent the whole ding dong day getting everything you need to be Pocahontas and me a nondescript cowgirl with cool boots, so we're *going*." It's always interesting to think back on how an evening of seemingly no consequence actually turns your life in a new direction.

This was a cocktail and buffet affair with dancing to follow. After a couple of glasses of champagne, I looked around for Nancy to hit the deliciously prepared buffet. I saw her coming my way with a "cowboy" wearing a similar hat and brown leather fringed vest like mine. He took my elbow and said, "Why don't the three of us get our plates and sit somewhere together for dinner."

We properly exchanged *first* names and loaded our plates with the spicy Moroccan fare. Paul Dopp was a most attractive blue-eyed man with white blonde hair. I learned he was Chairman of Butler Aviation, which owned Mooney Aircraft and other businesses. Nancy was more taken with him during their first conversation together, but later in the evening I found him quite appealing.

Months later he related to me that after dining, while he stood with the Moroccan Consulate Abdeslam Jaidi watching me dance, he said to Jaidi, "Now there is a woman I'd like to take out to dinner."

Jaidi's response was, "Paul, you're not rich enough or famous enough to get a dinner date with that little lady." It was not the sort of statement Mr. Dopp accepted.

Nancy left the party before me because Paul and I had become involved in a long conversation. When it was time for us to leave, he asked if he could drop me at Nancy's apartment in a taxi. I thanked him, but said that I had my former boss's car since the Senator was in Florida and that I would drop *him* off.

He kissed me goodnight outside his hotel, and it was chemically explosive enough that we ended up going to Nancy's. We sat on her couch simply talking until almost five A.M. At one point, he told me that he was flying to the Bahamas that morning with several Moroccan friends to look over a property investment for King Hassan. Then he asked if I would fly down with them. I laughed and advised him that his was the third invitation I'd received to make that trip and further informed him, I wouldn't consider flying to the Bahamas with any man I barely knew.

"But, it's *my* jet. I can't believe any one else had the nerve to ask you to join us."

"It was my party girl persona Paul. The truth is, I often play the *wild one* at a festive occasion, but leave that persona at the door at the end of the evening." He grasped my meaning and asked if he could call me when we were back in New York. I told him that was a splendid idea.

Sunday morning I read Betty Beale's social column in the Washington Post. A she recounted the lively party at the Moroccan Embassy Friday night, she mentioned several well-known guests along with a very flattering comment about my new friend.

"Paul Dopp, the incredibly handsome, now eligible bachelor and Chairman of Butler Aviation, came down from New York for this party. . . . etc."

Late afternoon on Sunday, I was up on a ladder painting Nancy's foyer ceiling with an artistic glazing, when the phone rang. It was Paul calling to tell me he had dropped off his guests and was refueling his Learjet at

Butler Aviation's base at National Airport. He asked if I would like a lift back to New York City and if so, he would be happy to wait for me there.

I sensed that this was a man used to getting what he wanted, and there had been no shortage of beautiful women in his life since he and his wife separated. Even though I would have loved a lift back to NY, I did what a smart woman would do when she was interested in a spoiled man . . . I lied.

"Thank you so much for your generous offer Paul, but I'm doing my nails just now as I have a social engagement in an hour." Definitely not true. "I'm not returning to New York until tomorrow evening." Which *was* a true statement.

"Tell me what flight you'll be on and I'll have my driver pick you up at the airport," he quickly offered.

"You are *so* thoughtful, but the man I'm seeing for dinner *tomorrow night* is sending a car for me." These being lies number two and three. I had no Monday night dinner plans, and I was taking the bus back into the city from the airport.

At this lovely age of thirty-three, I was already dating two corporate CEOs, and I needed to start thinking more seriously about my future. Bob Wetenhall had no ex-wife and expressed several times his intent on marrying me.

Hugh Knowlton Chairman of Smith Barney was perhaps rebounding too quickly with me, but was divorced. We were seeing one another quite a bit, and he had asked me to move into his eighteen-room condominium on Park Ave. Uh uh, that wouldn't have been smart.

I had to carefully plan my next few months, if I was going to add a third attractive and intelligent CEO to my social calendar. Plus, I wanted to be *very* in love with whomever I chose, and Paul might possibly become the right one for me.

When Paul called on Tuesday, I told him I'd very much enjoy having dinner with him the following evening. I learned he had a townhouse in one of the most charming and unusual settings in New York City. Off East 36th Street, there is a narrow, quite chic cobblestone alleyway that accommodates four tall townhouses on each side. Sniffin Court is chained off, but you can look down at all the lovely flower boxes adorning each townhouse. There are "horse hitches" a century old, outside. It is quite English in feeling and appearance. I never even knew it existed, but immediately fell in *like* with it.

Its' immediate charm slid away from my psyche when I also learned he had been steadily dating a German gal who spent quite a bit of time there with him. That is, when they were not in the Mediterranean on his yacht, or in Europe.

We enjoyed an elegant dinner at a restaurant on the west side. We ate in a flower laden garden area off the interior room. As on most first dinner dates, we shared information about our lives and friends within the *choose to share*, or perhaps the *impress* category. We hadn't covered all the interesting things about our lives the night we met, so we explored more territory here.

When we met, he was very successful. His divorce papers were in hand shortly afterward, so only the German was in my path. One night we actually sat through a movie two times, so we could hold hands and spend more time together. The German was at his townhouse, and we couldn't go there! "Butch Cassidy and the Sundance Kid" was a great movie, but even I had gotten my fill of Paul Newman and Robert Redford that night.

Paul and I first made love at my old apartment on East 46th Street. Bill Fugazy had leased the apartment from me when I moved back to Washington in 1965 and loaned it out to his clients on their NYC business trips. I was able to borrow it once in awhile if I needed to be in NYC after a flight and it happened to be empty.

I had sold the furniture from the apartment to Bill, and that included the two "three quarter" sized beds Kelly and I had used. They were half way between the width of a single and double bed, which is perfectly roomy for *one* person. It was quite crowded for two, and particularly if those two people are performing the rituals of sex for the *first time*.

We knew we had good chemistry when we found ourselves on the floor entangled in the covers that plunged off with us. One of my legs was wedged under the bed. Neither of us could stop laughing until passion triggered a second and third assemblage! I know that neither of us slept until daylight emerged and we were totally debilitated.

After that night together I thought, *this is the one*. Having absolutely no interest in a ménage à trois, the German would have to be extricated from Paul's house as well as his social life. This was not a venture I had ever needed to initiate, and I would need advice!

Fortunately, I was scheduled for several trips to Paris with Pan Am and Eugenia was now married and living there with *that* Italian. She was still modeling for Channel. I had dinner at their apartment each time and for the three of us, the dining room served as a "war room." I received both a man's view and a woman's outlook, neither of whom had my emotional involvement. Poor Paul, he was quite out flanked and the German girl would soon be a memory on the horizon of his present life.

In April of 1970, Paul invited me to go over to Pennsylvania for the Reading Air Show. It was stimulating to spend time with some of the well known stunt pilots and even barnstormers who provided thrilling rolls and diving back flips.

Barnstorming became big in America after the First World War when the military sold all the $5,000 Curtis JN-4s nicknamed "Jenny" bi-planes for $200. Pilots who had trained in them for the war felt comfortable and used them to make a living by entertaining in makeshift country airfields near barns, hence the name. In the 60's and 70's, that entertainment died out, but was still available at U. S. Air Shows. Bob Hoover was probably the best known stunt pilot of all time. He was a fearless world class test pilot in larger, faster aircraft than the Jenny and worked in several Hollywood movies. There is film of him pouring a glass of ice tea sitting on the dash board while doing a roll and not spilling a drop. That is pulling a lot of "G's."

Following the air show in Pennsylvania, Paul had me flown back to NYC in a Mooney aircraft in time to change for my scheduled working flight to Rome. That evening after boarding all our passengers, the ground assistant asked me to hold the door open for just a minute longer as a newly ticketed passenger was about to board. Much to my surprise, Paul Dopp came aboard! He had decided at the last minute to accompany me, as I was working First Class and had a two-day layover in Rome. This was the first of many surprises to come from this man who enjoyed doing the unexpected.

We had a fun flight over and before landing, Paul invited me and the other flight attendants to fly over to Malta and spend the night aboard his yacht. I discouraged the other gals of course, but said that I would certainly enjoy it. Being in the aviation business as well as on the Aviation Council of New York, he could pull a few strings at airports.

I learned how much he could organize when after disembarking the passengers, he had already arranged for me to forgo customs and simply board his Learjet, which was waiting right next to where our Pan Am Boeing parked! He had also convinced the PAA Station Manager to let him fly me to Paris from Malta, as my crew was deadheading up there on Air France anyway to work our flight home in two days.

Flying over the shimmering Mediterranean Sea that day, I totally forgot that neither of us had slept crossing the Atlantic the previous night. There was only a curtain between the cockpit and our cabin, but Paul decided that it was past time that I join the "mile high" club. I was nervous about the pilots, but after we began making love, I totally dismissed them from my mind.

Malta is directly south of Italy beyond Sicily and it is a spectacular place. I had previously seen it only in the movie "Popeye" with Robin Williams romping about.

Paul's Captain met us at the airport, and we drove to the docks where we boarded one of the two launches that were kept aboard his yacht. When we arrived off shore and pulled up next to the "Asmeda Hope," I was astounded at the size. I didn't know she was 120 feet long with a 28 foot beam. I felt like Jack looking up at the Beanstalk.

She carried ten crewmen because there was so much teak wood to keep up, as well as many brass railings to polish. Paul told me he had named her by using the first letter of the middle name of each of his six children. This was definitely a party boat, and we enjoyed cuisine prepared by ex-Queen Juliana's former chef. The formal dining room had a huge solid teak table, lit by an exquisite crystal chandelier.

The Captain had the onboard motorcycle put in the launch for the shore, and we used it to tour the island. The sheer beauty of this place is further enhanced by an aqua blue sea, almost Caribbean clear as far as my eyes could see. What a pity it is off the beaten path because more people would totally enjoy seeing it. The Capitol town of Veletta had stone or brick roads, some so narrow we had to walk. We stopped in quaint cheese shoppes and bakeries for snacks and selected goodies to take back to the boat.

Paul delivered me to Paris in his Learjet after two days of absolute heaven. Yes, I admit that I was a bit blown away by his attention and his toys. I don't know if I was really in love on that working trip home from Paris, or just simply overwhelmed. But he certainly knew how to *court* a woman in whom he was interested.

The German blonde gal was still in his life and living in his NYC townhouse part of the time when Paul asked me to go to Tokyo with him. He had to meet with the Chairman of Mitsubishi Aircraft, whose planes he was distributing through Mooney aircraft in the U.S.

At that time, he had a loyal Brazilian manservant. Joseph acted as his valet at home as well as his chauffeur when needed. The morning we departed NYC, the German was giving him a kiss goodbye at Sniffen Court, and I was waiting on the sidewalk outside Barbara Klenk's apartment in Peter Cooper Village fifteen blocks south. Of course I gave him a big hug before I entered the car. Joseph must have thought that Paul was indeed living the American dream.

We traveled first class west to Tokyo stopping briefly in Alaska where I once again almost had frost bite within minutes. A representative of Mitsubishi Corporation met us at the airport and without even realizing, because it came about so gracefully, I found myself walking several steps behind Paul and his Japanese greeter. This would remain our formation whenever we were with his Japanese hosts on this visit.

Paul began his meetings regarding Mooney Aircraft and Mitsubishi the next day while I caught up on my sleep and enjoyed one of the best massages I had ever had in the comfort of our room. He returned that afternoon as well as the next two, quite frustrated.

"Layte, you know how much I read about Japanese business customs with foreigners before we came, but I cannot believe how difficult it is to get these people to discuss business! I talk about my four sons and barely mention my two daughters so they can see I'm a virile sort of guy. But, I bring up manufacturing, and I'm back to zero. I've had tea and good manners up to my eyeballs at this point."

"Paul, you're here, just go with 'their' flow. It's really a different culture in so many ways! You've perfected your bowing from the waist and I hope you show me that same courtesy when we get back to New York! And, please enjoy my walking behind you everywhere here 'cause that little custom isn't going to make it back across the ocean."

Several evenings during our stay, we ventured out to discover the local fare and at the suggestion of our driver, we totally enjoyed our introduction to *sushi* and *sashimi*. Sitting at the sushi bars gave us more pleasure than at a private table as we could watch all the preparations for our dishes. We both fell in love with this native Japanese cuisine, and it became like a drug for us back home. We just *had to have it* at least once a week.

While Paul was in his all day meetings, I was riding their *bullet* trains to explore Kyoto and Osaka. After three days, Paul finally got his business associates to discuss *business*. Pure joy emerged from him when he arrived back at our suite that evening.

"Screw the sake, I feel I should open a bottle of champagne to celebrate such a breakthrough."

On the flight home I made the demand. "The German goes!" When we stopped for fuel in Alaska, Paul made the long distance call to New York and advised her to *be gone*—with all her personal things before he returned home. It sounds harsh in the retelling, but she was not exactly a sweet young thing during their relationship.

Resignation From Pan Am

It was May of 1970 and Paul wanted me to cruise on his yacht with him and with his children in the Aegean Sea and the Bosporus up to Russia. In fact, he wanted me to quit flying period. Now that I had finally met the man I knew I would marry, I certainly could not ask for a three month summer leave of absence from PAA, as that was our busiest season.

So I went to Jim Kilites' office and told him why I had to quit. To my great surprise, he said he really didn't want the airline to lose me, and he would grant the three-month leave. "You must be kidding," I exclaimed. "I thought you really resented me."

> *"I have no idea what I'm doing, but incompetence has never prevented me from plunging in with enthusiasm."*
> —WOODY ALLEN

"No, I mean it," he replied. "You have certainly put me through the mill, Layte, but when you actually work your flights, you are one of the best stewardesses we have on the payroll."

He walked over to one of his file cabinets and pulled out a couple of very thick files with my name on them. A lot of the sheets concerned my political pulling of rank, but most of them he told me, were glowing letters from passengers. I had no idea that anyone, much less so many had taken their time to write that I personally had made their trips so enjoyable.

"You might have carried out some interesting Public Relations jobs for Bill Fugazy, but we benefited the most by your friendliness and concern with our passengers. If you change your mind at the end of the summer and want to come back, we will welcome you. "I would never REALLY have fired you, you know," he said sincerely. *Who knew?* I gave him a heart felt hug.

Leaving Jim's office, I thought this had to be one of the big surprises of my life. I thought he totally disliked me and would be thrilled to be rid of me. I actually cried in the hallway, because I knew I would marry Paul and never wear my Pan Am wings again. My carefree life of flying around the heavens, was incredible, but it was time to spend more time on terra firma and live a more normal reality.

When I told all my friends I was going to marry this man who had six children, half of them accused me of being on drugs. I thought it would be wonderful to become part of a big family having been raised as an only child myself. The children aged seventeen to four were so relieved he didn't marry the German, it took some of the edge off their acceptance of me as a step-mother.

On June 24, 1971 in the beautiful gardens at the Anstatt's home in Ridgewood, New Jersey, the omens were good before and during the wedding ceremony. I was as surprised as our guests to see the "blue meatball" on the tail of a Pan American jet as it flew overhead several minutes before a butterfly fluttered around me. Yes, it actually happened. We even had a short-lived rain sprinkle, also a sign of luck in some cultures.

Having been raised as an only child, I knew one thing for sure. Marrying a man who had six children and hoping for a couple more in our marriage together, my holidays would be filled with much more excitement and hopefully I would learn to be a *very good cook!*